CW00584576

THE ENTREPRENEURIAL SOCIETY OF
THE RHONDDA VALLEYS, 1840–1920

The Entrepreneurial Society of the Rhondda Valleys, 1840–1920

Power and Influence in the Porth–Pontypridd Region

Richard Griffiths

UNIVERSITY OF WALES PRESS
CARDIFF

© Richard Griffiths, 2010

All rights reserved. No part of this book may be reproduced in any material form (including photocopying or storing it in any medium by electronic means and whether or not transiently or incidentally to some other use of this publication) without the written permission of the copyright owner except in accordance with the provisions of the Copyright, Designs and Patents Act 1988. Applications for the copyright owner's written permission to reproduce any part of this publication should be addressed to the University of Wales Press, 10 Columbus Walk, Brigantine Place, Cardiff, CF10 4UP.

www.uwp.co.uk

British Library CIP Data
A catalogue record for this book is available from the British Library.

ISBN 978-0-7083-2290-1
e-ISBN 978-0-7083-2291-8

The right of Richard Griffiths to be identified as author of this work has been asserted by him in accordance with sections 77, 78 and 79 of the Copyright, Designs and Patents Act 1988.

Printed by CPI Antony Rowe, Chippenham, Wiltshire.

CONTENTS

Preface

With very minor exceptions, almost all that has been written about the society created by the coal industry of Wales has been about the workers and the unions, and there is a significant gap as regards the entrepreneurs of the Valleys. It is hardly surprising that so little work has been done in this area, given the reputation accorded in modern times to the nineteenth-century mineowners and their successors. Yet this gap is nevertheless a seriously worrying one, if a rounded picture of life in the south Wales valleys in the nineteenth and early twentieth centuries is to be achieved.

This book is an attempt at social history; it has no claim to be the kind of all-embracing economic history of Welsh entrepreneurism desired by the leading Welsh historian Chris Williams when he declared the pressing need for 'an even-handed approach to the entrepreneurial and business history of the coalfield'.[1] It is, rather, an attempt (hopefully an even-handed one) to enter the enclosed world of the entrepreneurial society of the Valleys, and to consider the collective existence of a restricted portion of society in the Porth-Pontypridd area via the details of the lives of individuals, as found in contemporary documentation. For this approach, I owe much to the late Richard Cobb ('Ancient Richard'), who taught me how much historical truth could be found by an examination of the individual experiences of people within a social system. The geographical area that will be dealt with is a narrow one, centred around Pontypridd, Porth and the Rhondda valleys, and the Taff valley from Pontypridd to Abercynon and Nelson.

---

[1] Chris Williams, *Capitalism, Community and Conflict: The South Wales Coalfield, 1898–1947* (Cardiff: University of Wales Press, 1998), p. 2.

The way into the close and almost claustrophobic middle-class society of this area of the Valleys has been facilitated by concentration on one extended family central to that society; in particular on the coal pioneer James ('Siamps') Thomas, his son-in-law William Henry Mathias, and his grandson Sir William James Thomas. These three men were intimately connected with most of the events and developments in this area of industrial south Wales between 1840 and 1914, and were an integral part of the society we will be examining.

Thus it is that Siamps Thomas, the founder of the clan, gives us a rags-to-riches story (graduating as he did from six-year-old doorboy to coalowner), and illustrates the attitudes of the early coalowners to the workers within their mines. His mixed experience of the Tynewydd disaster in 1877 (praised for bravery, sued for negligence) tells us much about relationships down the mines at that period, and about the Government's problems in bringing coalowners to book for negligence. Later, in the years of his great success as owner of one of the most successful steam coalmines in the Rhondda (the Standard Collieries, Ynyshir), amid the general trend towards limited liability companies and more distant management, he was one of the last outposts of the old methods.

The activities of Siamps Thomas's son-in-law, William Henry Mathias, and his father Richard Mathias, tell us much about the entrepreneurial activities of railway contractors in this period of rail expansion; and W. H. Mathias's later career as a mineowner shows us much that had changed in the coalfields over 25 years (while the disaster at his Albion mine, while highlighting those changes, also shows how difficult it was, still, to touch negligent owners). Mathias's activities during the 1893 and 1898 strikes, as magistrate and as owner, highlight the clashes of interest (in particular when the magistrates brought in the military) which seemed to matter so little in such circles. We shall also see some of the more questionable business practices undertaken by people like Mathias (two of the best examples being the backgrounds to the creation of the Cowbridge-Aberthaw Railway, and to the sinking of Windsor Colliery, Abertridwr and the development of workers' housing nearby). Mathias was in many ways a typical second-generation entrepreneur, surrounded by similar people to himself; his position was safeguarded by the mutual support given by the members of this 'acquisitive society', some of whom (e.g. Thomas Griffiths Maesgwyn, William Jenkins Ystradfechan, J. D. Williams Clydach Court, Walter Morgan Forest House, Walter Nicholas, the North

Lewis brothers, James Hurman and Henry Oakden Fisher) were close associates of his over many years. Mathias's prominent position in local government is also examined for evidence of some of the practices that existed in that area.

Sir William James Thomas, Bart (Siamps Thomas's grandson and Mathias's nephew) epitomizes a new generation of entrepreneurs. He built, via new mining ventures, on the fortune left to him by his grandfather. Having made this money, he, like many others, then withdrew from the mining industry, thus avoiding in time the economic difficulties of the inter-war period, and became part of the 'escape to the coast'. He also shows us the way in which some of the beneficiaries of the coal industry used their money in good works, such as supporting hospitals; and how charitable munificence could reap its rewards. Made a baronet by Lloyd George in the 1919 New Year Honours, he became part of the Cardiff-based aristocracy of the new rich.

These men act merely as the foredrop to the close-knit and mutually supportive society formed by the new middle classes within the townships of the Valleys. The acquisition of wealth, within this society, had not been achieved only by entrepreneurial ability; some of the most prominent people we shall be seeing were, for example, brought to their prominence by their families' possession of land, usually farms, at the point where mines were to be sunk or townships built. Wealth was also to be made, in the Valleys, from ventures other than mines or railways. There was a whole substructure which thrived on the new society: contractors and builders; property developers; grocers (ranging from the vastly successful William Evans of Thomas and Evans, creators of Corona mineral waters, to the prosperous owners of corner shops) and so on.

The success of such people as the Thomas/Mathias clan was facilitated by the networks of local worthies by which local society was ruled. The magistracy, the local councils, the County Council, the Boards of Health, the Boards of Guardians, the entrepreneurs, were all part of a highly effective network of interest. It was the mining entrepreneurs, however, who had created the opportunities on which all this activity thrived and it was the railways which were the essential support to these efforts. It was in these two areas that the Thomas and Mathias families gained prominence.

I am in fact a descendant of this family (through W. H. Mathias's daughter Lizzie and her husband Lemuel Griffiths, my grandparents). In the process of looking into the family, I have discovered much which has discomfited me. My effort, at all times, has however been to find the truth and to state it.

The book starts, after an introductory chapter on the coal industry in the period, with a study of the major figures from this family, and of their friends, collaborators and contemporaries. There then follows an examination of specific aspects of their activities, in the business and the political worlds, and in relation to two major mining disasters and two major strikes. We then come, with the new century, to the activities of the last important member of the clan, Sir William James Thomas, as he withdrew from the coal industry and, like so many others, settled on the coast. The three generations involved cover the whole of the coal boom, from the 1840s to the 1920s.

I am grateful to a number of people, both living and dead. For genealogical and other information about the Thomas/Mathias clan I am indebted to Michael Mathias, Mary James and to the late Derek Williams; for information about John Roskill to Nicholas Roskill; for information about Mrs Elizabeth Miles to the late Spencer Miles; and for information about property dealings in the Cowbridge area to Philip Riden and Brian James. More generally, I am grateful for help, information or fruitful discussion over the years, to a great many people, including Geoffrey Alderman; Tony Atkins; Stefan Berger; the late Ivor Bulmer Thomas; the late Richard Cobb; the late Sir William Crawshay; Andy Croll; the late Mr Davies Bryn-y-Groes; Ivor England; Neil Evans; André Gren; Dominic Griffiths; Roger Griffiths; Teifion Griffiths; Patrick Ground QC; Ursula Henriques; David Jenkins; Bill Jones; the late David Joslin; Harry Judge; Russell Lewis; Kenneth Morgan (Lord Morgan of Aberdyfi); Prys Morgan; the late Emrys Pride; the Revd Chris Reaney; the Revd Huw Rhydderch; Caroline, Lady Rhys Williams; Peter Roberts; Dai Smith; Richard Spencer; Peter Stead; Meic Stephens; the late John Thomas ('Johnny Millions'); Steve Thompson; the late Philip Weekes; Arthur Williams; Chris Williams; Hywel Williams; and Laurie Williams. The staff of the various libraries and archives that I have used (the National Archives, the National Library, the Colindale Newspaper Library, the Glamorgan Record Office, Cardiff City Library, Bridgend Library, the Rhondda Cynon Taf Library Service, etc.) have been unfailingly helpful.

I am grateful to the Honourable Society of Cymmrodorion for permission to re-use my article 'The Rhondda connection and the Cowbridge-Aberthaw railway', which appeared in its Transactions in 2006.

Also to the Coal Mining History Resource Centre, to Picks Publishing and to Ian Winstanley for permission to quote from the Report of the Children's Employment Commission 1842; to the Rhondda Cynon Taf Library Service for permission to use two photographs from their collection; to the University of Wales Press for permission to use a map of the south Wales coalfield; and to Anna Ratcliffe for permission to use her map of the railway system in the Vale of Glamorgan.

Above all, I am grateful to my wife Patricia for helping me to distinguish the wood from the trees, and also for her patience.

Illustrations (pp. 139–45)

Family Trees (pp. 319–20)

Maps (pp. xxi–xxiii)

xiii

Abbreviations

GCC	Glamorgan County Council
GRO	Glamorgan Record Office
GWR	Great Western Railway
M&SWCA	Monmouthshire and South Wales Coalowners' Association
OUP	Oxford University Press
PRO	National Archives (Public Record Office)
RAVGWC	Rhymney and Aber Valleys Gas and Water Company
RUDC	Rhondda Urban District Council
TVR	Taff Vale Railway
UWP	University of Wales Press
YLGB	Ystradyfodwg Local Government Board
YUDC	Ystradyfodwg Urban District Council
YUSA	Ystradyfodwg Urban Sanitary Authority

A note on the attachment of place-names to people's surname

The frequent recurrence of the same first names and surnames in south Wales at this time – John Thomas, William Morgan, David Williams, etc. – meant that (as indeed nowadays) various strategies had to be developed to differentiate the people concerned. One strategy was to make extensive use of people's second names (e.g. David *Watkin* Williams, William *Henry* Mathias). Another, even more frequently used, was to add either the name of a town or that of a mine with which they had been associated (e.g. David Williams Ynyscynon, Thomas Jones Ynyshir, Daniel Thomas Brithweunydd), or, in the case of successful people who lived in notable houses, to add the name of their house. Even here, however, because house-names were also frequently the same, difficulties could occur. Thus, William Thomas and James Thomas (who were in no way related) both lived at houses called Brynawel, one in Aberdare and the other in Ynyshir. The only solution, a clumsy one, has been to call one James Thomas Brynawel (Ynyshir) and the other William Thomas Brynawel (Aberdare). (The same problem is caused by the two 'Clydach Courts', one in Trealaw and the other in the Taff Valley opposite Cilfynydd). In this book, the names used in this way include:

David Davies Llandinam (also known as 'David Davies Ocean Collieries')

David Davis Ferndale (and his heirs Lewis Davis Ferndale and Fred Davis Ferndale)

Thomas Griffiths Maesgwyn

David Jenkins Glanffrwd (also known as 'David Jenkins Timberyard')

William Jenkins Ystradfechan

Thomas Jones Ynyshir

Thomas Jones Porth Farm

Henry Lewis Tŷ Nant

Mrs Miles New Inn

Evan Morgan Tynycymmer

Walter Morgan Forest House

William Morgan Tynewydd

Moses Rowlands Penygraig

Daniel Thomas Brithweunydd

Edmund Thomas Llwyncelyn

James Thomas Brynawel (Ynyshir)

John Thomas Fernbank

Samuel Thomas Ysguborwen

William Thomas Brynawel (Aberdare)

Charles Williams Roath Court

David Williams Ynyscynon

David Watkin Williams Fairfield

Gwilym Williams Miskin Manor

Idris Williams Brynglas

J. D. Williams Clydach Court (Trealaw)

To the memory of
Ancient Richard

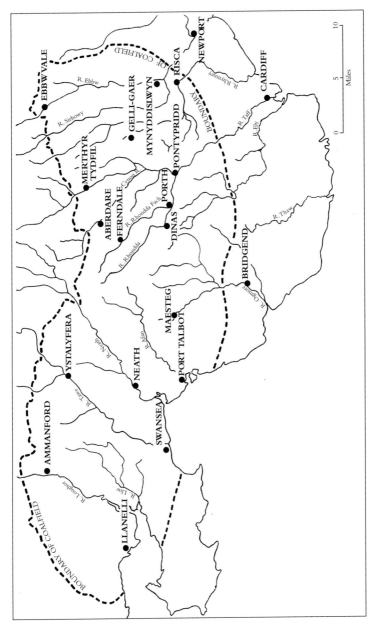

The South Wales coalfield.

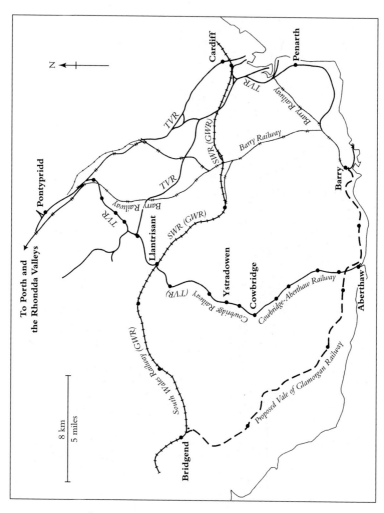

The Cowbridge–Aberthaw Railway and
the rail network around it.

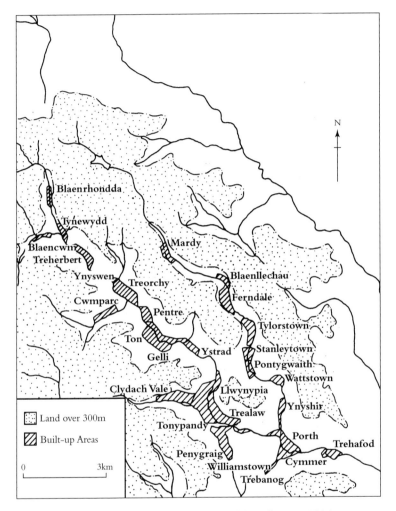

Major settlements in the Rhondda Valleys, *c.* 1920.

Introduction

1

The South Wales Coal Industry

The growth of the industry[1]

It was in the early 1840s that the activities of the south Wales coalfield started expanding at an explosive rate. There had, of course, been extensive exploitation of the resources of the coalfield (which extends in a swathe from the Ebbw valley in the east to beyond Llanelli in the west) before this time. This had, however, mainly been for the benefit of the metal industries on its periphery, which had flourished from the mid-eighteenth century onwards: the extensive iron trade at the heads of the Valleys (Merthyr, Blaenafon, Tredegar, etc.) and the copper industry in the Swansea area. In both areas, the employers had been predominantly English incomers.

These various copper and iron companies developed their own mines. The coal concerned was bituminous coal, suitable for coking. At the same time, in these areas, coal that was surplus to iron founding requirements was produced for sale as house-coal. Very little coal was exported, partly because of the problem of transporting it to the coast. What coal was exported was mainly to the areas around the Bristol Channel and to southern Ireland, transported by the coastal vessels which had plied their trade there over the centuries.

This picture was changed in the early nineteenth century by a number of factors. Firstly, the transportation of coal overland was facilitated by new methods, the canals and then the railways. Secondly, the opening of capacious docks in Cardiff in 1839 provided the possibility of major shipping having access to the coal supply. Thirdly, the importance of steam engines meant that there was a new need for steam coal (found in seams way below those of the bituminous coal that had up till now been mined), for the steam engines of the railways and for the shipping of the world. This opened up a vast and completely new market.

The first new form of transport was the canals, built as part of the canal boom of the 1790s. Of the four canals built in Glamorganshire, the two that will interest us most are the Glamorganshire Canal built in 1794 from Merthyr to Cardiff, and extended four years later to a new sea lock at the mouth of the Taff, and the Aberdare Canal, opened in 1812, which ran the length of the Cynon valley from Aberdare to Navigation (the modern Abercynon), where it joined the Glamorganshire Canal. The main shareholders in both these canals were the great ironmasters and the transportation of iron was their main purpose.

It was not until the 1840s that the railways came to Glamorgan. In 1840 the first major line, the Taff Vale Railway (TVR), linking Cardiff and Merthyr, opened as far as Navigation (Abercynon), and in 1841 the line was completed to Merthyr. Though ironmasters were prominent among its directors, and though iron was at first, in continuation of what had been the case with the Glamorganshire Canal, the main commodity carried on the line, a major aim of the new railway was also to carry coal. Indeed, two major coal pioneers, Walter Coffin (who had from 1809 onwards mined at Dinas in the Rhondda valley) and Thomas Powell (who from 1829 onwards had mined extensively in the Gelligaer area), were on the first board. They were responsible for two important extra features of the original layout of the railway: a branch line up the lower Rhondda valley as far as Coffin's pits at Dinas, and another branch line from Navigation (Abercynon) to Llancaiach (in the vicinity of the modern Nelson), to link with Powell's Gelligaer mining interests.

The TVR was merely the start of the extensive rail exploitation of the south Wales valleys, with a plethora of different companies vying for the trade – but its pre-eminence, and Cardiff's new dock facilities, meant that, though Newport (serving the Monmouthshire valleys) and Swansea (serving the western valleys) were also major coal exporting ports, Cardiff became the most successful of them all. In 1839, the Marquess of Bute (who owned most of Cardiff, and whose estates in the rest of Glamorgan contained much of the land where coal might be expected to be found) had opened the West Bute Dock, which could accommodate major seagoing vessels. This was just in time to cope with the trade provided two years later by the TVR. Three further major docks were to be built at Cardiff between 1859 and 1907, and rival docks at Penarth (1865), and Barry (1889) added further to the capacity for export from the central part of the south Wales coalfield. By 1862, two million tons of coal were being exported annually from Cardiff Docks and by 1913 this had risen to over ten and a half million. Very large amounts were by now being exported from Barry and Penarth as well. Those three ports, serving the central part of the coalfield, were in 1913 exporting 19.3 million tons, compared with Swansea's 4.7 million and Newport's 3.5 million.[2]

It was, then, in 1839–41 that the enormous Glamorganshire coal boom of the mid-nineteenth century started. At first, a large part of that boom consisted of small mines still producing bituminous coal; but soon the demand for steam coal for the engines of industry and transport took over, and coalowners sank deeper and deeper mines in order to reach its rich seams. The use of steam for shipping was soon to be the major driving force in the development of the coalfield, and this was given an even greater boost when, after a series of trials in 1847–51, the Admiralty declared that Welsh steam coal was the best available. From then on, Admiralty orders were given almost entirely to Welsh suppliers. Despite desperate efforts from the coalfields in the north-east of England to stem this, a further report in 1860 came down even more strongly in favour of Welsh coal. And it was not just the British Navy that chose Welsh coal; the same was true of the navies of the world.

The Rhondda Valleys [3]

There are two Rhondda Valleys, the Rhondda Fawr (big Rhondda) and the Rhondda Fach (little Rhondda). The two rivers flow down from the mountain range at the top of the coalfield, and join at Porth, the 'gateway' to the Valleys. From there the Rhondda flows south-east for four miles to Pontypridd, where it joins the river Taff. This stretch is known as the 'lower Rhondda'.

Walter Coffin from Bridgend had, in 1809, started mining at Dinas, just a mile up the Rhondda Fawr from where the town of Porth was later to grow. He had started by mining the No. 2 Rhondda vein, which was bituminous coal of excellent quality. But in 1812 he sank a pit to a lower seam called Bodringallt, or No. 3 Rhondda, 'very superior coal',[4] which speedily became known as 'Coffin's coal'. This coal gained an enormous reputation, 'especially for coking purposes and smith's work'.[5] In the succeeding years, Coffin sank further shafts to the No. 3 seam. Until the mid-1840s there was little other mining in the Rhondda, apart from a few small levels in the Hafod area, below the confluence of the two rivers. The opening of the TVR branch line to Dinas in 1841, however, 'stimulated the interest of mining adventurers',[6] who began to operate in the vicinity of Porth and the lower Rhondda valley. One of the first of these was George Insole, a Cardiff coal-shipper who had been mining at Llantwit Fardre, and who now, having leased 375 acres from Evan Morgan of Ty'n-y-cymmer Farm, started his extensive operations in Cymmer, on the south-west side of the river at Porth, with his first mine, the South Cymmer Level, in 1844. This was to be followed by Cymmer Old Colliery in 1847, Upper Cymmer Colliery in 1851, and New Cymmer Colliery in 1855. Meanwhile another pioneer, John Calvert, sank the Newbridge Colliery in the lower Rhondda Valley, at Gelliwion near Pontypridd in 1845. Most of this early activity, however, was in an area within a mile or so of the centre of Porth. In 1845, Leonard Hadley, a Caerleon miller, sank the Troedyrhiw Pit just a short distance up the Rhondda Fach, while just beyond it, about a mile from the centre of Porth, Shepherd and Evans sank the Ynyshir Pit, also in 1845. Meanwhile, David James had sunk the Porth Colliery (1845) and was soon to sink Llwyncelyn Colliery (1851), while in 1852 Thomas, Cope and Lewis sank the Tynewydd Colliery, right in the centre of Porth.[7]

At this stage, however, Rhondda mining represented 'no real break with the past', the bituminous coal produced being 'mainly for domestic purposes or to provide coke for industrial use',[8] with little effort being made to reach the deeper steam coal seams. This was in part because the seams of steam coal were much nearer to the surface in the Aberdare valley, where the main effort with regard to steam coal had up to now been made. It was also because, thanks to Coffin, the Rhondda was so highly reputed for the numbers 2 and 3 Rhondda seams, which produced 'housing and coking coals of the highest quality.'[9]

In this first stage of Rhondda expansion little effort was made to move further up either valley (the highest point, up the Rhondda Fawr, being Coffin's Dinas pits, and, up the Rhondda Fach, the Ynyshir pit, about a mile from the confluence in each case). This was in part due to the caution shown by the TVR, whose directors had been reluctant to undertake the great cost of building a line beyond Dinas until they knew what mineral prospects there were in the region. In 1850, however, the TVR offered £500 to anyone who would sink an exploratory pit in the upper Rhondda Fawr. This offer was taken up by the trustees of the Bute mineral estates, who decided to try to sink a pit there to the steam coal seams. A trial pit was sunk in September 1850 at Cwm-Saerbren, near Treherbert, right at the head of the Rhondda Fawr valley, and in 1851 it reached the Upper Four Foot seam of steam coal. The Cwm-Saerbren mine started production in 1855,[10] in an area that one contemporary observer described as having been until then 'a desert, as far as the working of coal is concerned'.[11]

However, with the great success of the Aberdare valley as a steam coal provider, there did not at first seem much reason for the Rhondda to ape its success. Later, however, the picture changed. By the mid 1860s, the steam coal seams of the Aberdare valley were almost entirely worked out. This was the point at which the Rhondda valleys took over the baton. From 1864, the steam coal industry in the Rhondda underwent a vast expansion, with mines sunk at Ystrad, Pentre and Llwynypia in that year, at Tydraw, Treherbert, Treorchy, Cwmparc and Ton Pentre in the following year, and with continuing expansion thereafter. A small number of people, showing considerable foresight, had however moved into the production of steam coal in the upper Rhondda Fawr and the Rhondda Fach ahead of this 'gold rush' of the mid-1860s: Carr, Morrison and Co. at the Tylacoch Colliery in Treorchy in 1855; David Davis at Ferndale in the Rhondda Fach in 1857; T. Wayne at Pontygwaith in the Rhondda Fach in 1858; and Siamps Thomas, with his partners William Cope and John Lewis, at Ynysfeio near Treherbert in 1859.[12]

Immigration to the valleys

The coal boom attracted great numbers of workers to east Glamorgan and to Monmouthshire. Initially, the vast majority came from other parts of those counties, and from other parts of Wales (and also a certain number from the west of England), often from the rural areas where, amid a severe agricultural depression, the prospect of work, and the higher wages provided by the coal industry, were a powerful incentive to move. As Chris Williams has put it:

> In comparison with other manual workers of the late Victorian and Edwardian era, albeit in scant compensation for the awful dangers they faced, coalminers were well paid, and those of south Wales better paid than most of their British counterparts.[13]

In later years, however, the fluctuations in the coal trade meant at times that wages went down rather than up, as we shall see.

As the century wore on, immigration from England became more common, particularly from the South West (Somerset, Devon, Gloucestershire and Cornwall). There were also other minorities, such as the Scotsmen who accompanied the Scottish coalowner Archibald Hood to Llwynypia in the 1860s, and a number of Irish coalworkers (though Irish immigration was mainly restricted to the navvies used in the building of the railways and the urban substructure).

The Rhondda is a very good example of the dramatic rise in population in the coalfield in the nineteenth and early twentieth centuries. Between 1841 and 1924, the number of people in the Rhondda rose from less than a thousand to almost 168,000, which was 'more than the combined populations of Cardiganshire, Breconshire and Radnorshire'.[14]

For most of the nineteenth century the predominant language in the Glamorganshire valleys was Welsh. Many of the coalowners were Welsh-speaking, and Welsh was the language of the vast majority of the workforce. It was used at home, at work, and of course in the chapel. It has been noted that 'English workmen were obliged to acquire a smattering of Welsh in order to work alongside their more numerous Welsh colleagues.' It was only later, from the last two decades of the nineteenth century, that a greater influx of English workers made a difference to this. Although at first it remained on the whole true that 'the Welsh language was still supreme in the home, at work, and in general intercourse',[15] there nevertheless eventually came a significant decline in use of the Welsh language.

Many other workers, apart from those who came to work in the mines, were attracted to the Valleys. Many came to work on the development of the railway system. Others were employed by contractors on roads, bridges, and the large amount of housebuilding needed for the expanding community.

The major contributors to the prosperity of the area were the coalowners. Except in the ironworking areas, the south Wales valley communities depended almost exclusively on this one industry, on the back of which all these other activities flourished. The precariousness of this economy was to be shown in the coal slump of the twentieth century, when the prosperity vanished almost as suddenly as it had appeared.

Unlike the ironmasters, the majority of south Wales coalowners were Welshmen. There were the famous exceptions, of course: Archibald Hood from Ayrshire, John Calvert from Yorkshire, John Nixon from the North of England, George Elliot and Edmund Watts from Northumberland; but they were the exceptions that proved the rule. The coalowners, mining coal for sale and export, were of a different breed from the ironmasters, and came from a variety of backgrounds. In the distinction which Outram draws between 'gentlemen' and 'players' among the United Kingdom coalowners,[16] the vast majority of the first generation of Welsh coalowners were definitely 'players'. Alongside the Cardiff coalshippers who decided to invest in the mines that provided their cargoes, one finds a large number of people who came locally from the Valleys, most of whom had already made a certain amount of money (whether as shopkeepers, contractors or landlords) in the area that had originally been made prosperous by the iron industry, and who now decided to invest in mining. As John Williams has put it:

> The men who developed [the industry] were themselves a by-product of the earlier activities of the London and Bristol merchants who had become the ironmasters of Glamorgan. The industrialization that had

already taken place in the county during the first third of the nineteenth century had produced a group of solicitors, mining engineers, shopkeepers and others with modest resources which they wished to employ. The iron industry was beyond their grasp: wherever iron companies were started . . . they still largely raised their capital from outside.[17]

Another area from which some of the coalowners stemmed was that of railway contracting. David Davies Llandinam was the most famous of those who, having made money from railway contracting, moved into coalmining. But there were many others, including John Calvert and William Henry Mathias.

There were also, in the first stages of the expansion, a small number of men who worked their way from lowly employment in the mines to the position of coalowner. This was because, as Williams puts it, 'local knowledge was at a premium in the coal industry'.[18] As the century wore on, however, such modest entry into the coalowning fraternity became less and less common, as the directors of the limited liability companies which had become the norm tended, more and more, to be Cardiff-based and London-based exporters and docksmen, with at most one or two directors in each case who had experience of mining (one of whom usually held the post of 'managing director'), and with the day-to-day running of the mines being left to professional managers.

The Landowners

The role of the landowners was crucial to the development of the industry. They fell on the whole into three categories (though those categories occasionally overlap). There were the absentee landlords, mainly aristocratic estates which until now had been on the whole agricultural; there were a number of small landowners, including farmers who had owned their own land; and there were those who, aware of the possibilities of the new industry, invested heavily in land in the areas where mining was expected to take place.

The greatest of the aristocratic estates was that of the Marquess of Bute, who held not only the freeholds of great portions of land in the mining area, but also owned the minerals beneath the commons within the basin of the river Taff.[19] His shrewd advisers ensured, however, that he expanded his holdings by further purchases of property. It is interesting to note, for example, that the property of Cwm-Saerbren at Treherbert, where the Bute estate successfully sank the first steam coalmine in the upper Rhondda in 1850, had been bought only two years before.[20] Other extensive estates in the coalmining area included that of the Earl of Dunraven, and that of Griffith Llewellyn of Cwrt Colman and Baglan.[21] Bute's action in sinking his own mine at Cwm-Saerbren was, however, untypical of such owners (and, indeed, untypical of his own estate's activities: the pit was sunk mainly to prove the presence of steam coal at reasonable depths in the upper Rhondda, and was leased out within two years of its sinking). Such landowners in the main preferred merely to receive the extensive royalties on the mines that were sunk, and the ground rents from the housing that was built on their land. As John Davies has pointed out, 'by the early nineteenth century active participation by landowners in the exploitation of minerals had ceased to be common in the south Wales coalfield . . . [and] by 1919 less than two per cent of Welsh coal output was mined from freeholds'.[22]

There were, of course, a number of farmers and other assorted lesser property-owners who possessed the freehold of their own properties. Though such holdings were often comparatively small, they were sometimes at crucial sites where coal was to be extracted. These owners, who usually continued to live in the Valleys, thus became among the new rich of the area. Typical examples are William Morgan of Tynewydd Farm, Treherbert; Evan Morgan of Ty'n-y-cymmer Farm, Cymmer; the Williams family of Porth Farm; and the Revd David Watkin Williams, who owned most of Ynyshir.[23]

The third category consists of those people who speculated by buying land which seemed likely to be developed for coal. They were the equivalent of those people, in the twenty-first century, who look for land which, though at present restricted, appears likely eventually to get planning permission. And, as with the twenty-first century, so in the nineteenth century the term 'speculation' was at times an inaccurate one, in that many such people relied on 'insider knowledge' when making their purchases. Many of them, having made their money in other areas of industrial south Wales's activities, made extensive purchases over many years. It was, to use a modern term, 'a recipe for printing money'.

What were the advantages of owning land from which coal was to be extracted? The first was that, having leased the land to those who were to sink the mine, you were entitled to a royalty for every ton of coal extracted. You were equally entitled to a royalty if a mine sunk on neighbouring land extended beneath your property, and to wayleaves if extracted coal crossed over or under your land. You were also, irrespective of the amount being extracted, entitled to a 'dead rent' based on the amount of ground involved.[24]

There were other advantages to the landowner, too. One was, that extensive colliery villages were built on the land, either by the landowners themselves, or by the coalowners, or by other speculators, bringing in each case substantial ground rents to the landowner. Another was that, in a narrow valley, the extent of your estate could mean that there was no way for the railway to get through except across your land – and in such cases, a hard bargain could be struck with the railway company. When the Marquess of Bute bought the farm of Cwm-Saerbren, for example, among the enthusiastic advice he was given was that the farm 'extends across the valley, so that no railway may be taken up without crossing it'.[25]

All in all, the relationship between landowners (whether old-established families or speculating newcomers) and coalowners was crucial to the development of the south Wales coalfield. Landowners were also at the heart of the development of the new settlements for the mineworkers, and also benefited greatly from the need for railways in the narrow valleys. It is small wonder that so many people who had made money in other activities during the coal boom should have used that money to invest in land in crucial areas.[26]

Dramatis Personae

2

'A dogged will, a fixity of purpose, a tenacity of spirit': Siamps Thomas (1817–1901)

Early years

James ('Siamps') Thomas was to become one of the most influential figures in the Rhondda Valleys. His origins, however, were very humble. He is an example of the 'rags-to-riches' opportunities that existed for a number of people in the south Wales coalfield in the mid-nineteenth century. He was born in 1817, in a small farmhouse in the parish of Mynyddislwyn, Monmouthshire.[1] His father, Thomas John Thomas (1781–1851), a farmer and farrier, had six sons and two daughters by his wife Mary (née Smith, 1785–1859),[2] and their financial circumstances were poor. This was the time of a considerable agricultural depression in south-east Wales,[3] and many small farmers were finding it impossible to make ends meet. In the circumstances, the Thomases did what many other people who were in the vicinity of the new industries did. They sent all their sons, in turn, out to work in local coalmines. Young James, their third son (and fourth child) was six years of age when he first went down the mine.[4]

Mynyddislwyn itself is a tiny village in a remote mountain area, and the Thomas's farm, Hen Graig Penna, was near the hamlet of Clawr-y-Plwyf, just to the west of it.[5] The church of St Tudur, beside the old road which crosses Mynyddislwyn mountain, had from medieval times been the centre of a large parish, covering 17,984 acres of land, and measuring ten miles by eight. Like so many of the formerly rural Welsh parishes before the redistributions later in the century, it contained by the early nineteenth century a good number of conurbations in the surrounding valleys, which far outweighed its rural village centre.[6] Iron had been produced there as early as the beginning of the eighteenth century, and by the mid-nineteenth century the main employment of the inhabitants of Mynyddislwyn parish was in collieries and ironworks.

The mine where James Thomas was first employed was the Waterloo colliery[7] just north of the hamlet of Penmaen (and in the region of present-day Oakdale). This mine, as its title suggests, had been sunk in 1815, the year of the great battle, by the Tredegar Iron Company, which was at that time sinking a good number of mines in the Sirhowy valley in order to provide coking coal for its ironworks. The mine was not a large one. Even by the 1840s, it was to employ merely 57 adults, 26 boys under eighteen, and seven boys under thirteen.[8] When James went down in 1823, he was not at the youngest age for being sent down the mines. As the reports of the Commission of Enquiry into the Employment of Children and Young Persons in the Mines disclosed in 1842, it was not unusual for children to be employed at the age of four, and one witness stated that 'young boys are taken down as soon as they can stand on their legs'.[9] James, like most of the youngest children, served as a 'door-boy'. His job was to look after one of the underground doors designed to stop wastage of ventilation. He had to open it when anyone, or the coal-trams, passed through, and then, as quickly as possible, let it close again. His time was passed in total darkness, and usually alone. The shift was usually one of twelve hours. One of the commission's inspectors described the life of one such boy:

> He sets himself in a little hole, about the size of a common fireplace, and with the string in his hand; and all his work is to pull that string when he has to open the door, and when man or boy has passed through, then to allow the door to shut of itself . . . He may not stir above a dozen of steps with safety from his charge, lest he should be found neglecting his duty, and suffer for the same . . . He sits solitary by himself, and has no one to talk to him. He, however, sees every now and then the putters urging forward their trams through his gate, and derives some consolation from the glimmer of the little candle which is fixed on their trams. For he himself has no light. His hours, except at such times, are passed in total darkness.[10]

The evidence given to the commission on or by the individual boys stressed, among other things, their lack of any formal education (the quotations from the boys themselves were either translated from the Welsh, or improved by the inspector as far as English grammar was concerned):

I am the oldest of the hauliers and I can't say when I began work, it was so long ago. I never went to school and can't read either Welsh or English. (*David Jones, aged 17, haulier, Waterloo colliery*)

I have been at work for four years. I work 12 hours, 7 in the morning till 7 at night. I have never been to school but gets plenty to eat. (*David Morgan, aged 13, collier, Dinas colliery*)

I have been driving horses below ground for three years and was 12 months before at a trap-door. When at the traps I used frequently to fall asleep. I work 12 hours, I would go to school if the work were not so long but I cannot go now as I have to work all night as well as the days shifts . . . I never was at school. (*Philip Davis, aged 10, haulier, Dinas colliery*)

I never get beaten but sometimes feel hungry and I work 10 hours a day and have been below ground about one year. I never was at school and speaks Welsh only. (*Richard Richards, aged 7, collier, Top Hill colliery, Gelligaer*)[11]

In his later life, when he was a powerful figure in the coal trade, 'Siamps' Thomas (as he became known) felt keenly this lack of formal education. But, as one of his obituaries put it:

As a youth Mr James Thomas exhibited a mind of peculiar strength and receptive faculties of a somewhat rare order, and though in later life he felt the disadvantage of his scanty learning, he competed successfully with men who had had all the advantages of the tuition afforded by the high-class schools of the country. His chief characteristic early in life was his desire to get on, and to shoot ahead of those around him, both in reference to the work done and income earned. Although it seemed at the outset that his life was ever to be one of toil and hardship, he persevered, and was never discouraged.[12]

Siamps gradually rose up the ladder of the underground workers, and by his early twenties he was an overman, a position of considerable responsibility, looking after an area of a mine, directly under the manager and under-manager. We do not know in which mines he worked after Waterloo, but he gained a great deal of practical experience in the process, and was soon known as someone with considerable mining knowledge and expertise, 'his ability [becoming] known throughout south Wales'. He was soon to occupy 'very prominent [i.e. managerial] positions in connection with several collieries'.[13] Such a progression into management was not uncommon in the early days of the mining boom, in the case of intelligent workers who had gained their expertise at the coalface itself.

In the early 1840s, his home was still in the Mynyddislwyn parish. We find him in 1841, aged 24, living in the vicinity of New Bethel Congregational chapel, with his newly-married wife Elizabeth (1817–60) and their first child, a son of 9 months called Thomas James Thomas.[14] New Bethel, which lies on the mountain road just a mile or so north of the village of Mynyddislwyn itself, was to have considerable importance for Siamps and his family. This was one of the first Independent chapels to have been founded in the area, dating from 1758.[15] The connection was to be a lasting one. Despite Siamps Thomas's later career outside the area, his family, and he himself, were to be buried in a family vault in its graveyard, while his grandson, the future Sir William James Thomas, was to be educated in the little chapel school (which served both as a Sunday school and as a day school)[16] on the other side of the road from the chapel.

The move into coalownership

In 1850, when Siamps was 33 years old, there came the first great opportunity of his career. William Cope,[17] a wealthy brewer in Newport who had become a coal exporter, had just moved to Cardiff,[18] which he rightly saw as the port of the future for the expanding coal trade in the Taff and Aberdare valleys. He decided to invest in a mining enterprise himself, the Troedyrhiw mine at Porth in the Rhondda valley. Like many of the enterprises in those days, it was at first a modest one, the two partners who put in most of the capital being Cope and his brother-in-law John Lewis, an Aberdare grocer.[19] As was usual in such partnerships, they needed a further partner with mining expertise – and they invited Siamps Thomas, who as we have seen had by now achieved a considerable reputation as a mining expert. As John Williams puts it, 'This kind of marriage between mining knowledge and finance was quite common, and one that was well liked by landowners.' And a number of the new coalowners came from similarly humble origins to those of Siamps Thomas:

> The diverse and occasionally humble origins of the coal owners arose primarily from the ease of entry into the industry. Thus it was at all times possible to secure at least a toe-hold in the industry on the basis of very meagre resources.[20]

Elizabeth Phillips tells us that Thomas, being 'of a most saving – not to say parsimonious – disposition', had 'by dint of strenuous work and the most rigid self-denial … gathered together a small amount of capital'.[21] While this may well have been the case, there is no doubt that Cope and Lewis could well have managed without any financial contribution from Thomas, and that any such contribution may have been purely nominal. What they were getting, by choosing him as a partner, was the expertise that they themselves lacked.

Years later an inhabitant of Porth, Idris Williams Brynglas, was to describe the impression that Siamps Thomas had made when he first came to the Rhondda valley, accompanied by his brother Thomas John Thomas:

> He could recall the appearance of Mr Thomas and his brother – well-known at that time as 'Twmi Shon Thomas' – when they came. Others came to the neighbourhood wearing black coats, stuck-up collars, gold chains, and fully equipped for sinking pits, but Mr Thomas came not on horseback, but in a brown coat and working clothes … The men with the gold chains had since gone away, while Mr James Thomas remained, and had been remarkably successful.[22]

So it was that Siamps Thomas came to Porth, which was to be the centre of his operations for the rest of his life. The Porth to which he came in 1850 would be fairly unrecognisable to those who know the major town which eventually grew up. The area had originally consisted of two large farms – Porth Farm, on the north-east bank of the river, owned by Thomas Jones and his heirs the Williams family, and Ty'n-y-cymmer Farm, on the south-west bank of the river, owned by Evan Morgan. Mines had by now been sunk on this land, and a certain amount of workers' housing erected, but in 1850 what was eventually to be the commercial centre of Porth (which developed around Hannah Street, famous throughout the valleys) was still farmland, and Porth Farm continued its existence there, despite being cut in half by the railway line.[23] At the beginning of the Rhondda Fach, between the centre of Porth and the Troedyrhiw and Ynyshir mines, there was some scattered housing, but nothing on the scale of later developments.[24]

The Siamps Thomas who came to Porth in 1850 was to remain the same throughout his, from now on, highly successful life. Success did not change either his character or his behaviour. Elizabeth Phillips, in a series of panegyrics of the Welsh coalmining pioneers in the *Western Mail* in 1925, gives us a picture which, despite her evident *parti pris* in favour of her subject, is nevertheless in some of the personal aspects a convincing one:

> He amassed a large fortune, but never changed his humble habits. His lack of education, which he had never been able to remedy, prevented him from taking much part in public life, and political matters had no interest for him … He was quite illiterate and full of harmless eccentricities, which made him a somewhat quaint figure in that age of rapid progress. In his dress he was quite original – having a great liking for large black and white checks and a gaily coloured shirt finished off with no collar, but a knotted handkerchief of bright red … He will always be remembered in the coalfield as a vigorous, stern, and determined personality, who had no time to waste upon the frivolities or the graces of life.[25]

He was a non-smoker, a teetotaller, and very abstemious. A story is told of him, which may well not be true; but it is one of those stories which are so authentic in relation to character that they deserve to be true. Apparently, if anyone came to do business with him, he put on the table bread, cheese and butter. If the man took butter with his cheese he 'was eschewed as a lover of the "flesh-pots of Egypt"', and Thomas would have nothing to do with him.[26]

All in all, Siamps Thomas conformed very much to the type of Welsh coalowner, in this early period, whom Morris and Williams have described:

> Their faults were largely the faults of their virtues. Industrious themselves, they tended to drive others; thrustful, they resented opposition; thrifty, they could become avaricious . . . Nevertheless, their relations with their men were usually best when they resided in the district and had personal contact, and their inflexibility towards their workmen was often tempered by a paternalistic outlook.[27]

A description by a *Western Mail* reporter of some of the coalowners at the time of the 1875 lockout, as they 'jauntily' arrived for their talks in Cardiff, is rather less flattering, but also rings true in some respects of Siamps Thomas:

> As you scan their countenances, they appear by no means an intellectual set of persons. Many are awkward, burly and dull-looking; persons who tread clumsily, as if the smooth floor beneath them were furrowed by plough-shares. Probably not a few were once upon a time much lower down the social ladder than now, for now – their personal defects notwithstanding – you see clearly enough something that bespeaks in them a dogged will, a fixity of purpose, a tenacity of spirit.[28]

Thomas's whole life centred around coal:

> He had no interest in anything but coal or a coal pit, varied by the evolving of ingenious and original methods of economy. To the latter he gave quite a large portion of time and thought.[29]

Career as a coalowner

Cope, Thomas and Lewis started by buying in 1850 the Troedyrhiw colliery, which lay beside the Rhondda Fach a little north of its confluence with the Rhondda Fawr, from Leonard Hadley, who had sunk it in 1845.[30] Though they were soon to become among the most adventurous pioneers in the Rhondda, expanding into a number of other ventures, they started by developing the Troedyrhiw mine itself. As one commentator has put it, 'The Troedyrhiw Colliery . . . was a diminutive concern and the real growth of the enterprise occurred when it was taken over by James Thomas.'[31] Up until then, the mine had only reached the Rhondda No. 2 seam, but Thomas sank a new pit in 1854 to gain access to the highly prized Rhondda No. 3 seam.

Meanwhile, within two years of buying Troedyrhiw, the partnership, calling itself the Troedyrhiw Coal Company, had sunk in 1852 a new pit in central Porth called Tynewydd, south of the Troedyrhiw mine, beside the Rhondda Fawr on the tongue of land at the confluence of that river and the Rhondda Fach. Here 'the No. 3 Rhondda seam was immediately struck and a number of coke ovens were established'.[32] At Tynewydd both No. 2 and No. 3 seams were worked.

Then in 1854, a mere two years after sinking Tynewydd, the partners took a daring leap to the Upper Rhondda Fawr valley, immediately after the Bute estate had, in response to the TVR's challenge, sunk the Cwm-Saerbren mine up there. In that year they leased Ynysfeio Farm from the Griffith Llewellyn estate, at Ynyswen near Treherbert, and sank the Ynysfeio mine there.[33] They were the first, apart from the Marquess of Bute, to mine in that area. Initially, however, the Ynysfeio mine produced merely bituminous coal (the Rhondda No. 3 and Abergorci seams). At that stage the partners were content to continue raising bituminous coal, without making the considerable extra effort needed to access steam coal.[34] In 1859, however, somewhat in advance of the 'steam coal rush' of the mid-1860s, they sank a new, deep shaft at Ynysfeio (the sinking, as with all their other ventures, being under Thomas's 'direct supervision'),[35] and reached the Gorllwyn and Two Feet Nine seams of steam coal. 'A period of steady prosperity followed.'[36]

Meanwhile Siamps had turned his attention to the Caerphilly area, and opened as his own concern, without his Troedyrhiw partners, a colliery called Energlyn[37] to the west of that town, which mined bituminous coal and provided work for several hundred workmen. He remained living, however, in the Porth area, at a substantial house between the Troedyrhiw and Tynewydd mines called 'Mount Pleasant'[38] (which later gave its name to a whole area of Porth). He was to remain in that house until the early 1880s.[39] Like many 'active' partners in colliery enterprises in those days, he acted as manager as well as part-owner of the mines, and he was manager of the Tynewydd and Troedyrhiw mines right up to about 1880.[40] The management of Energlyn was deputed to others (including Henry Lewis Tŷ Nant,[41] and eventually his own son Thomas James Thomas).

In 1874, he turned once more to the Rhondda, and more specifically to the Rhondda Fach, in search of steam coal. He leased, from the Revd David Watkin Williams of Fairfield, Pontypridd, a large mineral tract at Ynyshir,[42] about half a mile north of his Troedyrhiw mine, and just north of Thomas Jones's Ynyshir mine (the one originally sunk by Shepherd and Evans in 1845). Calling his new mine the Standard Collieries, he sank, in collaboration with Daniel Thomas Brithweunydd,[43] two shafts in 1875–6. The Four Foot Seam of steam coal was finally struck, 377 yards down, in 1877. This was to be the most successful of all his ventures, and the colliery with which his name will always be associated. With remarkable acute business acumen, he succeeded in buying Daniel Thomas out of the partnership at this stage, for the sum of £18,000.[44] The coal from Standard became highly thought of, as some of the best coal in south Wales, and demand was great, both from the Admiralty and from France.

By a quirk of fate, however, 1877, the year in which this coal was reached, was the same year in which Siamps Thomas faced the greatest crisis of his career. This was the famous Tynewydd Disaster of April of that year. Siamps, as manager (as well as part-owner) of the Tynewydd mine, found himself firstly in the position of an acclaimed rescuer, and then, after the inquest, in that of a man accused of manslaughter, responsible for the deaths concerned through his own negligence. At his trial, in August, the jury was unable to agree on a verdict. A second trial was held in April 1878, at which he was, rightly or wrongly, exonerated. This twelve-month saga must have been a time of considerable tension for him and the eventual outcome was uncertain right to the last.[45]

Nevertheless, Siamps from now on single-mindedly continued with his successful career, devoting most of his personal energies to the Standard collieries, while gradually withdrawing from the day-to-day activities of other mines. He remained part-owner of the Ynysfeio colliery, and also continued to own the Energlyn colliery, Caerphilly, but left the running of them to others. While he also retained part-ownership of the Tynewydd colliery, he soon handed over the managership of it to his younger brother Zephaniah.[46] The Troedyrhiw colliery was another matter. In 1882 it was renamed 'the Aber Rhondda Colliery',[47] and was now leased to other interests, though Siamps Thomas and his fellow-directors of the Troedyrhiw Company retained the head lease.[48]

Standard continued, throughout the rest of Siamps's life, as a highly successful concern. True to his former reputation for care for safety, which had been dented only by the Tynewydd Disaster, Siamps kept the mine remarkably free of major accidents.[49] In later years, he relied heavily on his manager John Thomas Fernbank, who shared in these concerns for safety.[50] The Ynyshir Steam Coal Company, through which Siamps ran the Standard Collieries, was by the last decades of the nineteenth century the only major mining concern in the Rhondda Fach to remain entirely under family control, and not to have become a limited liability company.[51]

During the industrial troubles of the early 1890s, Siamps Thomas kept his mines out of membership of the Monmouthshire and South Wales Coalowners' Association, and took a far more conciliatory line with his workers than that association had proposed to its members. The 1893 strike hit his mines, of course, but immediately afterwards he was able to declare that work went on as usual.[52]

Unlike so many other coalowners (even those from as humble origins as himself), Siamps never moved to a grand house in the Vale of Glamorgan or in one of the coastal towns. He did eventually build a large house, Brynawel, in the early 1880s; but it was on the hillside above the Standard mine, where he could keep an eye on his coal.

Among the many panegyrics which were bestowed on him in his later life, one of the main causes for praise from his workmen was that, though 'he had worked his way up from a workman to the position of a gentleman', he 'never forgot that he had been a workman.' As one middle-class observer noted, 'it was extremely satisfactory to find employers of labour residing amongst their workmen, as the Thomases of Ynyshir had done.'[53] In this Siamps was not alone. Kenneth Morgan has described early coalowners such as him, these newcomers to the already-established industrial scene in south Wales, contrasting them with the ironmasters who had preceded them:

> Many of the later industrialists, particularly the coalowners and their managers . . . were Welsh in speech and nonconformist by religion, preserving an intimate, personal relationship with their employees, with whom they could combine against the anglicized squires who ruled Welsh society.[54]

A man like Thomas, living alongside his workmen, speaking the same language and attending the same chapel as many of them, working down the mine himself, was fairly typical of his generation. But he was vastly different from the next generation of coalowners, many of whom had little experience of underground life, and left the direction of the mines to trained managers.

Siamps and his extended family

Siamps remained, throughout his life, close to his brothers and sisters. Many of his brothers worked, like him, in the mines, several of them achieving comparative success (though nothing to match his). Many of his close relatives eventually came to work for him, often in positions of responsibility. His brother Thomas, as we have seen, accompanied him to Porth. His much younger brother Zephaniah, after some years in mining, came to live in Ynyshir in the 1870s and worked in the Standard collieries, later succeeding Siamps as manager of the Tynewydd colliery.[55] His elder brother John had been an overman at Waterloo colliery (the pit in which Siamps had started his career), before moving to Church Pit, Gelligaer, then to Caerphilly (where he worked in his brother's Energlyn mine), and finally to the Rhondda.[56] John's son, also called John (later to be known as 'John Thomas Fernbank', after the house in which he lived in Ynyshir), was born at Waterloo in 1856, and went to work underground in Church Pit Gelligaer when nine and a half years old. He then worked at Energlyn at the same time as his father. When the family moved to the Rhondda, he started work in his uncle's Tynewydd mine, then went to Standard, where he was appointed fireman. Having in 1887 achieved a First Class colliery manager's certificate, he was taken on, in 1893, as manager and agent of Standard, a post in which he was a considerable success, also becoming a substantial figure in the local community, and eventually a councillor on the Rhondda Urban District Council. He was manager of Standard from 1893 to 1914, under first Siamps Thomas and then Siamps's grandson William James Thomas.[57]

Siamps's cousin, Michael Thomas (1838–1911), had started life, as an orphan, as an underground haulier at the age of eight. In 1857, he moved to Porth to work at his cousin's Troedyrhiw colliery, and there married Siamps's niece Margaret (daughter of 'Twmi Sion Thomas'). Before the age of 21 he moved away again to become manager of Daranddu colliery, but he returned to Porth, to the Tynewydd colliery, as under-manager in about 1869, when he was 31 years old (and responsible for surface operations at the time of the Tynewydd Disaster in 1877).[58]

But Siamps's relatives served, too, in more humble employment in his mines. We shall see that one of the colliers at the coalface who were trapped in the Tynewydd mine in 1877, George Jenkins,[59] was a nephew of his from Mynyddislwyn (he was the son of Siamps's elder sister, Ann).[60]

Siamps's closeness to his roots in Mynyddislwyn remained strong throughout his life. He appears to have made frequent visits to friends and family there. In the 1851 census, for example, we find him visiting his elder sister Ann (b.1808), her husband Richard (a haulier at the Waterloo colliery), and their family. They were living in a lodging-house or hostelry called Waterloo House, in Penmaen hamlet.[61] Ann Jenkins's five-year-old son George was destined, four years later at the age of nine (his mother having meantime been widowed),[62] to go to work down Siamps's Tynewydd mine. Siamps's attachment to his home territory is further shown by the fact that the graveyard of New Bethel Congregational chapel was chosen by him, despite its distance from Porth, as the place where he buried almost all the close members of his family, including his wife, Elizabeth, and three of his children who died within months of their birth.

Siamps's children

Siamps's wife Elizabeth had died in 1860, when he was 43 years of age. By her he had had seven children, only four of whom survived into adulthood: Thomas James Thomas (b.1841); Rachel (b.1843), who married the successful contractor William Henry Mathias; Mary Ann (b.1846), who married the accountant Richard Packer, who was for many years to act as Siamps's right-hand man; and Elizabeth (b.1854), who married another successful contractor, David Jenkins.

By 1881, his four children having married and flown the nest, we find him alone at his house Mount Pleasant, with merely a housekeeper and a domestic servant for company.[63] In the early 1880s, however, he settled down in the large and imposing house, Brynawel ('breezy hill'), that he had had built in Ynyshir overlooking the Standard mine. Here he was joined by his son Thomas James Thomas and his family.

Thomas James Thomas was a mining engineer. He had spent most of his early adult life in Caerphilly, where he worked for his father's Energlyn colliery, eventually becoming manager. By his first wife, Jane Phillips, who died in 1869 at the age of 27, he had one surviving child, a son, William James Thomas (b.1867). He then married Rachel John, daughter of a boatman from Upper Boat, who had been brought up by her uncle Thomas Isaac of Castle Farm, Caerphilly.[64] By her he had three daughters, Elizabeth ('Cissie'), Rachel and Sarah Maud.

In the early 1880s, he and his family moved to the Rhondda, for him to become manager of his father's Standard collieries. Originally, they lived in a large house in the Ynyshir area called 'Danygraig House',[65] but they soon came to live at the newly-built Brynawel. Siamps saw Thomas as his successor in the business, and, in his possessive way, wished to keep him and his family under his wing. It was an appalling shock when in 1885, at the age of 43, Thomas James Thomas unexpectedly died of pneumonia.[66]

The grieving father determined to erect a suitable memorial to his son. In the graveyard of Groeswen chapel[67] in the hills near Caerphilly (which was the chapel where the family of Thomas's second wife, Rachel John, worshipped – her uncle Thomas Isaac having been deacon there for forty years),[68] there was an Isaac family vault, above which there were simple memorials to the Johns and the Isaacs. Baulked of his desire to bury his son in the Thomas family vault at New Bethel Chapel, Mynyddislwyn (and it says something for Rachel's strength of character that she successfully resisted that desire), Siamps decided to make his mark nevertheless upon Groeswen. The simple memorials were now removed, and superseded by a vast monumental structure in white marble which still dominates the graveyard, with three pillars surmounted by urns. This monument must be what John Newman, in *The Buildings of Wales: Glamorgan,*[69] is above all referring to when he describes the Groeswen burial ground as containing 'an array of monuments, some of them grossly displayful'. The Johns and Isaacs were commemorated on the two outer pillars, with the much larger central pillar containing the name of Thomas James Thomas, of 'Brynawel, Ynyshir'. The inscriptions were naturally all in Welsh.

What was Siamps like as a father? 'In his household as well as at his collieries, his word was law, and he ruled his family with an iron hand. All had to work from morning till night, and little time or money was allowed for pleasure or outward adornment.'[70] Siamps was a powerful and possessive father and grandfather, who believed in keeping his family around him. His son's family lived with him at Brynawel after his son's death, and all three of his daughters and their husbands lived within a short distance of Ynyshir.

As a Welsh-speaking Congregationalist, Siamps brought up his children in that faith.[71] He and his grandson William James Thomas both attended Saron Welsh Independent chapel, Ynyshir (of which William James Thomas was to be a considerable benefactor), while his brother Zephaniah was a deacon there for many years.[72] Siamps's four children and their spouses were all prominent worshippers at various Welsh Independent chapels: his son Thomas James Thomas and his second wife Rachel at Groeswen Independent chapel; the Mathiases and the Jenkinses at Porth Welsh Independent chapel (of which William Henry Mathias was a prominent benefactor); and the Packers at Cymmer Welsh Independent chapel, Porth, of which Richard Packer was a deacon and W. H. Mathias's close friend, Thomas Griffiths a prominent member of the congregation.[73]

Siamps's heir

After Thomas James Thomas's death, all Siamps's hopes now rested on his grandson, William James Thomas (b.1867) (known to family and friends as 'Willie'). Willie, his stepmother Rachel, and his three half-sisters Elizabeth, Rachel and Sarah Maud, all continued to live at Brynawel with the old man. Willie was 18 at his father's death, and already following in his father's footsteps as a mining engineer. His early education had been at a local school in Caerphilly, and also at the small school opposite New Bethel Chapel in his grandfather's old home of Mynyddislwyn.[74] His father and grandfather, grooming him as their heir, had sent him down the mine, in his teens, to work as an ordinary collier, in order to understand the mine's workings from his own experience.[75]

The newspaper accounts of the ceremonies for his coming-of-age in March 1888 show us not only Siamps's affection and possessiveness towards him, but also give first-hand evidence of the public esteem in which Siamps was held by that time.[76] The event was held in Saron chapel, Ynyshir. The guest of honour was the miners' leader William Abraham, the local MP (always known by his bardic name of 'Mabon'). Siamps's nephew, John Thomas Fernbank, the manager of Standard collieries, 'took the chair', supported by Mrs Williams, the wife of that prominent local figure the Revd David Watkin Williams (Fairfield), who was the ground landlord of Ynyshir. Many local worthies attended (including Idris Williams Brynglas, who made a lengthy speech), as did representatives of the workmen, who had contributed to a collection which provided for the young man 'a library of over 200 books, and a suite of magnificent furniture.' Much was made of the good industrial relations that existed at Standard. John Thomas declared, to much applause, that 'Labour must have its Mabons, and capital must have its James Thomases.' Thereafter, there was much 'forelock-tugging'.[77] A representative of the surface workmen spoke of the young man's deceased father as having been 'one of the kindest men he had ever seen or worked for'. Much was made of Siamps's origins, and his life among the workmen, with a comparison being drawn between him and his grandson. One of the workmen said that they 'rejoiced to think that the young man who would be their future employer was one who had lived amongst them, and knew the position and modes of life of the workmen.' He also said, however, how little they wished to lose their old employer (applause) because, though the colliery had not been entirely free of troubles, 'he believed no colliery had given less trouble to Mabon'.

Mabon himself now spoke. He started by drawing a parallel between the circumstances of Siamps's early life, and those of his own, and then marvelled at how Siamps, with no educational advantages, had 'been able to attain a very high and most honourable position through his intelligence and perseverance, and had been the means of helping others to attain a good position in life'. He said that if Siamps's grandson William James did not attain high things, 'it would not be the fault of his grandfather, of his late father, or his kind mother, or apparently the workmen and tradesmen of Ynyshir, for Mr W. J. Thomas was the man whom they delighted to honour'. They honoured him, said Mabon, not just for the good qualities he had already shown he possessed, 'but for the good old stock from which he sprung'. He hoped William James Thomas would 'rise as high as the highest in the good family to which he belonged'.

Mabon's attitude was not as unusual as it seems to modern eyes. It was typical of an age in south Wales when the affinity between the productive classes, employers and employed, seemed greater than it would to later generations.

After William James Thomas had made a short speech of thanks, Mabon prevailed upon Siamps to speak. It is the only example we have of his public speaking. The speech was short, to the point, and not without humour. Siamps thanked the workmen for the library and furniture, and (making it clear where he wanted and expected Willie Thomas to continue to live) said: 'The library and furniture were elegant, and the recipient would not want a house to take them to so long as he (the speaker) had one (Applause)', and, referring again to his desire for his grandson to stay with him, said that 'he hoped Mr Willie Thomas would live long there, and think as much of the workmen as he (the speaker) thought of them (Great cheering)'. Siamps then seconded the vote of thanks to Mabon, which had been proposed by the Revd David Williams's nephew, Mr Whitting, and the meeting adjourned.[78]

Mrs Mary Thomas, and Siamps's last years

In about 1877 Siamps started a relationship with a woman over 25 years younger than himself, Mrs Mary Thomas (b.1843). Mary was the wife of a miner, Evan Thomas (b.1843). They lived very close to Siamps Thomas's house Mount Pleasant, in the Troedyrhiw area.[79] At this stage Evan and Mary had five children: Thomas (b.1864), John (b.1866), Elizabeth (b.1868), William (b.1874) and Mary Ann (b.1876). Three further children were to be born to Mary Thomas – Jane, or Jenny (b.1878), Edward (b.1881) and Margaret, or Maggie (b.1883).[80] These three were to be singled out as beneficiaries under Siamps Thomas's will, and it appears likely that they were his children.

During the course of the 1880s, Mary was installed, without her husband, in a substantial house in Cardiff (31 Fitzhamon Embankment, then a fashionable area overlooking the river Taff), where she lived with all but her two eldest children, Thomas and John, who were already working down the mine in Porth with their father.[81] This house was a considerable change from the workman's 'cottage' she and her husband had inhabited in Porth. Siamps Thomas appears to have spent considerable time in this Cardiff house, as a 'boarder', as he was described in the 1891 census (in which, as he was not at home at Brynawel when the census was taken, his daughter-in-law Rachel was described as 'Head' of the family there).[82]

Somewhere in the mid-1890s, when Siamps was approaching his eightieth year, he decided to stand down from the day-to-day running of his mines. We are told that he now decided to devote himself to farming, and that 'as he succeeded in other things, so he succeeded in this'.[83] He had bought a lot of land in Glamorganshire and Monmouthshire, and spent his last years at Cross Farm, Llanedarne (now known as Llanedeyrn), near Cardiff. He left the running of the Standard collieries to his manager John Thomas Fernbank, who was also expected to train up young William James Thomas for his future role as owner.

The move to Cross Farm was probably taken for other reasons as well, however. His relationship with Mary Thomas had continued to flourish. He now decided to install her at Cross Farm with him, in the ostensible role of housekeeper. That their relationship was more than that is shown, however, by the 1901 census return, in which Mrs Thomas is not given as 'servant' or 'housekeeper', but as the 'Head' of the household, which consisted of her children Elizabeth (now 32, with the surname 'Hollingshead'), William (26), Jennie (23), Edward (20) and Margaret (18), her granddaughter Janet (7), and her 'uncle' James Thomas (listed as 'colliery proprietor'), the 'family' being served by four servants (cook, groom, housemaid and stable-boy).[84]

Death, and a disputed will

'Being a non-smoker, very abstemious, and exceedingly fond of outdoor exercise, his health was always of the best, and prior to 1901 he experienced hardly any illness.'[85] In early April 1901, however, Siamps fell seriously ill. Though by 20 April the *Porth Gazette* was able to report that his illness had 'taken a turn for the better',[86] his condition deteriorated over the next few months, and he died on 29 July, 'from a complication of pneumonia and bronchitis',[87] at the age of 84.

The obituaries were many, and effusive. It had been decided that he should be buried in the family vault at New Bethel Congregational chapel in Mynyddislwyn, and so, after a short service at Cross Farm, the cortège started at noon on 3 August, for the train journey via Caerphilly and Tredegar Junction. The listed mourners consisted of his immediate family: his daughter-in-law, his grandson and his three granddaughters from Brynawel; his three daughters and their husbands; his four Mathias and Packer grandsons; his younger brothers Zephaniah Thomas (Ynyshir) and David Thomas (Gelligaer); his younger sister Harriet Matthews (Cadoxton); and his niece and her husband, Mr and Mrs Evans (Ynyshir Hotel). There were also a good number of prominent figures of the coalfield, including his partner Matthew Cope, and Ebenezer Lewis. On arrival at Tredegar Junction, the mourners were joined by nearly 1,000 employees and friends from the Standard Collieries, 'who had been conveyed by two special trains'.[88] Siamps Thomas was buried next to his wife Elizabeth, who had been interred there 41 years before. An impressive monument, bearing a massive statue of him in Italian marble,[89] was eventually raised over the grave by his grandson William James Thomas (impressive even among the many other vast and tasteless memorials raised by the Thomas and Mathias families). In *The Buildings of Wales: Gwent/ Monmouthshire*, John Newman notes that the statue on this 'presumptuous memorial . . . overtops the chapel roof'.[90] It is situated so as to look out over the valley in the direction of Waterloo Colliery,[91] where, all those years ago, Siamps Thomas had started out as a doorboy.

It is calculated that Siamps left almost £500,000. That would, in modern terms, be about £31.5 million. Like almost all his contemporaries, he believed in the principle of male primogeniture, and he left the main bulk of his fortune to his grandson William James Thomas. When it came to the minor bequests, however, there was trouble in store. He left money to Mrs Thomas's three youngest children, Edward (£5,000, modern equivalent c.£314,500), Jennie and Maggie (£4,000 each). To Mary herself he gave all his household furniture and effects, and six cows of her choice, plus the income from £4,000 'for her sole and separate use from the control, debts or engagements of her husband and so that she shall not have power to anticipate the same.'[92] When it came to his legitimate children, however, Siamps was in the event far less generous. In a will drawn up in 1892, he had proposed to leave his three daughters (W. J. Thomas's aunts) £6,000 each, plus a set of silver plate each. In March 1901, however, just before his fatal illness, he changed all that: 'He said he wanted to give his daughters six pounds each, instead of what he had left in his former will. He wanted the solicitor also to take out the gifts of silver.'[93] The new will was witnessed by William James Thomas and Mrs Mary Thomas. One can only presume that the three daughters had annoyed him in some way, to the extent that he not only deprived them of their inheritance, but also clearly insulted them in the process. The fact that his grandson and his 'housekeeper' were prepared to witness the changes, making a special visit to the solicitor's office to do so,[94] seems to suggest that they were in agreement with him on this. May it have been that, hearing of the bequests to Mrs Thomas's children, the daughters had cast aspersions on the relationship? Certainly, W. J. Thomas appears to have had considerable affection not only for his grandfather but also for Mary Thomas,[95] whom he would have been keen to defend.

The new will must, after Siamps's death, have come as a considerable shock to Rachel Mathias, Mary Ann Packer and Elizabeth Jenkins. They decided to contest the will, claiming that it 'was obtained by the undue influence of the plaintiff [William James Thomas] and Mary Thomas'. The hearing of Thomas v. Mathias took place on 18 March 1902, at the Law Courts in London before Sir Francis Jeune. The court was packed with the Welsh 'great and the good', including Mabon, who struck quite a figure in the courtroom. There were seven barristers, including four KCs. Rhys Williams, the son of Judge Gwilym Williams of Miskin Manor, held a 'watchdog brief' for Mrs Mary Thomas (presumably retained for this purpose by William James Thomas).

There appeared little hope of an agreement being arrived at, until Sir William Thomas Lewis (the future Lord Merthyr) came on the scene. This consummate 'fixer' took the various parties into 'the dark, dismal corridor outside', and worked towards an agreement. Finally, the proceedings were halted with the news that Mathias, Packer and Jenkins unreservedly withdrew their charges; in return, William James Thomas (who had been obdurate 'so long as there was any suggestion that he had acted improperly in regard to [the will]') announced that 'with a large sum of money like this coming to him, there were two aunts, two daughters of the testator, whose circumstances would make it reasonable that something should be given to them, and he had wisely agreed, with regard to Mrs Packer and Mrs Jenkins, that he would deal with them according to the advice of Sir William Thomas Lewis, whose advice he would be prepared to take in the matter.' He wished that 'it should not be said that he had been unjust, inequitable and unfair to the relatives'. [96]

Pointedly, he made no mention of the formidable Rachel Mathias, who received nothing. This could, of course, have been because of William Henry Mathias's already considerable fortune, which would have made any bequest less necessary; but if their main reasons for taking up the case had been the insulting nature of the sums given to them, the insult remained for Rachel Mathias. She had, of course, been the moving force behind the action (given her strength of character – comparable with her father's), and W. J. Thomas may well have not only seen her as the ringleader, but also borne a grudge against her for whatever she had done to cause Siamps Thomas's anger. At all events, Siamps's death had brought as much controversy as his life. And Rachel Mathias had shown herself to be her father's daughter.

How typical was Siamps

Siamps Thomas was not only one of the outstanding examples of success within the south Wales coal industry, but his career also showed how it was possible for someone to climb from the lowest rung of the ladder to a position of extreme wealth. How typical was this of coalowners in this early period? It is true that there were one or two similarly striking examples of changes of fortune. David Williams Ynyscynon (1809–63), for example, was born in Ystradowen in the Vale of Glamorgan, at a time of severe agricultural depression, in which his family lived in great poverty. When David was twelve years old his family moved to Aberdare, which was already a flourishing iron town, in search of work. Father and son became sawyers at the Abernant ironworks. Soon, however, David went into coalmining as a working haulier at nine shillings a week. Gradually, like Siamps Thomas, he worked his way up the working hierarchy of the mine, and eventually, 'with marked ability, grit, perseverance and a large measure of luck he soon attained a prominent position in the coalmining world of south Wales.'[97] In 1842, he sank a mine at Ynyscynon. There followed further mines (all in the Aberdare Valley): Williams's Pit in Aberaman, Deep Duffryn at Mountain Ash, and Cwm Dare.[98] He invested extensively in land in Glamorgan and Carmarthenshire, and left a fortune to his heirs, Judge Gwilym Williams and his brother Gomer. Another similar figure was William Thomas Brynawel (Aberdare), who like Siamps had worked underground as a child.

John Williams, however, has been right to point out that there is a danger of exaggerating the degree of social mobility in the Valleys, which was for most people 'severely constrained.'[99] The vast majority of coalowners, even in this early period, had made money elsewhere before venturing into mining, even if, in the early stages, such contributions could be comparatively modest. Alongside the Cardiff shippers who decided to invest in the mines that provided their cargoes, one finds examples of the new rich of the Valleys, including the local tradesmen such as grocers (who were among the most prosperous people in the valleys' towns). There were, for example, the Aberdare grocer John Lewis of the Troedyrhiw Company, the Merthyr grocer Samuel Thomas Ysguborwen (father of Lord Rhondda, and founder of the family fortune), and the Aberdare draper David Davis, founder of the prosperous Ferndale collieries. Others came from successful careers in other areas of south Wales's expanding economy.

Later in the century, it was much harder for people of moderate means to make their way into the ranks of the coalowners, as the deeper workings and much larger mines needed far greater inputs of capital, much of which was by then being raised through shares in the companies which now ran most of the mines.

3

'A blunt, straightforward, and from head to feet an honest man': Richard Mathias (1814–1890)

Richard Mathias, the father of William Henry Mathias (who became one of Siamps Thomas's sons-in-law) is typical of another important element in the development of the Valleys. He originally came to south-east Wales as an itinerant builder, but was to become a highly successful railway contractor, in the period of the great railway expansion of the mid-nineteenth century. His success story mirrors, in a different field and on a different scale, that of Siamps Thomas.

Of the great influx of people who came to south-east Wales in the mid-nineteenth century, spurred on by all the opportunities provided by the explosion of industry in that area, the vast majority came in the early years from other parts of Wales, one of the main areas being west Wales. Not all of them were, however, agricultural workers aiming to become miners. The ancillary work needed in order to support the mining and iron industries was an area of opportunity for those who possessed the basic skills required – and moreover provided rich pickings for those with an entrepreneurial flair. Nowhere was this more so than in the areas of transport and housing. The development of the Taff Vale Railway (TVR) and its various branch lines, together with the work of the other railway companies, was one of the main areas of such employment, while the work of providing new roads and new housing was another.

Richard Mathias was one of the builders, engineers and contractors who made their way from the rest of Wales to east Glamorgan and Monmouthshire in the 1830s and 1840s. He came of a family of builders, or 'masons', who had originally lived in the little village of Llangendeirne, Carmarthenshire. His father William, born in 1782, moved from Llangendeirne to Tenby on the Pembrokeshire coast in the early 1800s.[1] Tenby had been a thriving seaport in the Middle Ages, but had gone into some decline from the sixteenth century onwards. Now, in the Regency period, it had begun to take on a new life as a fashionable resort. There were assembly rooms, a theatre, and a thriving social life. The large old houses from the successful seaport days, which had fallen into ruin, were rebuilt in Regency style. William's move to Tenby is explained by these developments, as Tenby must have been a Mecca for the builders of Pembrokeshire and Carmarthenshire.

On 30 August 1809, at the age of 27, William married Elizabeth Griffith, and in January 1814 Richard Mathias was born, and was baptized in St Mary's Church, Tenby. His mother died shortly afterwards, and his father remarried a year later, on 16 March 1815. Richard's half-brother William, who was to accompany him to the south Wales coalfield, was born in 1820.[2]

Richard became a builder like his father. And like his father, he seems to have had an eye for areas of opportunity. At some time in the late 1830s or early 1840s, when in his twenties, spurred on like so many others by the vision of industrial south-east Wales as a place in which fortunes were to be made, he moved to the area on the border between the parishes of Llanfabon and Gelligaer, near modern Nelson. On 6 February 1844 he married Margaret Evans, the daughter of a Newport carpenter, in Gelligaer parish church,[3] and when his first child, William Henry, was born on 5 January 1845 he was baptized at St Mabon's Church, Llanfabon. On William Henry's baptismal record, the home address of Richard and Margaret Mathias was given as 'Llancaiach Colliery', which lay in the parish of Llanfabon, and was just to the north-east of modern Nelson.[4]

The mention of parishes, in records, can often be misleading to the modern eye, as we have already seen with Mynyddislwyn. One must remember that the old parishes, created when this was a mainly rural area, were often very large, and that the influx of industry had not as yet led to the redistribution of parish boundaries. The result of this was that, though often still based on country churches outside the main areas of population, the parishes now tended to contain large urban areas where the new industries had formed. Thus, within the parish of Llanfabon (Llanfabon being a small hamlet in the hills just south of Nelson) we find not only Nelson and part of Navigation (the modern Abercynon), but also a number of other industrial centres, including Llanbradach and Ystrad Mynach.

The reference to Llancaiach Colliery gives us a useful clue as to why Richard Mathias had come to this specific area. His 1891 obituary was to refer to him as having been 'for forty years a contractor to the Taff Vale Railway Co.' before he retired.[5] It appears likely that his relationship with the TVR goes right back to this time in the early 1840s, because the important Llancaiach branch, from Navigation to Llancaiach colliery and Thomas Powell's collieries in the same area, had been built at the same time as the TVR's main line from Cardiff to Merthyr, in 1841.[6]

One of the key places on the Glamorganshire Canal had been Navigation House (around which the town of Navigation – the modern Abercynon – eventually grew), at the junction of the Aberdare and Taff Valleys where the Glamorganshire Canal was joined by the Aberdare Canal.[7] Eventually, it became an important junction on the Taff Vale Railway.

Thomas Powell's Gelligaer mine had been sunk in 1829, to the east of Navigation and of modern Nelson, and had been followed by Beaumont's Tophill Colliery, and by the Llancaiach Colliery of Duncan and Co. Powell, as we have seen, was the moving force behind the creation of the Llancaiach branch line. In the November 1835 Notice for the Bill for the TVR, the following was provided for: 'A branch railway ... to or near the collieries called Llancaiach, near Pontysquire, in the parish of Gelly-gaer.'[8] The eventual line, built in 1841, stretched for four miles, from a junction with the TVR main line about half a mile below Navigation, to Llancaiach, passing through what was to become Nelson. The original plan had been for it to have extended beyond the Llancaiach Colliery, but that was not done at this stage.

It is worth noting that what was to become the major conurbation in the area, Nelson, was not mentioned in any of these contemporary documents. Indeed, it was the coming of the coal industry, but above all the coming of the railway, which was to enlarge the little village of Ffos-y-Gerddinen ('marshy ground of the mountain ash') into the township of Nelson. It is said that the change of name occurred because the railway navvies from Ireland and the West Country could not pronounce the original name, and found it easier to give the village the name of its pub, the 'Nelson'.[9]

What is significant is that in 1845, the very year we find Richard Mathias giving Llancaiach Colliery as his residence, the TVR, in face of many competing railways, was examining various possibilities of new lines in the area, including the extension of the Llancaiach branch 'as far as the terminus originally authorised by the TVR Act of 1836'.[10] If, as one suspects, Richard Mathias was in the area because he was involved in this work, it would only have been in a relatively minor capacity. Six years later, at the 1851 census, when he and his family – now including a son, William Henry, and a daughter, Mary Ann – had moved to live at the Nelson Inn, he was to describe himself as a 'builder, master employing 6 men'. One of those men was his half-brother William, who was staying at the Nelson Inn at the same time.[11]

Richard Mathias remained in this vicinity, at various addresses, during the period 1844–51, and possibly earlier, and during this period the TVR was fairly continuously at work in the area. Richard's fortunes clearly improved in the years thereafter, during which he became a major contractor for the TVR – so much so, that in the 1861 census, when living in the hamlet of Garth, south of Nelson and not far from Llanfabon Church, he was able to describe himself as a 'contractor employing 40 men'. The family continued living in the Nelson area until at least 1864,[12] and moved to a grand house in Navigation, Cynon House, some time shortly after that.[13]

Unlike the Thomases, the Mathias family was Anglican, and had close connections with St Mabon's Church, Llanfabon. All the successive family baptisms took place there, from 1845 onwards, and Richard placed the family burial vault in that churchyard. He also took on the duties of a churchwarden there for over twenty years.[14]

Through his TVR work, and other contractual work undertaken by his firm, Richard and his family prospered, as is witnessed by the impressive house to which he and his wife went to live in Navigation – and by the magnificent monument to him and his family above the family vault in Llanfabon churchyard, in which he is proudly proclaimed as 'Richard Mathias, of Cynon House'. Manifestly, his work had led to material success and social position. Our evidence of the actual work that he did is sparse. We know that he built the station at Treherbert, which opened in January 1863, and the new passenger station at Porth, which opened on 1 July 1876, because we are informed in W. H. Mathias's obituaries that he assisted his father in these contracts.[15] We also know, from the same sources, that Richard worked on the Cowbridge Railway, having been brought in as a major contractor when in 1875 the TVR finally took over the workings of that railway, which had existed as an independent body for a number of years. His work on this branch line has been described as the work 'for which he was best remembered'.

The projects which Richard Mathias the elder undertook were not exclusively concerned with the railways. He did a certain amount of work, too, for the embryo local authorities. Much of this was concerned with the building of bridges – a natural concomitant of his work for the railways. In the 1870s, for example, in Pontypridd District No. 2 alone, he tendered for three bridges and a retaining wall.[16] Presumably there would have been similar tenders for the other local highway boards. Mathias undertook extensive work to do with roads as well, and with the provision of stone for making roads. In 1875, for example, he successfully tendered for the provision of 'materials' in Llantrisant;[17] and in 1878 we find the surveyor for the Ystradyfodwg Urban Sanitary Authority (YUSA) reporting that the Mathias firm had contracted to supply limestone to Pandy, Penygraig and Ferndale.[18] One year later, the firm tendered for the provision of 'curb channel stone ware drains' at Treherbert.[19]

Richard Mathias became a pillar of local society. He was appointed churchwarden of St Mabon's Church in about 1867, serving in that post for 23 years. His professional expertise and advice must have been most useful to the parish in the period, as a church school was built in the late 1860s, and in 1887–9 St John's Church, Nelson, was built to serve one of the main areas of population in the parish.[20]

He also served on the Llanwonno School Board for a number of years, from 1880 to 1889. This board had been founded in 1871 as a result of the Education Act of 1870, and was responsible for setting up board schools in the parish of Llanwonno, and for administering them. Certain specific schools run by the Llanwonno Board catered for children from neighbouring parishes as well as Llanwonno residents, and so the board had seven members from Llanwonno parish, and two each from the 'contributing districts' of Ystradyfodwg, Llanfabon and Llantrisant. Richard Mathias was one of the two members for Llanfabon, which had a specific interest in the board school at his home town of Navigation, a town which was partly in Llanwonno parish and partly in Llanfabon (the river being the boundary). He turned out to be an extremely useful member of the board. He became a member both of the Finance Committee and of the Building and Sites Committee, where his professional skills were brought into play. In particular, amid the extensive building of new schools, and extending of others, which was undertaken by the board during this period, he was often sent, accompanied either by the chairman of the board or by the vice-chairman (the ubiquitous Idris Williams Brynglas of Porth) to inspect the way in which projects were proceeding. His judgements were at times damning, as in the case of a visit to Penrhiwceiber schools in 1881, where, expressing surprise at the slow progress and the standard of work, he also managed to show that the architect had been misleading the board. The architect was dismissed.[21]

Like his near-contemporary, Siamps Thomas, Richard Mathias appears to have been something of a rough diamond. His obituary described him as 'a blunt, straightforward, and from head to feet an honest man'. While blunt and outspoken, he also seems to have had a kindlier side: 'In whatever position, social or official, he always spoke his mind with a fearlessness which won for him universal respect, while his kindliness of heart and simplicity of character secured for him a large circle of admiring and loving friends.'[22]

He had nine children of whom seven (two boys, five girls) survived beyond childhood, the firstborn being William Henry (January 1845). They were all baptized in Llanfabon Church. All those who reached adulthood were to marry, except one daughter, Mary Anne, who lived with her parents. William Henry Mathias married Rachel Thomas, the daughter of the veteran coalowner Siamps Thomas. Richard James Mathias (b.1861) married a girl called Catherine. The four remaining daughters all married doctors: Dr Thomas Jones of Glasgow (later of Harlesden, London); Dr Rees Griffith Price of Carmarthen; Dr Rees Morgan of Llandeilo; and Dr Owen Williams, of Burry Port.

The last named, Dr Owen Williams, was distinguished enough to figure in the 1920 *Who's Who in Wales*, where we learn that he had published important articles in *The Lancet* and the *British Medical Journal*, and in 1919 had become president of the South Wales and Monmouthshire Branch of the British Medical Association. He was a JP, and a Unionist (Conservative). His religion he gave as 'Churchman', which meant Anglican. And he proudly declared that he had married 'Emily, youngest daughter of the late Richard Mathias, Cynon House, Llanfabon, Glam'.[23]

All this is a long way from the humble starting-point of Richard Mathias as a 'mason' in Tenby, or as an itinerant 'builder . . . employing six men'. By the standards of his time, his daughters, by marrying into the professional class, had consolidated the social position he had by now created for himself; while his son William Henry, by marrying the daughter of another 'self-made man' – albeit a 'self-made man' on a scale far outdoing Richard's more moderate success – had laid the foundation for a position of eminence among all the other second-generation members of the entrepreneurial class who were to dominate the Valleys in the late nineteeenth century.

It is interesting to note that when Richard Mathias died (strangely enough, intestate) on 31 December 1890, he left only £8,793 (of which the modern equivalent is about £575,000).[24] While this was in some respects a substantial sum, it pales into insignificance when compared with the eventual wealth of his son William Henry. The assets making up the £8,793 were divided equally among his surviving children.[25]

Richard was buried at a private ceremony, at Llanfabon. Those present were his widow and his daughter Mary Ann; his sons William Henry and Richard James; and his four other daughters and their spouses. 'The remains were deposited in the family vault, Llanfabon Church',[26] in which his son John Evan had preceded him in 1868.

There were many other 'self-made men' of the calibre of Richard Mathias in the Valleys at this time – and many of them had come, as he had, from rural west Wales. A very good example is the father of David Jenkins, another son-in-law of Siamps Thomas. Charles Jenkins had come to Glamorgan from Cardiganshire, where his family were farmers. The upward curve in his fortunes was swift. Between 1851 and 1861 he was working as a carpenter in Aberdare. By 1871, he had become a timber merchant in Porth. By 1881, he was a 'Timber Merchant and Contractor, employing about 80 men'.[27] The firm, 'Charles Jenkins and Co.', was then to go from strength to strength under his son David, not only holding a pre-eminent position among Rhondda contractors,[28] but also, later, working all over Glamorgan.[29]

Richard Mathias and Charles Jenkins are two fairly typical examples of the west Walian contractors, both railway and civil, who made their fortune by coming to the south Wales coalfield. By the turn of the century, their heirs, David Jenkins and Richard James Mathias (William Henry's brother, who had taken over the firm when William Henry retired from contracting in 1891) ran the two most prominent firms in the Porth area.

4

The Rhondda Second Generation: William Henry Mathias (1845–1922), a Rhondda Notable

Richard Mathias's eldest child, William Henry, was in many respects typical of the second-generation entrepreneurs of the Valleys. By his middle age, he had already become what the French would call a Rhondda '*notable*' – part of that inter-relating, networking group of prominent figures whom we find involved in almost every event or project of importance in the Valleys in this period. His financial success was enormous. Little of it can have come either from his father (who left a moderate amount of money, which was shared between his seven children) or his 'economical' father-in-law, who left only six pounds to his daughter, Mathias's wife Rachel. In his later years, William Henry Mathias was to be a byword for power within the Rhondda Valley, with his interests extending to railway contracting, coal-owning, quarry-owning, property development, directorship of companies ranging from electricity to flour mills to insurance, and – the basis for much of his power – a prominent position in local government, both on the Glamorgan County Council and on the Ystradyfodwg (later Rhondda) Urban District Council.

Early life

He was born on 5 January 1845, and baptized at St Mabon's Church, Llanfabon. Throughout his childhood, the family was living in or around Nelson. Between 1849 and 1858 five sisters were born, and then, in 1861, his brother Richard James. Though there were sixteen years of age between William Henry and Richard James, they were to work closely together at various stages of their lives.

In the 1861 census, at the age of 16, William Henry, living with his parents in the hamlet of Garth, near Nelson, was described as a 'carpenter'.[1] But Richard Mathias clearly intended his son to be properly trained for work as a contractor in a way that he, the father, never had been, and in July 1861, at the age of sixteen, William Henry was apprenticed, for a period of fifteen months, to George E. Chittenden, a Cardiff surveyor, who for the sum of twenty pounds agreed to 'teach and instruct' the apprentice in 'the Art of a practical surveyor'.[2] Chittenden signed William Henry off on 30 November 1862, declaring that he had been 'diligent and trustworthy during his term with me'.[3]

Richard Mathias took his son into his contracting work from an early age. During the latter part of his apprenticeship, William Henry worked with his father on the building of Treherbert station.[4] Though the line to Treherbert had been opened for coal traffic as early as 1856, it did not open for passenger services until 1863, with the resultant need for a suitable station building. This was built in the last months of 1862, opening on 7 January 1863. For the next few years, William Henry was to be closely associated with his father's work.

On 25 May 1865, at the age of twenty, William Henry married Rachel Thomas (aged twenty-two),[5] the eldest daughter of Siamps Thomas. We do not know how and when they met. This marriage can be seen as the starting-point of Mathias's exceptional career, and of the social status that he was to create for himself in Valleys society. The young couple went to live near Siamps in Porth. In the first years of their marriage they appear to have lived first in Siamps's house Mount Pleasant (where their first child James was born in 1866),[6] just north of the Tynewydd mine, and then, by the 1871 census, in a house nearby in the district of Troedyrhiw.[7] Eventually, in the mid-1870s, as Mathias's career took off in a big way, they moved into a handsome house, Green Meadow,[8] on the Aber Rhondda Road, which led out of the centre of Porth into the Rhondda Fach valley. Green Meadow was just south of Siamps's mine, the Troedyrhiw (later renamed the Aber Rhondda).

Rachel was a powerful woman, very much a chip off her father's old block, described in her *Rhondda Leader* obituary as having always been an 'energetic lady'. She had worked for her father, acting as cashier of the Tynewydd colliery, and paying the workmen herself on pay-day.[9] The only portrait we have of her is a photograph taken in later life; but it is a formidable one.[10] The influence either of his wife or of his father-in-law appears to have persuaded William Henry to change his religion, leaving the Anglican Church of which his family had been such staunch members, and becoming a Congregationalist, attending with his wife the Porth Welsh Independent chapel, of which they were to become prominent members and benefactors.

One must not, however, think that the marriage partnership was an unequal one. William Henry Mathias himself possessed great strength of character, in his dealings both with politicians and businessmen, and with his own family. He was also a flamboyant, confident, extravagant character, who enjoyed the good things of life, being in this a considerable contrast to his father and to his frugal father-in-law Siamps Thomas. Photographs of him in later life show us a handsome, distinguished-looking man with a fashionable goatee beard[11] (a far cry from his rough-and-ready father-in-law in his loud checks and neckerchieves).

The first child of William Henry and Rachel, James Henry Thomas Mathias, was born on 4 April 1866, followed by eight further children between then and 1884 (5 girls and 3 boys).[12] The family was to remain staunchly Welsh-speaking, in this generation and the next.[13]

The contractor, 1865–1891

We have little evidence of William Henry Mathias's activities between 1865 and 1875, though we know that in the 1871 census he was describing himself as a 'contractor employing twenty men', and in 1881 as a 'railway contractor employing seventy men'. Clearly, his career was flourishing. Though he had struck out on his own as a contractor by 1871, we know that he also continued, in the 1870s at least, to work alongside his father on certain contracts. He was certainly occupied with him in the extensive work on the Cowbridge Railway which took place in 1875–6; and for the TVR he and his father together built the new station at Porth,[14] which opened on 1 July 1876, replacing the original station which had been built in 1863.

None of this, however, explains the evident prominence that Mathias held in Porth society by the late 1870s, and the regard with which he was viewed. Such prominence will not seem out of place later in his life, when his outstanding entrepreneurial exploits would seem to have justified it; but it is surprising at this stage in his career, when he was thirty two. Be that as it may, the Tynewydd disaster of 1877 provides evidence of such prominence. When the Daily Telegraph Disaster Fund was seeking local worthies to help it in its choice of recipients of awards, the worthies concerned turned out to be three already prominent local figures (the Revd David Watkin Williams of Fairfield, the well-known local doctor Henry Naunton Davies, and the manager of the largest bank in Pontypridd, the West of England Bank) – and William Henry Mathias.[15]

Like so many of Siamps's other relatives, Mathias was himself involved in the Tynewydd rescue. The mine was very close to his house, and he appears to have been on the scene fairly early. He was also among those commended for his part in the rescue. His role, however, appears to have been a minor one.

From 1877 onwards, Mathias was working for Siamps Thomas in Ynyshir, clearing land and providing the substructure (drains, access roads, etc.) for the workers' housing that the old man was providing for those working in his newly-sunk Standard Collieries.[16]

In 1882, he was accorded a major contract, that for the Treferig Valley Railway.[17] The Treferig valley, leading north from Llantrisant, had at various times been considered as a prospect for mining, but the geological conditions in the lower part of the valley (where steam coal was at far too deep a level) had appeared to make it too difficult a venture. The upper part of the valley was a different matter, and in the mid 1870s the Glyn colliery, near Tonyrefail, was successfully sunk. The lack of a railway leading to it, however, limited its potential. Interested parties, including the lessees of mineral rights in the valley, were convinced that the Glyn's success would lead to others, and a Bill was therefore deposited in November 1878 for the Treferig Valley Railway, which would run up the valley from a junction with the Llantrisant and Taff Vale Junction Railway at Llantrisant Common.

The venture was essentially a Pontypridd one, and some of the main people involved in it were already-established acquaintances of Mathias's. The main promoter of the prospective railway was Tudor Crawshay (b.1850), son of Francis Crawshay of Forest House, Treforest, the owner of the extensive ironworks and tinworks in that suburb of Pontypridd. The secretary to the company was Walter Morgan, the Pontypridd solicitor. One of the five original directors was William Thomas, managing director of the Mardy collieries (later known as William Thomas Brynawel) who had been a close associate of Siamps Thomas (of whom he was, despite his surname and the name of his house, no relation).[18]

Though the TVR agreed to back the venture, they did not commit their own capital, and the line had to be built by the Treferig promoters. The contract was given to Mathias. The construction of the line eventually cost £3,000 more than the estimates (which, as we shall see with the Cowbridge-Aberthaw Railway as well, appears to have been a constant where W. H. Mathias's contracts were concerned). Progress in the construction was delayed because of a dispute with the local highway board about the design of two of the bridges. Mathias took part in these discussions, and his attitude when dealing with the Pontypridd District Highway Board and its chairman the Revd David Watkin Williams appears to have been characterised by the rather grand high-handedness that was typical of him in his prime.[19]

The opening of the Treferig line took place in August 1883. Already, a financial crisis was brewing. Not enough had been raised from the shares, and the company already owed substantial sums. Prominent among the creditors was W. H. Mathias.[20] The TVR, on 7 December, agreed to lend £2,500, but the financial problems continued. Finally, on 30 June 1889 the Treferig Valley Railway Company was dissolved, and amalgamated with the TVR.[21] Though the Glyn colliery had provided considerable trade for it, the hoped-for mineral exploitation of the rest of the valley did not materialise, and the venture was never the success that had been predicted. Unlike the company, W. H. Mathias did well out of the Treferig Valley venture, earning a great deal of money from the contract.

Throughout the 1880s Mathias maintained close contact with George Fisher (the chief engineer of the TVR Company),

J. H. Brewer (a roving chief engineer for the TVR's client companies, including the Treferig Company), Henry Oakden Fisher (son of George Fisher, and himself one of the company's major engineers) and James Hurman (the traffic manager). In the late 1880s, Mathias did extensive work for the TVR, particularly on such projects as the widening of the span of the road bridges in the Rhondda, when the TVR decided that they wanted to have three lines passing under them instead of two,[22] and the building of new stations (such as the Church Village station, in 1887).[23]

Finally, in 1889–91, Mathias undertook the last great contract of his career, the Cowbridge–Aberthaw Railway. The series of manoeuvres which surrounded this venture, which are in many ways typical of Mathias and his friends, present an extraordinary picture.[24] As with Treferig, the authorised capital was exceeded on the contract, and the company eventually foundered, being taken over by the TVR. As with Treferig, Mathias himself came out of it extremely well financially, being paid in all £76,845 (almost £5 million in modern terms).

This was William Henry Mathias's last piece of work as a contractor. Thereafter, his brother Richard James Mathias took over the family firm, renaming it 'Richard Mathias'. He was to make of it one of the leading firms in the Rhondda.

Councillor, alderman, justice of the peace, 1886–1922

By the time of his death in 1922, W. H. Mathias was above all associated in the public mind with local government, in which he had played a prominent role for over 30 years. Our first evidence as to that career dates from the year 1886, though one of his obituaries stated that 'as far back as 1866 he was a member of the old highways board authority under the Board of Guardians in Pontypridd'.[25] If this were so, he would have taken up such a position at the age of 21 – a remarkable achievement. Sadly, it has been impossible to find any record of his activities on the highways board at that time.[26]

The first recorded local government activity by Mathias comes on 2 July 1886, when he was co-opted to the Ystradyfodwg Local Board.[27] Mathias speedily became one of the most powerful and influential persons on the Board, and on its successor, the

Rhondda Urban District Council (RUDC) (of which he became the first chairman).

In 1889, Mathias was one of the first batch of members of the new Glamorgan County Council (GCC), for which he had stood in the Liberal interest. In 1893, he was created an alderman, a position he was to hold for over twenty years. On the GCC, too, he exerted great influence, particularly on the Roads and Bridges Committee. The balance of power nevertheless gradually changed, but it was only in the post-war period that this 'grand old man of the County Council' was to lose his seat, in 1919, to a Labour candidate. The RUDC, and the GCC, served as a potent power base for Mathias, and for his other activities.

In April 1893, Mathias became a justice of the peace.[28] Among his colleagues on the bench of the 'Lower Miskin Petty Sessional Division' were a number of old friends and acquaintances: Dr Henry Naunton Davies, William Jenkins Ystradfechan, Theophilus Hamlen-Williams, Thomas Jones Ynyshir, Ebenezer Lewis, William Morgan, Gwilym Williams, Rhys Williams, and William Abraham MP (Mabon). Mathias appears to have been a conscientious magistrate, even though, at the time of the 1893 and 1898 strikes, he seems at times to have been unaware of potential conflicts of interest.[29]

Coalowning, 1886–1922

In the mid-1880s, Mathias's career took on a new turn. While continuing as a contractor, he also undertook various entrepreneurial ventures in his own right, in particular within the coal industry.

In 1886, he entered on his first coalmining venture, joining with Daniel Owen of Ash Hall, Ystradowen, and with various colleagues from the TVR, to form the Aber Rhondda Coal Company Ltd, which leased the old Aber Rhondda mine (formerly the Troedyrhiw) from Siamps Thomas and the Troedyrhiw Company. The formation of this new company was in part connected with the manoeuvres pertaining to the Cowbridge–Aberthaw venture.[30] In its own right, however, the Aber Rhondda Company can be counted as something of a success. Admittedly, this mine was no longer at the forefront of the Rhondda mines. It was not a steam coal mine, and of the house coal for which it had been reputed the

No. 3 seam had now run out. The No. 2 seam was still active, however,[31] and it could be considered quite a shrewd move to lease the mine for a reasonably short period (taking advantage, in the deal, of its lesser value in the long term) and continue to extract the valuable coal from the No. 2 seam while the supply lasted.

The connection with the Aber Rhondda mine, on Mathias's part, was to last for some years.[32] As the only local director (the other three lived in Llanishen, Penarth and the Vale of Glamorgan), he played a major part even when Daniel Owen was chairman, though the day-to-day running of the mine was entrusted to a professional mining engineer, David Jones. After Owen's premature death in 1895, Mathias became chairman of the company. As we shall see, at times of industrial unrest it was to Mathias that the workforce and the unions looked for negotiation.[33] The company lasted till November 1901, when it was wound up because of the imminence of the expiry of the lease, and the mine was taken over by the Ynyshir Steam Coal Company, which was now owned by Siamps's grandson William James Thomas (Mathias's nephew). By this time, however, the Aber Rhondda Company was small beer, overshadowed by other major mining interests of Mathias's.

The first of these had been the famous Albion colliery, Cilfynydd – one of the major colliery undertakings of the 1890s. It was situated in the Taff valley a few miles north of Pontypridd. The relative decline in coal production in the Taff valley in the 1870s and 1880s (coinciding with the rapid development in the Rhondda valley) had now been overcome by new techniques which enabled deeper sinkings to the steam coal measures here and in Abercynon.[34] The entrepreneurs who had seized on this new area of expansion were among the most seasoned veterans of the Valleys: Matthew Cope, Ebenezer Lewis and Henry Lewis Tŷ Nant. As with many of Matthew Cope's (and his father, William's) other partnerships, at Albion one partner, in this case Henry Lewis, provided much of the mining and engineering expertise, with Cope providing capital and the Cardiff outlet (the Albion Steam Coal Company Ltd's offices being at his address at 12 Bute Crescent Cardiff, as were the Troedyrhiw Coal Company's).

When, in April 1891, the Albion Steam Coal Company Ltd was registered, William Henry Mathias became one of its most prominent shareholders.[35] Within a year, in 1892, he was on its board of directors. He found himself in the company of some of his father-in-law's closest associates: Matthew Cope (son of one of Siamps's first partners, nephew of the other, and Siamps's current partner in the Troedyrhiw Company); Henry Lewis Tŷ Nant (nephew of Siamps's first partner John Lewis, and formerly consulting engineer for the Troedyrhiw Company at Ynysfeio, and Siamps's manager at his Energlyn mine);[36] Alfred Cheney (agent for the Troedyrhiw Company in the 1870s);[37] and Ebenezer Lewis (uncle of Henry Lewis Tŷ Nant and of Matthew Cope, and brother of the John Lewis who had partnered Thomas and William Cope in their early ventures).[38] Clearly Mathias's relationship to Thomas had had some effect on his acceptance on what was a fairly exclusive board.

The Albion colliery was to become a large and successful mine, which in 1893 produced 534,000 tons of coal. It had shafts 646 yards in depth, which reached the famous (and fiery) Upper Four-Foot Seam of steam coal.[39] A branch of the TVR was opened to serve it, and by 1898 it was to have a siding capacity of 725 waggons.[40] By 1893, it was employing about 1,700 men.[41] Mathias was soon one of its most important directors, and as the most local of the directors was to be at the forefront of a number of its greatest vicissitudes in the next few years: the Albion disaster of 1894, and the major strikes of 1893 and 1898.

An interesting but abortive venture in which Mathias involved himself around this time shows the extent to which his appetite for mining activities had been whetted. At a sale between 24 and 28 July 1893, we find him buying up the fixed plant and machinery of the old Dinas colliery (which had just been forced to close), at a cost of nearly £20,000, 'with a view, if possible, of resuming operations'. Coffin's old colliery had mined the Rhondda No. 3 seam of bituminous coal, and that had in large part been worked out. Mathias's aim, as declared to the newspapers, was to 'penetrate to the lower measures and work those rich seams of steam coal which hitherto have been untouched.' For this purpose, he would be endeavouring to obtain the necessary powers from the local landlord. The *Pontypridd District Herald*, welcoming the 'enterprise of a local gentleman', described the great satisfaction this news had given to the inhabitants of Dinas; much local depression had been caused by the stoppage of the colliery.[42] Sadly, however, nothing further appears to have come of this. This may have been because Mathias became aware that his project to develop Dinas as a steam coal mine was impractical; or it may have been that the great strike which, within a few days, was to engulf the south Wales coalfield, brought home to Mathias some of the risks pertaining to such a venture.

In 1901, Mathias became a director of another major colliery enterprise. This was the newly-formed Windsor Steam Coal Company (1901) Ltd, formed to mine and sell the coal from the Windsor colliery at Abertridwr in the Aber valley between Caerphilly and Senghenydd.

This was an Insoles project, the mine having been sunk in 1896 by Thomas Griffiths, manager of Cymmer (Porth) and a director of the parent company, who now also became manager of Windsor. The board of directors was a small one. Insoles were represented on it by George Insole (chairman) and William Henry Lewis, both directors of the parent company. Then there were W. H. Mathias and a further two directors: Robert Forrest, agent to the Earl of Plymouth, who had sat with Mathias on the Glamorgan County Council for the past twelve years; and J. Forster Brown, the well-known mining engineer. In 1908, the latter was succeeded by another prominent mining engineer, Ithel Treharne Rees (who had been closely associated with the Albion colliery), while William North Lewis took the place of his recently deceased father W. H. Lewis on the Board. In 1909, Thomas Griffiths became an additional director.[43] The secretary throughout this time was Alfred North Lewis, William North Lewis's brother (who was also son-in-law of Mathias's intimate friend and colleague James Hurman, traffic manager of the TVR).[44]

Mathias continued as an active director of both Albion and Windsor until his death in 1922. At Albion, dramatic changes took place in 1910. In that year, D. A. Thomas's Cambrian Combine obtained a controlling interest in the Albion Company, as part of its great expansion in this period. The board just before this had been: Matthew Cope (chairman), Henry Lewis (managing director), Alfred Cheney, William Henry Mathias, and William Cope

(Matthew Cope's son, who had joined the board in 1907). After the Cambrian Combine's takeover, however, a complete change in the board occurred. All the current directors, apart from W. H. Mathias, disappeared, and Mathias became chairman and managing director (he appears to have met that demanding man D. A. Thomas's exacting criteria for a good chairman). Four new members of the board appeared, part of the close-knit world of Cardiff coal-exporting, whom one would be tempted to call the 'Penarth mafia', in that they mostly lived in large houses in the prosperous little town at the entrance to Cardiff Bay: John Andrews, who lived at Rogermoor House, Penarth; Stephen O'Callaghan, a Cardiff businessman of Irish origin, who lived at Dros-y-Môr, Penarth; Charles O'Callaghan, his brother; and Graeme Forrester.[45]

Whatever the politics involved in the changes, W. H. Mathias came out of it well, with his position considerably strengthened, while the rest of his colleagues had to leave.

Other business interests, 1900–1922

W. H. Mathias's exposure to the Cardiff business world, occasioned partly by his links through the Albion and Windsor companies and partly by the contacts he was able to make on the Glamorgan County Council, seems to have encouraged him to extend his commercial interests outside the closed world of the Valleys. One of the people who appears to have acted as a contact for him in this area was Alfred North Lewis, his colleague in the Windsor Steam Coal Company (1901) Ltd. One of the first opportunities to which Lewis alerted him was in the world of flour milling.

Alfred North Lewis was a director (later managing director) of 'Spillers Nephews Ltd', a sister-company of 'Spillers and Bakers', a major milling company.[46] In 1903, a new company was set up, under the aegis of Spillers and Bakers, called Cardiff and Channel Mills Ltd.[47] It was the amalgamation of two concerns, based in Cardiff: the Phoenix Milling Company Ltd, and the New Cardiff Milling Company Ltd, the latter of which had been running at a loss for twelve years or so. The amalgamation with Phoenix was aimed at righting the situation. Spillers and Bakers must have seen potential in this, as must the various experienced and hardheaded people who were amongst the first subscribers to Cardiff and Channel Mills. They included Charles Williams of Roath Court (a major Cardiff landowner, who owned a considerable amount of land in the Roath area of the city, which had recently been developed for housing), and also a large number of people and firms experienced in the flour trade, who invested considerable sums in it. W. H. Mathias appears to have been enough convinced of the viability of the project to become the principal shareholder, with 9,600 shares. Apart from Mathias and Charles Williams, the other major shareholders were three firms of grain merchants from Bristol and Bradford-on-Avon, and three prominent Cardiff millers, Ernest Nicholls of Penarth, Edgar Nicholls of Llanishen, and Walter Allen of Llanishen, all three of whom were directors of Spillers Nephews alongside Alfred North Lewis.[48]

Mathias became one of the founder directors of the company. His fellow-directors were Charles Williams (chairman); William Garnett, a Bristol corn merchant; Ernest Nicholls; Edgar Nicholls; and Walter Allen. Mathias and Williams, neither of whom appears to have had a previous acquaintance with the milling industry, were presumably there because of their money and their business acumen. When Charles Williams died in 1908 he was not replaced on the board, and so Mathias became the only non-specialist director.[49]

It has to be said that Mathias's faith in the future of the business appears to have been justified. The professional input provided by Spillers was successful in turning around the business, and the shares rose steeply in value. Those who had invested in it had no cause for regret.

A year after joining Cardiff and Channel Mills, Mathias in 1904 became a director of another newly-formed concern, in a vital area of south Wales's expanding economy. This was the Treforest Electrical Consumers Company Ltd, a cooperative that had been formed to save the South Wales Electrical Power Distribution Company, a body which had been getting into serious financial difficulties.[50]

This company had had four power stations: Bridgend, Neath, Treforest and Cwmbran. In the area served by the Treforest station, which was situated in Upper Boat, there were a number of major consumers, including the Albion Steam Coal Company in Cilfynydd, the Lewis Merthyr Consolidated Collieries in Trehafod, the Great Western Colliery Company in Hopkinstown, the Windsor Steam Coal Company (1901) in Abertridwr, and the National Collieries in Wattstown.[51] These consumers, alarmed at the potential loss of their supply, and at the added cost the provision of another supply would doubtless entail, came to the rescue of the ailing company, forming the Treforest Electrical Consumers Company, which would take over the South Wales Company's distribution network, and at the same time rationalize its activities. Its remit, in an Act of 1908, was to 'work, maintain and manage the generation and supply of electrical energy within the area of supply of the Statutory Company.'[52]

Given that Mathias was a director of two of the major consumer companies (Albion and Windsor), and given his forceful and effective methods of management, it was natural that he should become a director of the new collective. He was joined on the board by two other representatives of Windsor, Alfred and William North Lewis; while his old friend and colleague Thomas Griffiths joined the board of the South Wales Electrical Power Distribution Company,[53] with which the Consumers' Association now worked in tandem.

Speedily, the enterprise was rationalised, initially mainly to the benefit of the area in which the major client companies were situated. The Bridgend and Neath power stations were sold to the local authorities, and activities centred on the Pontypridd district, served by Treforest, and on the area around Cwmbran. In the next ten years, the plant was continually added to, and the generating capacity was almost quadrupled. Then, during and just after the First World War, the network was extended to the Pontymister district (to serve steel plants and other concerns in that area), and to the Vale of Glamorgan.[54] After the war, there was a considerable growth in demand, much of it from domestic households. The consumers' collective wound itself up at about the time of W. H. Mathias's death in 1922, and handed the running of the enterprise back to the South Wales Electrical Power Distribution Company.

Another non-coal directorship of Mathias's was his membership of the Welsh Board of the Ocean Accident and Guarantee Corporation Ltd. It was a well-known and powerful insurance firm, and presumably he was chosen to serve on the Welsh board as the competent company man that he had become.

In the first decade of the twentieth century, W. H. Mathias expanded his interests into a great many new areas. Typical of his entrepreneurial flair was his involvement in the company formed to build a pier at Weston-super-Mare. This project had been under consideration since the early 1890s, but it took three South Wales entrepreneurs (Mathias, his close friend and collaborator James Hurman,[55] and Sir John Gunn), together with a Bristol landowner, Alfred Deedes of Frenchay Manor, to overcome all difficulties, including opposition from the local authority, and get the scheme off the ground. These four became the directors of the Pier Company. The first section of the pier was inaugurated with great celebrations on 13 June 1904.[56]

Property, 1890–1922

In the period from about 1890 to his death in 1922, W. H. Mathias bought a great deal of property. Much of this was in the form of land with mineral rights, where coalmining activities were either taking place, or might do so in the future. As we shall see in the case of the 104-acre Parc Newydd farm at Abertridwr, which he and Walter Morgan bought in or before 1892, leasing it thereafter to Insoles and to their Windsor Steam Coal Company (1901) Ltd,[57] such properties may often have been bought on the basis of insider knowledge as to mining intentions. Other properties of his included a half-share (again with Walter Morgan) in a 208-acre farm in Clydach Vale, leased from 1889 to D. A. Thomas's firm Thomas, Riches and Co.; two-thirds of a 240-acre farm at Maindy, near Llanharan, leased from 1909 to W. W. Hood of the Glamorgan Collieries, Llwynypia; the whole of an 86-acre farm near Gilfach Goch, leased from 1911 to the Britannic Merthyr Colliery Company Ltd; the whole of a 58-acre farm near Taffs Well, leased from 1912 to Baldwins Ltd; and the whole of another farm near Gilfach Goch, leased from 1919 to Glenavon Farm Collieries Ltd.[58] The royalties from these properties were considerable.

Mathias also invested in quarries, the most successful of which was the Fforest Quarry, Llanharry (just south of Llantrisant), on which both rent and royalties were paid by Glamorgan Quarries

Ltd.[59] A branch line from the Llantrisant–Cowbridge Railway was created to serve this quarry.[60]

He also bought agricultural properties, in Radnorshire and in the Vale of Glamorgan. He eventually owned seven farms in Radnorshire,[61] including Bryn-y-Groes[62] at Howey, near Llandrindod Wells. These he let to tenant farmers. Mr Davies, the last in the line at Bryn-y-Groes, described in 1980 how Mathias used to bring shooting-parties up to mid Wales. As a boy, he had seen and admired Mathias, who had appeared like a grand being from another planet. One thing in particular had taken his fancy: Mathias's habit of having his initials, WHM, engraved on the gates of each of his farms.[63] Lamb and mutton from Mathias's farms, here and elsewhere, found its way into the shops of Thomas and Evans, in the south Wales valleys.[64]

In Glamorgan, between 1891 and 1895, at the height of his association with Daniel Owen of Ash Hall, Ystradowen (near Cowbridge),[65] Mathias bought considerable land in the parish of Ystradowen. The purchases were large enough for Mathias to be listed, in the 1895 *Kelly's Directory* (and in succeeding volumes of it), as one of the three 'principal landowners' in the parish, the other two being Daniel Owen (succeeded after his death in 1895 by his son Tudor Owen) and Aubrey Aubrey Esq., of the prominent and ancient local family.[66]

The other major property investment that Mathias made was in grand houses. As a director of Albion colliery, he seems to have felt the desire to have, like his father-in-law Siamps Thomas, a great house overlooking his mine. An opportunity arrived at the death in 1898 of Colonel Grover, a prominent local figure who on his retirement from the army had become town clerk of Pontypridd, and who lived at Clydach Court in the Taff valley.[67]

This Clydach Court must not be confused with the Clydach Court at Trealaw in the Rhondda, owned by Mathias's friend and local government ally J. D. Williams. It was a large mansion in the Taff valley, on the west side of the river, situated at the junction of the road from Ynysybwl with the road from Pontypridd to Abercynon. 'The gardens were noted for their beauty, which was enhanced by a magnificent fountain on the lawn in front of the house ... The gardens, lawns, fountains and the rare trees attracted visitors from far and wide.'[68] The house was important enough to have given its name to the Clydach Court Halt (later Clydach Court Junction) on the Taff Vale line from Pontypridd to Merthyr. While the colonel lived there, the house had become known as 'Grover's'. It lay directly opposite Cilfynydd and the Albion colliery, whose workings extended below and beyond the Taff to the grounds of Clydach Court; this is borne out by the name of one of the main levels of the mine, 'Grover's Level'. Having bought this house, however, Mathias does not seem to have used it extensively himself. Occasionally it was let, but for long periods of time it remained uninhabited except for the caretaker, Thomas Price, who lived in a house, Clydach Cottage, in the grounds.[69] During the First World War, Mathias let the house, free of charge, to thirty-three Belgian refugees.[70]

Despite possession of this and other properties, Mathias and his family remained living in Porth. They did, however, move to a very much grander residence. This was Tynycymmer Hall, built by the Morgan Family of the Ty'n-y-cymmer estate in large grounds just up Cymmer Hill from the centre of Porth, overlooking Porth Bridge. When it became vacant in early 1906, Mathias clearly felt that it was a dwelling fitting to his new status, and bought it. He, his wife Rachel, and those of his children who were not yet married, moved there from Green Meadow some time between March and October 1906.[71]

Typically, Mathias kept Green Meadow but put it to practical use, developing its frontage on Aber Rhondda Road as 21 terraced houses (numbers 128 to 148) of which he retained the freehold, and leasing the house itself, with its stables, workshop and land, to the Rhondda Tramway Company.[72]

In 1911, he bought another large house, Great House, a seventeenth-century mansion in Llanblethian, next to Cowbridge in the Vale of Glamorgan. Its most recent owners had been Hancocks the brewers, whose chairman, Joseph Gaskell, lived there from 1893 to 1911.[73] It hardly seems a coincidence that Mathias's nephew, William James Thomas, had recently, in 1907, also bought an extensive property in Llanblethian, a great house in extensive grounds called Crossways (formerly owned by the Bassett family of Beaupre).[74] There is little evidence of Mathias having used his house, while Thomas seems to have bought his mainly for the use of his half-sister Cissie.[75] Their presence in the area was not a long one, and in Mathias's case (we have some evidence of previous financial transactions in the Cowbridge area, including the provision of mortgages to property buyers) the main motive in buying Great House may well have been purely speculative. Certainly he sold it in 1920 at a considerable profit (the price having doubled in nine years).[76] It was sold to the shipowner Owen Williams (to whom William James Thomas had sold Crossways three years previously).

Position in local society in Porth

W. H. Mathias, from the 1890s onwards, became a figure for adulation in the Valleys newspapers (and in the south Wales press in general). Much of this praise related to his work in local government. He was regularly described as 'Alderman W. H. Mathias, of Porth, one of Glamorgan's most useful public men.'[77] The *Porth Gazette* continually noted his virtues as a local politician, and his 'great practical and commercial knowledge', which '[has] been such an undoubted boon to the ratepayers.'[78] His obituaries in 1922 went even further. The *Porth Gazette*, for example, described him as 'the County's GOM'.[79]

From all we know of Mathias, he would no doubt have thoroughly endorsed these opinions of himself. He was never one to underestimate his own worth. In the years up to the First World War he held a very prominent position in Porth society. His status in the public mind, as early as 1894, is shown by an item in the gossip column of the *Pontypridd Chronicle*, which deplored the fact that the last train from Pontypridd, nicknamed 'Alderman Mathias's train', went only as far as Porth:

> The Rhondda people justly complain that the last train does not go further than Porth, and are making every effort to induce the Taff Company to run it as far as Treherbert. It was jocularly observed at Thursday night's meeting that the train was run for the convenience of Alderman Mathias! At all events it is called that gentleman's train, and I trust that he will lend the weight of his influence to get the company to accede to the prayer of the people.[80]

It is hardly surprising that he should have seen himself as one of the outstanding figures of the Valleys. Something of his self-importance comes out in a speech he made at a presentation in Porth to his old companion-in-arms Thomas Griffiths, in 1906:

> The oil painting was then presented to Mr Griffiths by Alderman Mathias, who remarked that it gave him very great pleasure to make the presentation, because Mr Griffiths was one of his oldest friends in the valley, extending back over a period of 42 years. They had always been friends, and had worked together on public bodies for many years. Mr Griffiths was the oldest public man in the district, and he (Mr Mathias) came second (Hear, hear).[81]

After his move to Tynycymmer Hall in 1906, Mathias took his new position as the 'squire of Tynycymmer' seriously, and took a prominent part in many local activities. In 1907–8, for example, he was elected president of the Porth Chamber of Trade,[82] a position in which he was succeeded for 1908–9 by his nephew William James Thomas.[83] At most gatherings of the worshippers from Porth Welsh Congregational chapel he, almost as of right, took the chair. He was also prominent among the subscribers to the various local charities, and at public meetings of all kinds. In these activities his name was often linked with his sisters- and brothers-in-law, the Packers and the Jenkinses, who shared the same social base in the Congregational Church, and also with his nephew William James Thomas.[84]

What is notable, in Mathias's relationships with his extended family, is the cordial terms on which he seems to have remained with the Thomas family of Brynawel, even after the acrimonious court case in relation to Siamps Thomas's will. This may well have been because Mathias was aware of the value of the Thomas connection, and because both he and William James Thomas realised that their common interests outweighed any personal animosities. It may also have been that W. H. Mathias had taken no part, nor wished to, in his wife's activities (there is no mention of him in the report of the court proceedings), and was seen by W. J. Thomas to be neutral in the matter. Whatever the reason, the two men appear to have worked well together, both on local bodies and on the county council. Mathias was a generous contributor, too, to the two hospital causes closest to his nephew's heart, the King Edward VII Hospital in Cardiff and the Porth Cottage Hospital.[85] All in all, the Thomases and the Mathiases kept up a close relationship and, though Siamps had tended to keep out of public affairs, after his death the two families were at the forefront of social events in the Porth area. Something of the position they (and Mathias in particular) had attained in the local community is shown by the prominent part they took in royal visits to the Rhondda – that of Princess Louise[86] and the Duke of Argyll in July 1909, and that of King George V and Queen Mary in June 1912.

Princess Louise's visit was devoted almost entirely to the area comprising Porth, Trealaw and Ynyshir. She and the Duke of Argyll arrived in Wales on 22 July 1909, and stayed overnight at Miskin Manor as guests of Rhys Williams. The 23rd was devoted to Williams family interests. The royal party was taken to Trealaw. There the princess opened 'The Judge's Hall' (or, more formally, the 'Judge Gwilym Williams Memorial Hall'), which Rhys Williams had presented in honour of his father to this township, whose coal-producing capability formed an important part of the Williams family's wealth. The other day of the visit, 24 July, was devoted to Porth and Ynyshir. The Thomas and Mathias families were both prominent in this. In Ynyshir, one of W. J. Thomas's sisters presented a bouquet to Princess Louise; in Porth, Gwen Mathias, William Henry's youngest daughter, aged 25, performed the same office. In Porth W. H. Mathias and Gwen were both members of the small platform party, together with Thomas Griffiths and his wife, William Evans (founder of the firm of Thomas and Evans), two officials, and David Jenkins, survivor of the Tynewydd Inundation (of which the shadow still remained central to Porth folklore). After Gwen had 'charmingly' presented her bouquet, 'Mrs Griffiths and Alderman Mathias were presented and introduced to the royal party.' David Jenkins then presented a miner's lamp of solid gold to Princess Louise, who had shown her profound knowledge of mining areas when she exclaimed, seeing some miners who had come straight from work, 'Oh, look at those black men!', at which 'the visitors laughed heartily as it was explained to them that the men were miners.'[87]

The King and Queen's visit in 1912 was a very much less leisurely affair. The time between their getting off the train at Trehafod and getting on it again at Porth to go further up the valley, was to be only thirty-five minutes, during which time they were to visit the Lewis Merthyr Colliery at Trehafod and the new Miners' Rescue Station at Dinas. They were accompanied on the train by Lord Merthyr (owner of the Lewis Merthyr mine) and by members of the Royal Household. Short as the royal visit was, however, William Henry Mathias managed to get in on the act. The party greeting the royals at Trehafod was listed in the *Porth Gazette*; Mathias's was the first name mentioned. The party again included William Evans, and also the redoubtable figure from the Labour movement, Councillor D. Watts Morgan:

> The Royal Party were met at the station by Alderman W. H. Mathias, JP, Porth; Councillor D. Watts Morgan, Miners' Agent; The Revs. John Williams, Trehafod, and W. Thomas, Porth; Councillor William Evans, Porth; Dr R. C. Joyce, Porth; Mr W. H. Bray, Head Surveyor of the Lewis Merthyr Collieries; and Mr Richard Evans, Traffic Manager of the Collieries.[88]

Final years, 1914–1922

Mathias's wife Rachel died on 1 July 1914, after five years of a serious illness that appears to have been a form of paralysis.[89]

We have little evidence, apart from his activities on the Glamorgan County Council, as to what Mathias did during the First World War. Unlike his nephew William James Thomas, he did not involve himself in fundraising for the war effort, nor did he, so far as we know, make any substantial contributions himself, though he did allow his house Clydach Court to be used free of charge by Belgian refugees.

He was, of course, almost seventy at the outbreak of war. There was, however, one new organisational role that he took on at this stage. He became chairman of the Welsh Committee of the Government's Road Stone Control Committee,[90] set up to ensure the proper use of, and stockpiling of, stone for use in roadbuilding, and further to ensure that enough manpower was available.

According to an official account in 1917, however, this committee had turned out not to be really needed, as 'the local authorities have now in stock such quantities of such stone as amount to over three times the total average pre-war requirements.' Also, 'there is a surplus of labour engaged in producing material for road repair, and no ground whatever for exempting men so engaged.'[91] Nevertheless, whatever the usefulness of the committee, the fact that Mathias was chosen to chair it shows how high his reputation was for expertise in such matters.

In the post-war period Mathias's defeat in the 1919 county council elections hit him hard, and he appears to have gone through a period of depression as a result, despite the fact that it might, at his age, have been reasonable to think of retirement at any rate. In April 1922, he fell seriously ill. It was hoped that, 'despite his advanced age, his wonderful physique and fortitude would once more serve to restore him to comparative health.' He was attended by his son-in-law, Dr George Dawkin, and by a Cardiff doctor.[92] Three weeks later, he died.

His eminence was shown not only by the extensive and fulsome obituaries in the Welsh national newspapers, the *Western Mail* and the *Cardiff Times*, but also by the fact that his death was reported in a short article in the *Times* of London.[93] His great services to the community were stressed on all sides. As the stipendiary magistrate D. Lleufer Thomas commented, 'It was as though a great landmark had been swept away from their midst.'[94]

Conclusion

William Henry Mathias is a prime example of those successful second-generation entrepreneurs in the Valleys who built upon, and further enhanced, the achievements of their fathers. One thinks of D. A. Thomas (Lord Rhondda) and his father Samuel Thomas, or of Matthew Cope and his father William Cope. Mathias had two formidable forebears – his father and his father-in-law. But, unlike those just mentioned, he did not inherit a great deal in monetary terms in the will of either, and he is unlikely to have received much from his tight-fisted father-in-law in the latter's lifetime. He did, however, inherit things of value from them: from his father, the skill of a highly-trained railway contractor; and from his father-in-law a whole range of contacts in the entrepreneurial world of the Valleys, and a reflection of the glory of the old man's reputation as one of the founding fathers of the steam coal industry in the area.

W. H. Mathias made great use of networking. This would, however, have been nothing without the evident flair he had for business affairs. Nobody would have bothered to put him on their boards unless that clearly would have been of advantage to them. No amount of contacts could make up for a lack of capability. Mathias was clearly an outstanding businessman. Starting out as a practical contractor and engineer, he gradually became more and more involved as a captain of industry. In the process, he carved out for himself a pre-eminent position in the society of the Rhondda Valleys. As the barrister Rhys Williams said of him at the House of Lords hearing of the Rhymney Valley Water Board Bill in 1911, he was 'a practical business man, and a man who is interested in a great number of undertakings in south Wales'.[95]

One important respect in which he differed from his father-in-law Siamps Thomas (and from his nephew William James Thomas) was in his relationship with his workers. Where Siamps Thomas seems genuinely to have seen himself as one of their fellow-workers (and indeed, as we have seen, his workforce actually included close relatives of his), Mathias saw himself as a cut above them. Indeed, it sometimes seems as though he regarded them as being of a different race.[96]

Mathias's attitude to the workforce was mirrored in the attitudes of the directors of the Albion Colliery in the 1893 strike, whose hard line was markedly different from that of Siamps Thomas's Standard Collieries. Mathias appears to have had much in common with the hardline Albion managing director, Henry Lewis Tŷ Nant. While admiring Mathias's energy and capability, we must never forget that much of what he achieved was at the expense of others. And while this was the common attitude of a whole class of people, his forceful character made of him one of the more ruthless operators of his time.

He was a man of great physical energy, even into comparative old age. At those disasters that he attended, his assiduity and capability for organisation of the rescuers were noted. He obtained a minor award for his activities at the Tynewydd disaster in 1877, and at Albion in 1894 he took charge of the rescuers on the surface from the start, his activities being widely reported in the newspapers. This capacity for organising rescues and making practical arrangements in the aftermath of a disaster remained with him right into his late sixties, when in 1911 he was one of the passengers on the train from Porth to Pontypridd which collided with a 'mineral train' in the vicinity of Hopkinstown. There were many deaths. Mathias, who had been travelling in a first-class carriage that had been untouched, was observed by a passenger from another train, as he 'rendered valuable assistance in directing the rescue work' and gave 'considerable aid to the injured.'[97] This observer noted the old man's evident expertise, as he gave advice 'how to shore up the debris while the searchers were trying to get out the injured and the dead'.[98]

Mathias had the self-confidence of so many of his entrepreneurial contemporaries. He felt that he held an important position in society, and had no qualms in saying so, and in behaving in ways that in any other context (and even in this context) would seem unbearably arrogant. But his own assessment of himself appears to have been typical of the way those around him thought of themselves. Not for them the understatement of the heirs of 'old money'; they had created their own 'new money', and were proud to let everyone know about it.

He was a forceful man, always determined, even in the most minor situations, to get his way, even if that involved the suffering of others (as in his dealings with the Rhymney and Aber Valleys Gas and Water Company, where he was prepared to cut off the water supply from his tenants in order to win a dispute over a comparatively minor sum of money).[99] This determination extended also to his dealings with his own family, with whom he was possessive and often domineering.

The way in which he differed from so many other people of his type, however, was the fact that he remained centrally based in the Rhondda – in Porth, the hub of the Valleys. Where so many others moved either to the Vale of Glamorgan or to the leafy suburbs of Cardiff, he appears to have had, like his father-in-law Siamps Thomas, no desire to do so. His family life continued to be

Welsh-speaking, his social life centred around the Porth Welsh Congregational Church. Within Porth middle-class society he held a pre-eminent place.

5

The Rhondda Second Generation:
Some Other Major Figures

Fortunes were made in the Rhondda by various means: by owning property which was used for mining; by owning or exploiting mines; by becoming major contractors on the railways or in the townships; by property development; by opening prosperous shops. The early pioneers built their fortunes often by risks and usually by unremitting hard work. Their heirs, those people who built on their successes, constituted the recognisable middle-class society of the valleys in their heyday – a society in which everyone knew everyone, and where mutual interest could govern most decisions and alliances. Certain figures recur time and again in the chronicle of that society in the Porth and Pontypridd area.

Idris Williams, Brynglas

Idris Williams (1834–94) at times seems to have been ever-present in Porth society, where he was a prominent and well-respected figure. At his sudden death in 1894, there was an extensive obituary of him in the Cardiff-based *Western Mail*, in which his death was described as having caused 'a void in the public life of the district which it will be extremely difficult to fill up'.[1] His funeral was 'one of the largest and most representative ever seen in the Valley', and was attended by about thirty-five nonconformist ministers, seven clergy of the Established Church, Alfred Thomas MP (the future Lord Pontypridd) and many JPs and other worthies, including the local county council aldermen Thomas Williams, Henry Naunton Davies, W. H. Mathias and William Morgan.[2]

Yet, at first sight, it is difficult to see what exactly had made him into such an important figure. He was employed as assistant overseer for the parish of Ystradyfodwg, with the task of overseeing the expenditure on poor relief. He was also registrar of marriages. But even that does not explain his involvement in all facets of Porth and Rhondda society. In voluntary work, he was a member, and then vice-chairman, of the Llanwonno School Board, and he eventually became a Glamorgan county councillor.[3] But, above all, he was always to be found in any gathering of the 'great and the good' of the area, and appears to have been a natural choice to serve on many committees such as that which dealt with the local fund for the Tynewydd disaster. Why was this?

The answer, I think, must lie partly in his wealth. Idris Williams was a part-owner, with his brother Levi, of the Porth Estate, the land of Porth Farm. As late as the 1841 census, when there had still been no sign that Porth was to grow into a town, the area where most of the future town would be was covered by Porth Farm, owned by Idris Williams's grandfather, the farmer Thomas Jones, and farmed by his son-in-law, Idris's father Edward Williams.[4] Porth Farm was just on the other side of the river from Ty'n-y-cymmer Farm, owned by Evan Morgan, which covered most of the land in Cymmer. By the 1851 census, there was already a certain amount of housing on Porth Farm's land, and mines had been sunk both on Ty'n-y-cymmer land and on Porth land. Living in the Porth farmhouse in 1851 were Idris's mother Jane Williams, now a widow (and described as a farmer), and her three children Levi (16), Idris (14) and Hannah (12). Still in the house was her father Thomas Jones, aged 72. Significantly, he was no longer described as a farmer, but as a 'landed proprietor'.[5] In later years the farm ceased to exist (though the farmhouse remained), and the land became almost entirely covered by terraces of houses; it eventually contained the whole of the commercial centre of Porth around Hannah Street. The former farmhouse was a large house right next to the railway station in the centre of Porth.[6]

On Jane's death, the inheritance was divided between Levi and Idris. Levi, as the elder, lived in the original farmhouse.[7] Idris built for himself a large house, Brynglas, on an elevated position overlooking the valley.[8] Not only was he henceforth known as 'Idris

Williams Brynglas', but his son Arthur and granddaughter Mary were to be similarly known, the latter right down to the 1960s, long after the family had ceased to live at the house.[9] The proceeds from their property made the brothers rich men, who need not have done any work for their living. After Levi's early death, his son Edward, a successful solicitor in Pontypridd and Porth, lived at Porth Farm, together with his two younger brothers.[10]

Idris was a fount of knowledge about the Rhondda, the family having of course been resident there before the coal boom. 'He witnessed the development of the district from containing scattered farmhouses and cottages, few and far between, to several populous towns.'[11] Though only 59 at his death, Idris seems to have become a well-loved old-stager in Valleys society.

Above all, he was an enthusiastic nonconformist, and a strong supporter of the temperance movement. At the Porth Welsh Congregational Chapel, which was also attended by the Mathias and Jenkins families, he sometimes preached, and frequently opened the services with readings and prayers.[12] He was well-known for his good works in many spheres.

He had two sons, Joshua and Arthur, and three daughters, two of whom married Congregationalist ministers. Joshua succeeded his father in 1894 as registrar of marriages for the area (though he died prematurely fourteen years later, in 1908).[13] Arthur, who married W. H. Mathias's daughter Louie, was to become a solicitor, joining his cousin Edward's Pontypridd and Porth firm. Edward (who had married another of Mathias's daughters, Maggie) left to extend the practice to Cardiff in 1901 (the house Porth Farm being taken over by William Evans of Thomas and Evans).[14] Arthur Williams remained in Porth, at Brynglas, and continued to work in the Pontypridd office of his and Edward's firm.

On 4 November 1894, while attending Porth Welsh Congregational Chapel, Idris Williams had a massive stroke, and died at his home shortly thereafter.[15]

The Revd David Watkin Williams, Fairfield

David Watkin Williams (1817–91) was one of the most colourful figures in the Valleys in this period. He was the eldest son of Edward

Morgan Williams, a native of Aberdare, who, after making money on the stock exchange, in 1817 bought the property of Ynyshir in the Rhondda Fach. David was born in the same year. He went to Trinity College, Cambridge, graduating in 1841. He was ordained deacon in 1841, and priest in 1842.[16]

In the same year, 1842, he was licensed as perpetual curate of the parish of Ystradyfodwg, which covered most of the Rhondda. In the meantime, his father, who like Idris Williams's family was benefiting strongly from the possession of land in an area which was to be the centre of the industrialisation of the Rhondda, had in the early 1840s leased land and mineral rights at Ynyshir to Shepherd and Evans,[17] whose Ynyshir Pit, sunk in 1845, was one of the first in the area.

Edward Morgan Williams died in 1857, leaving most of his fortune to David, who had now been curate of Ystradyfodwg for fifteen years. Within eighteen months, David had relinquished his living.[18] As the *Western Mail* reporter 'Morien' put it:

> He abandoned his clerical duties so far as not to associate himself with the constant practice of his profession. Throughout the rest of his life, he joined to his sacred character the habits of a country squire.[19]

He built himself a large house in Treforest called 'Fairfield' (described in the local Kelly's Directory as one of 'the principal seats' in the Pontypridd district),[20] 'a name which in due course came to be inseparably associated with him'.[21] He rode to hounds, and in every way lived the life of a country gentleman. He also joined the Cardiff and County Club, a gentlemen's club which, now situated in Westgate Street, Cardiff, continues to flourish. At the time of the Lord Mayor of London's visit to Pontypridd in 1877, to present the awards for the Tynewydd rescue, Williams not only, in a highly generous (but perhaps a little flamboyant) gesture, personally paid for a magnificent luncheon for more than 350 people, but also imported the maître d'hôtel of the Cardiff and County Club for the occasion.[22]

But Williams also showed himself to be very public-spirited, becoming not only a magistrate but also the first chairman of the Pontypridd Board of Guardians in 1863, and the first chairman of the Llanwonno School Board in 1871.[23] Above all, he seems to have been accepted as one of the major figures in the life of Pontypridd and the area around it, to the extent that he was called in whenever a figure of weight was needed. For example, he was the person chosen by the Lord Mayor of London to provide an initial list of names to benefit from the Mansion House fund for the Tynewydd Disaster,[24] was one of three (the others being Judge Gwilym Williams and the Chief Inspector of Mines, Mr Wales) to advise the Home Secretary on who should receive Albert Medals,[25] and was also one of the four people chosen to administer the *Daily Telegraph* fund on the same occasion.[26]

In his personal appearance, he could appear somewhat eccentric – but 'distinguished'. A contemporary described him as 'very leisurely ... tall with somewhat drooping shoulders, square felt hat, very open collar, long tail coat [with] black and white patterned trousers'.[27] When appearing as a character witness for Siamps Thomas at the 1877 Tynewydd trial, he described himself as 'a magistrate for this county, and a landed proprietor'.[28] He took both roles seriously. In the latter, he was continually looking to improvements in his property situation – whether it be leasing the mineral rights to further land owned by him (such as the land on which Siamps Thomas's Standard Collieries, Ynyshir, were to be sunk), or expanding his property portfolio, as he did in the Cowbridge area in the latter part of the century.

He remained a bachelor till the age of 63. By his late forties, however, he had begun to think of the question of an heir. His sister had married a man called Hamlen, who lived in Weston-super-Mare. They had nine boys and two girls. Williams decided that his heir should be one of the boys, and invited each of them in turn to visit Fairfield.[29] Thus it is that in the 1861 census we find 'David Hamlyn' (*sic*) living with him at Fairfield.[30] By 1868, however, he had decided on his heir, and adopted Theophilus Hamlen (1860–1905), then aged eight.[31]

In 1880 Williams married Mary Mostyn Renwick (b. 1860) from Bala, north Wales, who was forty-three years younger than him.[32] Her sister, Charlotte Mostyn Renwick (b. 1862), came to live with them and Theophilus at Fairfield, where she remained with them for many years.[33] They all spent much of their time at 'The Verlands', one of Williams's Cowbridge investments,[34] and one of the finest properties in that town.

After Williams's death in 1891, his adopted son, now calling himself Theophilus Hamlen-Williams, married his uncle's widow, who was the same age as himself. They inherited all Watkin Williams's estates. Theophilus became 'a man of considerable means, possessing much valuable freehold property, and receiving royalties on the coal produced at Ynyshir'.[35] He took on the same social role as his adopted father, becoming a prominent JP, and riding regularly to hounds.[36]

The couple had three children. Theophilus's wife predeceased him, whereupon he married her sister Charlotte.[37] On his death at the age of 45, in 1905, his widow sold Fairfield to the successful hotel entrepreneur, Mrs Elizabeth Miles.

Judge Gwilym Williams of Miskin Manor and Sir Rhys Rhys Williams

Gwilym Williams (1839–1906)[38] and his family are one of the best examples we have of a radical transformation of a family over three generations, typical of the fluid society of south Wales in the late nineteenth century. We have seen how Gwilym's father, David Williams (1809–63) rose from extreme poverty to become one of the most successful of Valleys coalowners.[39] Like many other successful coalowners, David Williams had invested extensively in land, both in the Valleys and in the countryside of Glamorganshire and Carmarthenshire. In the mining valleys he invested wisely in land where mining was likely to take place. At his death in 1863, these properties were divided between his two sons, Gwilym and Gomer. Gwilym inherited the Miskin Manor estate near Llantrisant, and much prime land in the Rhondda valley.

Gwilym, born in Ynyscynon in 1839, was educated at Cowbridge Grammar School, at the Normal College, Swansea, and in France. He became a barrister of the Middle Temple in 1863, the year he also inherited his father's Glamorgan estate. This included the farms known as Brithweunydd Uchaf, Brithweunydd Isaf and Ynysgrug in the Rhondda Fawr Valley, just west of Porth, and just opposite Dinas on the other side of the river. Gwilym

Williams, as ground landlord with mineral rights, did much to encourage the development of this area in the 1860s.[40] It was here that Daniel Thomas Senior opened up the successful Brithweunydd mine, which he left to his son Daniel.[41] Williams called the township which grew up there in the mid-1860s 'Trealaw' ('Alaw's Town'), in homage to his father (who had been a considerable poet in the Welsh language, and competed successfully under the bardic name 'Alaw Goch', in many *eisteddfodau*).

Gwilym shared his father's enthusiasm for the Welsh language and for Welsh literature. In 1872, after there had been an appeal in the House of Commons for bilingual judges to be appointed, he became stipendiary magistrate for Pontypridd and the Rhondda. Twelve years later, in 1884, he became a county court judge on the mid-Wales circuit. Within a year, however, he returned to south Wales as county court judge in Glamorgan, an appointment he held until his death in 1906, being chairman of the Glamorgan Quarter Sessions from 1894 to 1906. He played a dominant role in all areas of south Wales society from the 1870s onwards.

When Gwilym died in 1906, his estate was inherited by his 41-year-old son Rhys Williams (1865–1955).[42] Rhys was a typical third-generation member of an entrepreneurial family. The smooth transition from a working miner to an aristocratic landed gentleman had taken place from grandfather to grandson. Rhys was educated at Eton and Oriel College, Oxford. He became a barrister of the Inner Temple, in 1890. He often acted for Welsh clients (including William James Thomas and W. H. Mathias).[43]

Like his father, Rhys Williams lived at Miskin Manor, and became chairman of the Glamorgan Quarter Sessions. Their style, however, was quite different. Though he was, like his father, Welsh-speaking, Rhys, like so many of the new Welsh aristocracy, took on English manners. He entertained lavishly, and was host to the Royal Family on their visits to Wales (as we have seen on the occasion of the visit of Princess Louise. He was also host on several occasions to the Prince of Wales). In London, he resided at Charles Street (just off Berkeley Square) and at Mitre Court Buildings, Inner Temple. He belonged to some of the most prestigious of London clubs: White's, Brooks's, and the Guards Club.[44]

Rhys Williams was knighted in 1913. In the First World War, he fought in the Welsh Guards, becoming a lieutenant colonel in 1917. After the war, he became the Coalition Liberal MP for Banbury 1918–22, and was Parliamentary Secretary to the Ministry of Transport in 1919. Lloyd George had created him a baronet in 1918. With the fall of Lloyd George in 1922 and the resultant election after the coalition was dissolved, he lost his seat. In the same year, he became Recorder of Cardiff. As well as Miskin Manor, he by now also had a house in Eaton Place,[45] one of the most fashionable addresses in London. In later years, he added his first name to his surname, becoming Sir Rhys Rhys Williams.

Both his sons were educated at Eton. Sadly, his elder son Glyn David Rhys Williams was killed in action in 1943. His second son, Sir Brandon Rhys Williams, who like his father and brother had served in the Welsh Guards, succeeded to the title in 1955. He was Conservative MP for Kensington, 1968–88.

Thomas Griffiths, Maesgwyn

While, apart from the very early days, a rise from the ranks to coalownership was comparatively rare, the same was not true of a rise from the ranks to a professional managership in the heyday of the mining valleys. Here, the progression from doorboy to manager was still comparatively common. Philip Jones, for example, who became manager of that vast enterprise the Albion Colliery Cilfynydd, had started work as a doorboy when seven years old.[46] John Thomas Fernbank started work underground when nine years old, became a fireman, then achieved a manager's certificate before becoming manager and agent of Standard Collieries Ynyshir. But Thomas Griffiths's was the most remarkable of such careers. He achieved enormous influence on the life of the valleys, in a wide variety of roles.

He was born in 1849 at Bettws near Bridgend.[47] Shortly thereafter, the family moved to Hafod, just south-east of Porth. When he left school at the age of 11 in 1860, Griffiths started in Insole's Cymmer Colliery as a doorboy. Thereafter, he worked for ten years at the coalface, becoming a fireman in 1869. He had already determined to better himself, however, and to that end undertook part-time study, becoming a qualified mining engineer and securing a manager's certificate by examination.

In the early 1870s, he moved away from the area, but returned to Cymmer in 1875 as engineer for the sinking of Cymmer Old Pit to the steam-coal levels. Within two years he was the manager of the Cymmer collieries. His managerial qualification had served him in good stead, because the Mines Regulation Act 1872 had made this a stipulation for new managers.

By the 1880s, he was heavily involved in the whole Insole mining business, of which he had become a director. While continuing to serve them as a mining engineer (it was he who sank their new pit at Abertridwr, the Windsor Colliery, in the 1890s), he was also involved in their strategic thinking. Meanwhile, in Porth, he rapidly gained the reputation of one of the leading figures in local society. He lived in a large house called Maesgwyn. For over 40 years he was a close friend and associate of W. H. Mathias, and was part of the Welsh-speaking society which was at the centre of Porth life. In 1882, he became a member of the Ystradyfodwg Urban Sanitary Authority,[48] of which he was to remain a member, under its various guises culminating in the Rhondda Urban District Council, for about 40 years, and on which he was to exert enormous influence.

His role had long exceeded that of a manager and became in part that of an owner. His influence stretched throughout south Wales. By 1911, he was president of the South Wales and Monmouthshire Coalowners Association, and playing a leading part in the strike negotiations of that year.[49] He also became a life member of the South Wales Institute of Engineers.

In 1924, he retired to the Gower, where he died three years later at the age of 78.

William Jenkins, Ystradfechan

William Jenkins[50] benefited greatly from his family connections (though he also possessed great innate ability). Born in a small village in Breconshire, he was a nephew of the highly successful railway contractor and coalowner David Davies of Llandinam. His education started at a village school, but eventually he was sent to a school in Bristol, and then started work with his uncle at Cwmbach pit, Aberdare. Thanks to his uncle's influence, he was then articled to W. S. Clark, mining engineer to the Bute Estate. This training made of him an outstanding mining engineer.

Even before he had finished his articles, he was in 1861 appointed manager of the Bute Merthyr Colliery. Having held this post for one year, he then went to the Durham and Northumberland coalfields to gain further experience. On his return to south Wales, he did mining and valuation work for Samuel Dobson, before joining his uncle's firm of David Davies and Co. In 1871, he was appointed general manager of Davies's Ocean Collieries. He consolidated his position through marriage to the daughter of John Osborne Riches, commercial agent of Ocean Collieries and also a close associate of Samuel Thomas Ysguborwen.[51]

Jenkins, at the height of his career, was one of the most powerful figures in the coal industry, and a director of a number of major companies, including the Ocean Coal Co. Ltd, Deep Navigation Collieries Ltd (of which he was chairman), and the Barry Railway Company. His influence extended also into the field of local government, where he was a major figure on the Ystradyfodwg Local Board from the start, later becoming for many years the chairman. He also became a Glamorgan county councillor in the first intake of 1889, later becoming an alderman, and was a prominent member of the bench of magistrates. He thus wielded power in many of the interlocking spheres of influence in the Rhondda valleys.

As general manager of Ocean Collieries, he lived in a grand house in Treorchy called Ystradfechan House, and was popularly known as 'the squire of Ystradfechan'.[52] In 1915, he retired and thereafter devoted himself to farming in Herefordshire.

William Morgan, Tynewydd, and Walter Morgan, Forest House

William Morgan, like the Williamses of Porth Farm and Evan Morgan of Ty'n-y-cymmer Farm, benefited from owning a farm whose land became part of the industrial landscape of the Rhondda. His farm, Tŷ Newydd Farm, near Treherbert, consisted of 2,000 acres.[53] Most of the rest of the land in the Treherbert area was owned by absentee landlords: the Bute estate, which owned much of the central Treherbert area, the Dunraven estate, and the estate of Griffith Llewellyn of Cwrt Colman and Baglan, which owned extensive lands in the Rhondda Fawr.[54]

On the proceeds of his mineral rights (leased to Ebenezer Lewis, who sank the Tynewydd mine in the 1860s)[55] and his ground rents, William Morgan built himself a substantial house next to the farm, called Tynewydd House.[56] He devoted much of his time, in later years, to public work. He became a JP, and in 1889 a founder member of the Glamorgan County Council, for the Treherbert seat, listing himself (as in his census returns) as a 'farmer'[57] (his son Walter was elected to the council, for Pontypridd, on the same occasion). William speedily became an alderman. He was an active member of the county council, where he served with distinction on the Roads and Bridges Committee and the Local Government Committee.

William's son, Walter Morgan, is more central to the mid-Rhondda story. He was a solicitor, founder of the Pontypridd firm of Morgan, Bruce and Rhys. He was clerk to the Ystradyfodwg Board (which was later to become the Rhondda Urban District Council), and in 1889 became a Glamorgan county councillor, swiftly becoming an alderman and vice-chairman of the council. But this does not give all the story. Walter Morgan was a considerable 'operator', central to the networking involved in many of the entrepreneurial ventures that either took place in the Pontypridd area, or had Pontypridd figures at their centre.

He was also a keen entrepreneur as regards workmen's housing in areas which were being opened up to the coal industry, usually in collaboration with other members of what could be described as the 'Pontypridd and Rhondda network'. In 1884, for example (the Treferig Valley Railway having opened in 1883), he joined with several people (including the TVR officials, James Hurman and Henry Oakden Fisher) in forming the 'Rhondda and Treferig Workmen's Cottage Company'. On this occasion, however, the venture was an unsuccessful one. The hoped-for mineral exploitation of the central Treferig valley did not materialise, and by 1890 the Workmen's Cottage Company, which had carried on almost no business, had ceased to exist.[58] This did not deter Morgan, however. By 1892, he had joined William Henry Mathias in a piece of highly successful property speculation in the Aber valley.[59] This, and other such ventures in collaboration with Mathias, made him a very rich man.

At the height of his success, Morgan bought Forest House, Treforest, the mansion in which Francis Crawshay, owner of the Treforest ironworks and tinworks, had lived, and later his son Tudor Crawshay. Morgan stood for parliamentary seats on a number of occasions, in the Liberal interest, but was unsuccessful in those attempts.[60]

Walter Morgan, and his firm (which eventually, with the advent of Walter Nicholas, became 'Morgan, Bruce and Nicholas'), had another string to their bow. They represented the unions in many cases, so much so that Walter Morgan became known as the 'colliers' lawyer'. This tradition was later followed, after Morgan's death, by Walter Nicholas.

In August 1901, while on holiday in Llandrindod Wells, Walter Morgan suddenly died.[61] He was outlived by his father, who continued to serve on the Glamorgan County Council. His partner, Walter Nicholas, took over the firm, and also took on Morgan's role as clerk to the Rhondda Council.

Sir Walter Nicholas

Walter Powell Nicholas (1868–1926) was the fifth son of John Nicholas, a colliery manager of Brynamman, Carmarthenshire.[62] He was a brilliant lawyer, who after training in Neath and Newport offices obtained First Class Honours and the Law Society Prize in 1894. In 1897, he joined Walter Morgan's Pontypridd firm of solicitors as a partner. Within a year he had become solicitor to the newly-formed South Wales Miners' Federation, and also, like his partner Morgan, had become a Glamorgan county councillor (like Morgan, he was a staunch Liberal). In 1901, at the death of Morgan, he took over the clerkship of the Rhondda Urban District Council. As Chris Williams has put it, 'during the next two decades [he] established himself as "King of the Rhondda"'.[63] He was an outstanding figure in local government, both as an officer (where his influence was considerable, together with W. H. Mathias and

Thomas Griffiths) and as a county councillor. He became a particularly close friend and associate of W. H. Mathias.[64]

Nicholas also exerted much influence on a wider stage, as chairman of the Urban District Councils Association of England and Wales, and as a member of various royal commissions.[65] He was knighted in the Lloyd George New Year's Honours of 1919. Despite all his fame, Nicholas continued to live locally, at a large house called the Garth, Trealaw. He died in 1926, at the age of fifty-eight.

Dr Henry Naunton Davies

Henry Naunton Davies (1827–99) has been described as 'a foundation stone of the community'.[66] This remarkable medical man had a great effect upon the medical life of the valleys. He lived centrally in Porth, in a fine house called Glyn Rhondda House,[67] just by the bridge in the centre of town, for most of his working life. He came of a family dynasty entirely bound up with medical practice in the Rhondda region. His great-grandfather, Samuel Davies (1734?–1820), was described on his tombstone as 'surgeon'. His grandfather Henry Davies had had a wide country practice in the Porth area (and married the sister of Thomas Jones of Porth Farm – Henry Naunton Davies was thus a second cousin of Idris Williams). His father Evan Davies (1801–50) was the first of the family to specialise in a mining practice. He was medical officer of Walter Coffin's mine at Dinas.[68]

Evan Davies had married Catherine Naunton, daughter of David Naunton (1777–1849), Baptist minister at Ystradyfodwg. Henry, their eldest son, appears to have been much influenced by the example and teaching of his father (who had himself written on theology) and his maternal grandfather, as he attempted to come to grips with the medical problems of the mining community.

Henry graduated from Guy's in 1854, and immediately returned to practise in Porth. He eventually became surgeon to eleven local collieries and works. He came to widespread public notice throughout the United Kingdom at the time of the Tynewydd disaster in 1877, when he took the lead in the treatment of the rescued. It was this disaster, in which the injured had to be cared for in an *ad hoc* manner in a room in the Tynewydd Inn, that made

Davies realise, taking into account all the other local disasters, that something had to be done to provide proper medical facilities to deal with the results of one of the most dangerous occupations in the country. Over a number of years he tirelessly campaigned for a hospital to serve the needs of the community. In 1894 his efforts were rewarded by the foundation of Porth Cottage Hospital.

Henry Naunton Davies was more than this. He was a highly-regarded member of the local community, known wherever he went. He took on many public roles, not only medical (medical officer of health, factory surgeon, public vaccinator), but also serving the community as a justice of the peace and a county alderman. Locally, his advice to the Ystradyfodwg Local Board, and to its later manifestation the Rhondda Urban District Council, was of great influence in the gradual improvement of public health in the valleys.

He appears to have inspired his children and other younger relatives by his example. 'By the interwar period there were twenty-seven members of the Davies clan in medical practice within the region.'[69]

Henry Lewis, Tŷ Nant, and Ebenezer Lewis

Henry Lewis came of a family heavily involved in the coalmining entrepreneurial activities of the mid-nineteenth century. One of his uncles, John Lewis, who had married William Cope's sister, was a partner with Cope and Siamps Thomas in the Troedyrhiw Coal Company from 1850 onwards. Another uncle, Ebenezer Lewis, was however the greater influence upon him.

Ebenezer came to prominence in the steam coal bonanza of the Aberdare Valley, where he became the partner of Samuel Thomas Ysguborwen (father of the future Viscount Rhondda) and his brother-in-law Thomas Joseph in sinking their mine at Bwllfa Dare.[70] Like many others, he transferred his attention, in the 1860s, to the steam coal possibilities of the Rhondda Valley, leasing in 1865 from William Morgan the mineral property of Tynewydd, near Treherbert,[71] sinking there his Tynewydd mine.[72] Then in 1872 he sank, with his nephew Henry Lewis, the highly successful Fernhill Collieries at Blaenrhondda.[73] By the 1880s, he was undertaking further ventures with his nephews, Henry Lewis and Matthew Cope.

Henry Lewis trained rigorously as a mining engineer, and was to become regarded as one of the most accomplished engineers in South Wales. He had been articled to William Thomas Lewis (the future Lord Merthyr) in 1866, and immediately on completion of his three years of articles joined his uncle Ebenezer in sinking the Fernhill Collieries between 1869 and 1871,[74] and then went on to be the manager of the Rhondda Merthyr Colliery. In this period he also worked as a consulting engineer for the Troedyrhiw Company's mine at Ynysfeio. He then proceeded to become the manager of Siamps Thomas's Energlyn Colliery at Caerphilly.[75] At the Tynewydd disaster, he was among the owners and managers who helped in the rescue attempts, and was awarded an Albert Medal (Second Class) for his outstanding contribution.[76]

Once Matthew Cope had inherited his share in the Troedyrhiw Coal Company from his father William in 1874,[77] he and Henry Lewis joined with Ebenezer Lewis and P. A. Vyvyan-Robinson in a new venture, the sinking and development of the National Collieries at Ynyshir (about half a mile north of Siamps Thomas's Standard Collieries).[78] Then, in the late 1880s, they sold the National Collieries to Edmund Hannay Watts (the settlement around the colliery being rechristened 'Wattstown'), and moved on to exploit the Taff valley just north of Pontypridd, sinking the Albion Colliery at Cilfynydd.[79] By this stage, Ebenezer was taking more of a back seat, and did not become a director of Albion, though he bought a large number of shares in the new venture. Cope became chairman, and Henry Lewis managing director.[80]

In 1894, the Albion Colliery disaster took place. Lewis was heavily involved in the inquest and in the later hearing at the magistrates' court. Despite strong evidence as to negligence at the mine, the company was exonerated.[81] A year later, Lewis was returned unopposed to the Glamorgan County Council as the member for Cilfynydd.

Lewis, who was living in a grand house called Tŷ Nant, at Walnut Tree near Radyr, just outside Cardiff, had become a prominent figure in the coalmining community, and was reputed for his hardline attitude to industrial relations. He became chairman of the

Monmouthshire and South Wales Coalowners' Association just in time for the disastrous strike of 1898, which embittered relations between employers and employed for generations to come.[82]

He remained managing director of the Albion Colliery Company until 1910, when the Cambrian Combine took a controlling interest in it and replaced all the directors apart from William Henry Mathias, who became chairman and managing director. Henry Lewis retired to Tŷ Nant, where he died in 1917.[83]

Three major coalowners local to Porth: Daniel and Edmund Thomas, and Thomas Jones Ynyshir

The prosperity of Porth depended upon the local collieries: Cymmer and Tynewydd, centrally in Porth; Standard, Ynyshir and Troedyrhiw (Aber Rhondda) to the north, just up the Rhondda Fach valley; Llwyncelyn, Coedcae and Hafod to the south-east; Dinas and Brithweunydd to the west. By the 1870s, the major local coalowners were Insoles of the Cymmer Collieries (whose manager was Thomas Griffiths); Sir William Thomas Lewis of the Lewis Merthyr Navigation Collieries (the new name for Coedcae and Hafod); Siamps Thomas of Standard, Tynewydd, and Troedyrhiw; Daniel Thomas of Brithweunydd Drift and Dinas; Edmund Thomas of Llwyncelyn; and Thomas Jones of Ynyshir.

The two coalowning brothers Daniel and Edmund Thomas were very much at the centre of things in the Porth area. They were the sons of one of the pioneering figures in the coal industry, Daniel Thomas Senior, who was for 23 years the chief manager of Dinas Collieries, under Walter Coffin. After resigning from this job, he sank a colliery of his own, Brithweunydd Drift, on the opposite bank of the Rhondda Fawr from Dinas.[84]

Of his children, three were to be prominent in the coal industry: Daniel and Edmund as mineowners, and Isaiah as a successful manager. At an early age, Daniel (1849–84) became assistant to his father as manager of Dinas, and then in the Brithweunydd Drift Colliery. In 1870, his father fell seriously ill, and for the next two years, until he died in 1872, sole management of Brithweunydd fell upon Daniel Jr., who was in his early twenties. The old boy was so pleased by the way he did this, that he left the mine to him. Soon young Daniel was expanding his interests, and in 1877 he sank a new pit on Dinas Isaf Farm, in the Ely valley. He had also, in partnership with Siamps Thomas, leased the land in Ynyshir for the joint sinking of what were to be the Standard Collieries (though Siamps Thomas bought him out of these, at a very high price, before the production of coal started in 1877).[85]

In 1879, there was a terrible explosion at Dinas, after which between fifty and sixty men's bodies remained entombed underground. 'It was for some time feared that, owing to the terrible nature of the falls which the explosion had caused in the workings, the colliery would have to be abandoned altogether.'[86] In 1881, however, Daniel Thomas leased the Dinas collieries. He and his manager John Havard succeeded in recovering most of the bodies, and returning the mine into working order.

Meanwhile, his younger brother Edmund had become the owner of Llwyncelyn Colliery, Porth. In 1876, he sank the Tynybedw Colliery, and in 1877 the vastly successful Gelli Collieries in the Rhondda Fawr. He built for himself a grand house, Maendy Hall, in Pentre.[87]

One of the features of the mining community in this area was the way in which local owners and managers would gather to help in the major disasters that occurred. At the Tynewydd disaster, Daniel and Edmund Thomas, together with Thomas Jones Ynyshir, William Thomas Brynawel, William Davies of Coedcae, and many others took a prominent and in some cases heroic part in the rescue. Similarly, at the disaster at Moses Rowlands's Naval Steam Colliery, Penygraig, in 1884, the rescuers again included the Thomas brothers, together with Thomas Jones Ynyshir, William Jenkins Ystradfechan, W. Hood of Llwynypia, and Moses Rowlands himself. Edmund Thomas was described as 'the busiest at the top of the Penygraig downcast shaft', while Daniel's exploits were to cost him his life. The *Western Mail* noted that the Thomas family was well-known for its assiduity in such rescues: 'No disaster has been recorded in the annals of the district without the name of a Thomas being in some way connected with the perilous work of exploration and the noble efforts made to rescue any that may be alive.'[88]

Daniel died aged 34 in this disaster, as a result of the heroism with which he had penetrated too far into the mine to save a fireman who was an old friend and employee of his, only to be overcome by afterdamp.[89] The list of mourners at his funeral on 30 January 1884 presents us with a roll call of the society of the central Rhondda, including Lord Aberdare, Judge Gwilym Williams, the Revd David Watkin Williams, Dr Henry Naunton Davies, Moses Rowlands, Thomas Jones Ynyshir, William Jenkins Ystradfechan, Siamps Thomas, William Henry Mathias, Richard Packer and Idris Williams.[90]

Edmund Thomas was to live for many years more. We find his name in a great many contexts: in local government, on school boards, and on many social occasions. He was (as was Daniel) a keen member of the congregation of Cymmer Welsh Independent chapel, alongside Thomas Griffiths of Cymmer Colliery, Richard Packer, and many others. It was Edmund who, in the aftermath of the Tynewydd disaster in 1877, preached an address of thanksgiving at the service held in Cymmer chapel;[91] and Daniel's funeral took place there in 1884.

Another prominent local coalowner was Thomas Jones, who had in 1873 bought the Ynyshir Colliery. As well as this, Jones also owned the Tylacoch Collieries in Treorchy, and the Hafod Colliery. Like Siamps Thomas and many others of his generation, he was manager of his own collieries.[92] He has been described as 'one of the pioneers of the south Wales coal trade', and as 'a most striking personality'.[93] Certainly, he seems to have been at the forefront of most events, usually taking a very pro-active part in all that took place. His activities in relation to the various mining disasters have been described thus:

> In the terrible colliery holocausts which have from time to time caused such terrible devastation in the homes of hundreds of south Wales families, Mr Jones was always a conspicuous figure, and when the call for help came he was one of the first to volunteer in the work of rescue. At Tynewydd, Ferndale and Penygraig he displayed intrepid courage.[94]

He lived at Maendy Hall, Ynyshir, just across the Rhondda Fach river from his Ynyshir mine. An Anglican, he showed great interest in Church matters, and it was thanks to him that St Anne's Church in Ynyshir was built. (It was named after his wife.)[95] Jones died in April 1905.

William Evans

The new moneyed classes of the Valleys contained people from many other walks of life. Alongside those involved in the coal trade, the entrepreneurs who developed housing for the workers, and the multitude of small builders who carried out that and other aspects of urban development, there were also the shopkeepers. People came from far and wide, often from west Wales, to open shops in the Valleys towns, and in particular in the major centres such as Merthyr, Aberdare, Pontypridd, Treorchy and Porth. The outstanding example of a grocery entrepreneur was to be found in Porth: this was William Evans (1864–1934), born in Fishguard Pembrokeshire, who came to Porth in 1883 and by 1885, at the age of 21, had founded the famous Thomas and Evans store, which soon had grand premises on Hannah Street. In accordance with his nonconformist conscience, Evans soon hit on the idea of producing non-alcoholic beverages, 'fizzy drinks', to reduce the consumption of alcohol in the area. His 'Welsh Hills Soft Drinks' were soon to become the famous 'Corona' brand of mineral waters, which were sold throughout the United Kingdom. Thomas and Evans also opened many branches throughout south Wales. All this made of Evans a millionaire, who became a major benefactor to the local community.[96] He was an outstanding entrepreneur, but all those other grocers in the corner shops of the Valleys towns included many other highly successful and prosperous men. They and other shopkeepers were among those, in the first stages of the mining industry, who bought their way into the ranks of the coalowners; in later years, such men invested widely in stocks and shares, and also in major properties in the Vale of Glamorgan.

Mrs Elizabeth Miles

Mrs Elizabeth Miles (1847–1930) was an outstanding entrepreneur in a completely different field from those we have been examining –

the world of the hotel industry. Her origins did not give any sign of what the future would hold. She was born Elizabeth Spencer in 1847 in Treforest[97] near Pontypridd, the youngest of seven children of Francis Spencer, an innkeeper.[98] In 1869, aged twenty-two, she married a certain Shadrach Miles,[99] son of William Miles, grocer and draper of Llantwit Fardre.[100] Shadrach and his new wife set up in the grocery and drapery business in Clydach.[101] In the next two years, two sons were born to them: William (b.1870) and Francis (b.1871).[102] Then tragedy struck. Shadrach died. Elizabeth was never to remarry. She became an innkeeper, and was the tenant of the Bridge End Inn, Ystrad Road, Pentre, from 1877 to 1886.[103]

She must have gained a reputation for competence, because when the owners of the New Inn Hotel, Pontypridd, were looking for a new manager, it was she whom they chose. They certainly needed a new broom. It had until recently been one of the most prominent hotels in Pontypridd, and the proprietors had 'always desired that it should be the first commercial house in the town', but under the previous manager, William Morris, it had lost its 'well won reputation', and was 'suffering from premature decay.'[104]

Within months Mrs Miles had transformed the hotel. 'The New Inn, like a Phoenix from the ashes, rose to a newer and more vigorous life, to take its place as the premier hotel of advancing Pontypridd, under the benignant yet vigorous sway of that most genial and attractive of hostesses – Mrs Miles.'[105] The hotel was extensively used, from the late 1880s onwards, for important occasions. It was the natural place, for example, for the first luncheon of the new Glamorgan County Council in 1889; for the quartering of officers when the military came to Pontypridd during the strikes of 1893 and 1898; for the inquest for the 1894 Albion Disaster; and for the magnificent reception for Colonel Lindsay, a hero of the Boer War, in 1901. Often, on such occasions, Mrs Miles was specifically mentioned in the press reports as far afield as Cardiff. At the GCC luncheon, given by Alfred Thomas MP, 'the catering reflected the greatest credit upon Mrs Miles and her staff'.[106] At the Albion inquest, 'At the hands of Mrs Miles, the genial and kindly hostess, the bereaved mourners received the utmost hospitality, and all possible arrangements were made in the hotel for their temporary accommodation.'[107] At the Lindsay reception 'about two hundred sat down to an admirable spread, provided by Mrs Miles'.[108] And so on. She had clearly made a great impression upon everybody, including the press.

William Henry Mathias appears to have been among those who were impressed. He must have met her at the various functions he attended at the hotel, from the county council lunch onwards. One gets the impression that, like many successful entrepreneurs, he enjoyed the company of intelligent and capable women. Many years later, her grandson, Spencer Miles, was to describe their close friendship, which continued into comparative old age. In the late 1880s they were both in their early forties. Spencer hinted strongly that Mathias had bankrolled Mrs Miles's first entrepreneurial ventures,[109] as on a number of occasions did Mathias's grandson William Thomas Griffiths.[110] We have no documentary proof of this, but it would have been surprising if Mathias had not perceived the immense capability of Mrs Miles, and realised just what she might achieve, if given her head. The idea of his supporting her career financially at the start is not totally out of the question.

In the early 1880s, from being the manager of one hotel, Mrs Miles swiftly became owner of a number. Within a short space of time she was able to buy the New Inn Hotel from its proprietors, and to buy or lease a number of other hotels in Cardiff, Swansea and Caerphilly. Eventually she held the licences of ten hotels in south Wales.[111]

The place for which she became known (and is still remembered) was, however, Llandrindod Wells. This Radnorshire spa had been in existence for many years, but it was the coming of the railway in 1865 that had made the place much more accessible, and in the late nineteenth century it had become a flourishing watering-place. Though many people came from England, it was a highly popular resort among the new moneyed classes in Wales, many of them taking a regular holiday there every summer. Advertisements claimed that 'a decent class of people' were to be found there, 'chiefly upper class, professional and business people'.[112] It was generally regarded as 'the Harrogate of the Principality'.[113]

Among the many hotels and guest houses of varying sizes in the town, the largest at this stage were the Pump House Hotel and the Rock House Hotel. Mrs Miles clearly saw the need for another grand establishment. In December 1897, she bought a smallish hotel called the Bridge, the number of guests in which, during the season, was normally around thirty to thirty-five. Over the next few years she enlarged the hotel's capacity to over 100. By about 1910, it reached over 200, and became the largest hotel in the Principality at the time. Among the 1910 changes were the provision of a grand facade with twin turrets, very much in line with the grandiloquent style of so many Llandrindod buildings.

The venture was an enormous success. Despite the fact that a grand new hotel, the Gwalia, opened eight months after the purchase of the Bridge, there was enough custom for everyone, and Mrs Miles's hotel was always full in the season. A good number of people from the Pontypridd area were among the guests. In 1911, its name was changed to the Metropole.

Her perpetual desire for expansion of her hotel interests is shown by the fact that she leased the Angel Hotel, Cardiff, some time between 1895 and 1901.[114] She built a new facade for this, one of the major hotels of Cardiff.

Though the Metropole had become so central to her interests, Mrs Miles continued to live in the Pontypridd area, first at a house called the Grange, and then, after 1905, at Fairfield, the large house in Treforest where the Revd David Watkin Williams, and then his heir Theophilus Hamlen-Williams, had lived.[115] She also bought various properties in and around Pontypridd, including some quarries. One of her sons, Francis, never married, and lived with her in her Treforest house and at the Metropole. It was he who took over the running of that hotel from 1925 onwards. Her elder son William trained as a doctor at the Middlesex Hospital, but did not practise. Instead, he went into the beer industry, becoming chairman of the Ely Valley Brewery Company, and then, after its amalgamation with the Rhondda Valley Brewery Company, of the amalgamated firm.[116] He led the life of a country gentleman, riding to hounds with the Ystrad and Pentyrch Hunt, and becoming a prominent Conservative.[117] He sent his son Spencer to Harrow, and had his daughters educated privately. William died suddenly of heart failure in May 1922. Mrs Miles did not die until 1930, at the age of 84.

How unusual was Mrs Miles's career, for a woman, in the late nineteenth century? The first part of her career, as an innkeeper in

Pentre, accords well with the role of women in the period. Among the occupations undertaken by women in northern England in the late eighteenth and early nineteenth century, for example, Hannah Barker notes many examples of female publicans.[118] The same was true across Europe. In Vienna in 1910, for example, 32.3 per cent of those running restaurants and inns were women.[119] Many of these appear to have been widows,[120] like Elizabeth Miles, for whom innkeeping (usually as tenants) was often the best way of earning a good living. There were, of course, other occupations to which such widows could turn: confectioners, pastry cooks, milliners, sempstresses, etc.[121] In more middle-class areas, there were many such occupations available. In the Valleys society, however, such alternative occupations were rarer than the keeping of an inn or alehouse, or a hotel.

But what about Mrs Miles's later career, first as owner of the New Inn Hotel, and later as a major hotel entrepreneur right across south and mid Wales? Female entrepreneurs were a rare breed in the nineteenth century, and in most cases they built their careers on the already-established businesses left to them by their husbands or families. Even the pioneer coal entrepreneur Lucy Thomas (1781–1847), the 'mother of the Welsh coal trade', had benefited by her husband Robert Thomas's original development of the Waunwyllt mine, using it as the basis for her wide-ranging sales activities, undertaken with her son William.[122] Later in the century, Lady Charlotte Guest's industrial activities were a direct result of her late husband's ownership of the Dowlais works, and Amy Dillwyn took over her family's spelter works, admittedly turning an ailing business around in the process.[123] The situation was the same in other countries, too. Sophie Henschel, who aggressively expanded the Kassel locomotive firm Henschel und Sohn in the 1890s and 1900s, had been helped by inheriting from her husband this successful family firm. Her own entrepreneurial capabilities were enormous – but one asks oneself whether she would have had the opportunity of exerting them had it not been for these circumstances.[124]

Not only did Elizabeth Miles have no such family connections in the more prestigious side of the hotel trade; she was also unlikely to have had any of the initial financial advantages of the women just mentioned. This makes her rapid expansion of her business even more remarkable. Admittedly, there was another major female hotel entrepreneur in Britain who started her career shortly after her, in the 1900s – Lady Honywood, Managing Director of Honywood Hotels, which included the Angel Hotel Cardiff (which Mrs Miles leased from her for twenty years),[125] the Gloucester Hotel Weymouth, the Queen's Hotel Cheltenham and the County Hotel Malvern.[126] But Lady Honywood had the advantage of having a very wealthy husband, who could no doubt produce the venture capital she originally needed: Sir Courtenay John Honywood, 9th Baronet, of Kirby Hall, Essex, who owned 'about 5,700 acres'.[127]

Elizabeth Miles had no such financial start to her career. All this makes it more than likely that the family tradition that Mrs Miles had been provided with venture capital by William Henry Mathias has some truth in it. But this in no way detracts from the remarkable results she achieved through her own entrepreneurial activity. Mathias had known a winner when he saw one. Elizabeth Miles was one of the greatest entrepreneurs of late nineteenth-century Wales (a place and a time in which many entrepreneurs, mainly male, flourished). She deserves a prominent place in women's history of the period.

The Cardiff connection

Alongside all the people who were resident in the Valleys, there were, however, many equally influential people who, while living outside the area, wielded considerable influence within it, and were closely associated with the entrepreneurial activities of the area. Prominent among these were, of course, Cardiff docksmen of whom Matthew Cope and William his father were prime examples, as were the directors of many of the companies that ran so many mines in the later part of the century, such as Alfred and William North Lewis, John Andrews and the O'Callaghan brothers. Even more ubiquitous, however, were those people connected with the TVR, who not only pursued that railway's interests, but were also involved closely with the Valleys 'Taffia' in a number of their entrepreneurial schemes: George Fisher, chief engineer of the TVR; his son, Henry Oakden Fisher; James Hurman, traffic manager of the TVR; and others. Most of these people did not live in the Valleys, but instead inhabited the comfortable residential areas in and around Cardiff. For example, Matthew Cope lived in St Mellons; the O'Callaghan brothers and John Andrews in Penarth, James Hurman and the North Lewis brothers in Llanishen; George Fisher and Henry Oakden Fisher in Radyr and Llandough.

Much of our story will be centred around the relationships, and tensions, between these various groups of people, in the Valleys and on the coast.

Aspects of Business and Political Life

6

W. H. Mathias and Local Government, 1886–1919

The Ystradyfodwg Local Board
(later Rhondda Urban District Council)

This body had started life in 1877 as the Ystradyfodwg Urban Sanitary Authority (YUSA), dealing mainly with sewerage, drainage and water supply in the parish of Ystradyfodwg, which covered a large proportion of the Rhondda valleys. Its name was changed to the 'Ystradyfodwg Local Government Board' (YLGB) in 1881, when it took on additional duties in relation to planning and public works. In 1895, subsequent to the 1894 Act which attempted to standardise and simplify the ad hoc system of local government that had grown up over the years, it became the Ystradyfodwg Urban District Council (YUDC). Finally, in August 1897 its name was changed to the Rhondda Urban District Council (RUDC) (the name of the valley being much better known than that of the old parish). Its remit covered most of the Rhondda, and meetings were held at Pentre.

From its start in 1877, the YUSA was, like most public bodies in its day, a predominantly employers' body. Among its founding members were the coalowners Edmund Thomas Llwyncelyn and Moses Rowlands Penygraig, together with William Jenkins Ystradfechan, general manager of Ocean Collieries. Jenkins was to be one of the outstanding figures on the YLGB, becoming its chairman in the early 1880s, and continuing in that post for many years. The clerk to the board, from its foundation, was Walter Morgan.[1]

It was in July 1886 that W. H. Mathias was co-opted to the YLGB, to fill a vacancy.[2] Already on the board, since 1882, was Thomas Griffiths,[3] whom Mathias had known well since the 1860s.[4] Another local government colleague who was to be of importance in Mathias's life hereafter was William Jenkins Ystradfechan. They had closely parallel careers. They both became Glamorgan county councillors in the first intake of 1889, both became aldermen, and both became JPs on the same bench in 1893.

When Walter Morgan suddenly died in 1901, his place as clerk to the board was taken by Walter Nicholas, who had recently, in 1897, joined his firm. Nicholas was to become as close, if not closer, a friend and colleague to Mathias as Morgan, in many spheres.

Mathias appears to have taken a fairly prominent position on the YLGB from the start. At his fourth meeting, on 27 August, he took the chair in the absence of the chairman. Gradually, his influence seems to have grown. He soon became the most powerful member of the Roads Committee and of the Sewerage Committee, on both of which his professional skills were invaluable, and also of the Tenders Committee.

By the year 1891, Mathias was the obvious choice to chair the board whenever the chairman William Jenkins was absent, and did so on numerous occasions, becoming vice-chairman a year or so later. He was also the obvious man to deal with any questions to do with external authorities, such as Parliament. On 7 March 1890, for example, he was made a member of a three-man committee which was:

> authorised to employ such Counsel and Witnesses as they may think necessary in support of the opposition to the Ystrad Gas and Water Company's Bill, Bute Docks Company's Bill and the Rhondda and Swansea Bay Railway Company's Bill promoted in the present session of Parliament, and … authorised to attend in London if necessary with the Solicitors to watch the progress of the before-mentioned Bills.[5]

This was the first of many such commissions, in many of which it was solely he and the chairman William Jenkins Ystradfechan who were involved. In February 1893, for example (the YLGB having decided to prosecute the Ystrad Gas and Water Company for supplying unfit water), it was decided that Mathias and the chairman should attend the legal consultations in London, and the trial, with all their expenses being paid by the board.[6] (In view of Mathias's own later record in producing questionable water for his properties in the Aber Valley,[7] his involvement in this prosecution could be seen as ironic). In March 1894, Mathias, the chairman and the surveyor were requested by YLGB to attend in London to support its petitions against the Barry Railway Bill and the Taff Vale Railway Bill. These are just a few examples of his involvement over the years. As the *Western Mail* put it: 'He helped to pilot through Parliament measures of far reaching importance affecting drainage, water and tramways costing the Rhondda Council many thousands of pounds.'[8]

In 1896, W. H. Mathias became first chairman of the RUDC. His prominence on the board/council stemmed in large part from his obvious capabilities, not only in his areas of expertise which were so central to the board's concerns (roads, bridges, building materials, drains, etc.), but also in dealing with prominent people and those in authority. In his activities on the board we see continual evidence of that self-confidence which from henceforth was to mark all his public activities and statements.

His strength on the board was further enhanced by his close alliance with certain members – and in particular Thomas Griffiths and, from the mid-1890s onwards (he was elected to the board in 1893) J. D. Williams of Clydach Court, Trealaw, another prominent local figure. The voting-patterns, first of Mathias and Griffiths, and later of all three, were remarkably consistent, and constituted something of a power block on the board/council.

There is evidence, from the minutes and from newspaper reports, that W. H. Mathias was among those who worked strenuously to improve the sanitation and health of the Rhondda valleys, and to ensure that both public companies and private individuals conformed to the regulations regarding these matters. Public health had been one of the main areas of concern in the Valleys for many years. The environment had suffered from serious pollution caused not only by the detritus of local industry, but also by poor and often almost non-existent sanitation, and from casual methods of disposing of human excrement. The urban sanitary authorities in the Valleys had lagged behind those in other areas, and shown little urgency in dealing with these matters of sanitation and health. The lack of a proper system of drainage and sewerage had been pointed out by the Medical Officer of Health at one of the first meetings of the YUSA, in 1878, and the situation was still appalling fifteen years later when Dr Bruce Low, in a report to the YLGB, pointed out that the only main sewers in the district were the rivers. His report of the state of the river Rhondda gives some impression of the situation:

> The river contains a large proportion of human excrement, stable and pigsty manure, congealed blood, offal and entrails from the slaughterhouses, the rotten carcasses of animals, cats and dogs in various stages of decomposition, old cast-off articles of clothing and bedding, and boots, bottles, ashes, street refuse and a host of other articles . . . In dry weather the stench becomes unbearable.[9]

In such conditions, infectious disease was a perpetual danger. By the 1880s, the serious cholera outbreaks of the earlier part of the century were a thing of the past; but typhoid was ever-present, with serious outbreaks a frequent eventuality. Infant mortality was particularly high, as can be seen from the monthly medical reports to the board. It was almost twice as high as other areas of the United Kingdom.

The board employed 'nuisance inspectors' who enforced regulations to do with sanitation and hygiene. Their regular reports highlighted the areas of most concern: abattoirs, the sanitation of private speculative housing, the dumping of industrial waste, and so on. At times it was clear that their job was not always being carried out with the necessary vigour. Of the members of YLBG, William Henry Mathias appears to have had the strongest views on this. The local press often recorded his irritation with officials who failed to live up to his expectations. For example, in the *Pontypridd District Herald* for 10 September 1892 it was reported that 'Mr Councillor Mathias complained bitterly of the gross laxity of the Board's Inspectors in carrying out their duties.'[10] Another report of a board meeting, in the same newspaper on 23 September 1893, showed that the situation with which the board had to contend remained as serious as ever: a perpetual danger of diseases such as typhoid, and a laxity in relation to the most rudimentary rules of sanitation. Again, Mathias is described as someone who was perpetually trying to make sure that the proper duties were carried out: The report was headed 'Typhoid Fever in Ystradyfodwg':

> There is one fact that does not seem to have been regarded of sufficient importance in its effect upon the sanitary state of the district, and that is the irregular manner in which refuse heaps are formed and then left to play havoc upon the public health. Attention was called to the tipping of twelve loads of night soil on a refuse heap in front of the Ynyswen Board School without any attempt to deodorize the filth or disinfect it. Where was the Inspector of Nuisances on this occasion? It seems to us that the six nuisance officials paid by the Local Board are extremely supine in the discharge of their duties. One of the members of the Board, Mr W. H. Mathias, has more than once had to call the attention of these men to the want of energy and vigilance with which they discharge their duties. [11]

Mathias appears to have done no favours to those near to him, when they were in dereliction of duty on environmental matters. On a number of occasions, for example, his brother-in-law Richard Packer, as representative of his father-in-law James Thomas's Troedyrhiw Company, came in for censure, and was required by the board to put certain matters right, with on at least one occasion Mathias being the person who proposed the motion of censure. [12]

This places into context what might appear a certain laxity on his part in declaring an interest when relatives, or companies in which he had an interest, were concerned in matters before the board. It is clear that the prevailing culture was not particularly bothered by such matters. Indeed, the board appears to have chosen Mathias as its negotiator in certain cases precisely because he had knowledge of the situations and people concerned. Thus, when a dispute arose with the Administrator of the Aberthaw Pebble Lime Company in 1895, it was resolved that 'this be referred to Mr W. H. Mathias, with power to settle', despite his close connections with that company. [13] In the same year, he was made a member of a small sub-committee charged with organising the rebuilding of Rheola and Upper Eirw Bridges, and with '[waiting] upon the Colliery Companies who are believed to have caused the subsidences by their underground workings and [endeavouring] to come to terms with them as to the sum to be paid by them as compensation'. In the case of Rheola Bridge, the two companies believed to have caused these subsidences were Siamps Thomas's Troedyrhiw Coal Company (which still ran the Tynewydd colliery) and Mathias's own Aber Rhondda Coal Company. Furthermore, the three local landowners with whom the sub-committee were charged to negotiate for 'consent to erect the new bridge on their land' were the Troedyrhiw Company (in other words Siamps Thomas and his secretary Richard Packer), Mathias's other brother-in-law David Jenkins (owner of Rheola Timberyard), and 'the Executors of R. Mathias' (W. H. Mathias's father), all of whom possessed land in the vicinity of Rheola Bridge (and, as W. H. Mathias was one of the beneficiaries of his father's estate, he was in a sense being asked to negotiate with himself).[14]

When it came to the acceptance of tenders for building contracts, W. H. Mathias had close family connections with two of the most successful contractors in the area: his brother Richard James Mathias and his brother-in-law David Jenkins of 'Charles Jenkins and Son'. It would have been invidious, of course, if either of their firms had been deprived of business because a relative of theirs was on the local council. And they were in fact often the recipients of major contracts, without necessarily any suspicion of anything untoward. The major contracts for the Rheola and Upper Eirw Bridges, for example, approved by the Tenders Committee of which W. H. Mathias was a prominent member, and Thomas Griffiths the Chairman, went to Charles Jenkins and Son (Rheola) and Richard Mathias (Upper Eirw).[15] The only problem appears, to a modern eye, to be that W. H. Mathias neither stepped down from the Tenders Committee or the chair of the full Board, nor declared an interest, when his family was involved. And, though he only rarely himself proposed or seconded acceptance of their tenders, one occasionally gets the impression that Thomas Griffiths and J. D. Williams were only too happy to fill that role for him. A particular example of this was the occasion on the full Council, in

1896, when in the absence of the chairman W. H. Mathias, a critical motion was passed restricting the work being done by R. J. Mathias on Tylorstown road 'to the amount of the Surveyor's first estimate'. By the next meeting, W. H. Mathias was again firmly in the chair, and J. D. Williams and Thomas Griffiths moved and seconded motions rescinding the previous decision, and moving 'that the work be carried out by the Contractor down to the junction of roads at Tynewydd, Porth.'[16]

It is not certain whether the William Mathias of Treorchy, who was awarded several contracts, was a relation of W. H. Mathias's or not. He may have been his uncle, who had come to Glamorgan with his father in the 1840s. If so, it is interesting that W. H. Mathias occasionally proposed the acceptance of the tenders concerned.[17]

All this smacks not so much of corruption, as of a certain naivety, and of an acceptance of the prevailing culture. The contractors would no doubt have got the contracts without Mathias proposing or seconding them, or failing to record an interest. And Mathias appears to have been put on committees dealing with matters pertaining to his family or his business interests by the will of the rest of the board, and because they appear to have seen him as being particularly fitted to deal with the matters concerned. All this does not so much tell us something about Mathias, as something about the business and local government practices of the time.

All in all, W. H. Mathias's contribution to the work of the YLGB/RUDC appears to have been considerable. We are told that he was among those who were responsible for the development of the Rhondda communities from ill-drained, insalubrious collections of houses into, by the twentieth century, a society in which child mortality had been greatly reduced, and the standard of living greatly enhanced. As one of his obituaries put it, 'The health and convenience of the community have benefited greatly by his active interest and enterprising spirit.'[18] While he was prominent on the council, 'sustained and vigorous efforts'[19] had been made to grapple with the health problems of the Rhondda, with main and subsidiary sewers provided throughout both valleys by 1894.

Of course, by the nature of the original housing provision, there remained many houses that were substandard, and overcrowding remained a serious problem. Many private houses remained which had no water closets connected to the main sewers. As late as 1911, we still find people complaining that 'the housing conditions in the Rhondda are a grave menace to public health, and the overcrowding and filthy houses the people have to live in are questions calling for attention.'[20] The council made attempts to grapple with this problem. Properties declared substandard in the Medical Officer of Health's reports were listed either for demolition, or for improvement. But the scale of the problem was such that one gets the impression that the council could still only chip at the edges of it.

Mathias also took a prominent part in actions against the private company which provided water for the valleys, the Ystrad Gas and Water Company, which had failed to provide enough water, or water of proper purity, and in furthering a Bill in Parliament for the compulsory purchase of that company by the council. When the Bill came into force in 1911, Mathias became the first chairman of the new 'Pontypridd and Rhondda Joint Water Board'.

Mathias sat on the council for over 30 years. For many years he was returned unopposed, and, commenting on this in 1904, the local newspaper the *Porth Gazette* said that 'this shows that his services have been appreciated by the inhabitants whom he has served so well', and that it was 'gratifying to find that there are still men of experience and ability such as him, who will devote their time to serving the public.[21] Stories of his stern treatment of council staff, who ended up doing their job properly because of him, abounded. One such story, affectionately told when he was almost seventy, referred to him as 'the old tried and proved member, whose great practical and commercial knowledge have been such an undoubted boon to the ratepayers.' The story ran as follows:

> Only the other day an old lady walking through one of our main streets saw something flash by her, and on enquiring of a passer-by if it was lightning was astounded on receiving this reply: – No, it was one of the Council employees. What's the matter? enquired the old lady. The passer-by simply pointed to the old member, who was passing by at the time.[22]

By the early twentieth century, the four-seat Mount Pleasant Ward
(Ward No. 9, which covered the area at the start of the Rhondda
Fach valley as far as Wattstown and Tylorstown, containing not only
the Tynewydd and Aber Rhondda mines, but also William James
Thomas's Standard Collieries in Ynyshir) had become something
of a personal fief for the Thomas/Mathias interest. The seats on it
were held by W. H. Mathias and a number of his close associates,
including his cousin by marriage John Thomas Fernbank, manager
of the Standard Collieries. The candidatures were mostly
unopposed. Such a situation could not go on for ever, of course, in
the changing nature of south Wales politics. A good number of
Labour representatives had already come onto the council
(including for example the miners' leaders W. H. Morgan, Tom
Harris and Tom George), even if they had not yet penetrated this
ward. In 1905, for the first time, an official Labour candidate stood
in the Mount Pleasant Ward, against Mathias's friend Griffith
Davies. The attempt was unsuccessful, and the local paper (always
prepared to take the side of established authority) deplored the
attempt, stating that, 'considering the excellent manner in which
he, in conjunction with Alderman W. H. Mathias, had represented
the Ward', it had been hoped that Griffith Davies would be returned
unopposed.[23] In 1913, another official Labour candidate challenged
Mathias and John Thomas for their seats for the ward.[24] Again, the
challenge was unsuccessful. The writing was nevertheless upon the
wall and, though nothing was to occur as dramatic as Mathias's 1919
loss of his seat on Glamorgan County Council, he had by the
middle of the war withdrawn from Rhondda local government,
saving his energies for his work on the county council.

The Glamorgan County Council (GCC)

In January 1889, Mathias, who had stood, unopposed, for the
Ynyshir seat, became one of the first batch of incoming members
of the new Glamorgan County Council (GCC), formed as a result
of the Local Government (County Councils) Act 1888. Until then,
the counties had been governed by the magistrates, through the
quarter sessions. As most of these magistrates were landowners or
industrialists, the counties had thus been governed by what was in

essence a 'non-elected oligarchy'.[25] The Liberal government, subsequent to the 1884 Act, which had extended household suffrage for national elections to the inhabitants of the counties, realised the anomalous nature of such local government procedures, and decided to extend the vote to local elections as well. The 1888 Act, and the formation of the county councils in 1889, were the result.

It must be admitted, when we look at the first batch of representatives on the GCC under the new system, that the result appears in many ways to have been as 'oligarchic' as the old system. The two parties, Liberal and Conservative, had chosen the great majority of their candidates among the same kind of oligarchs as had governed via the quarter sessions. Where on many English county councils many of these people were the traditional landed gentry, in Glamorgan they were in large part industrialists, with major landowners and their agents restricted to the southern part of the county.[26]

Colliery proprietors were to the fore. Of the sixty-eight members of council, eight listed themselves as 'colliery proprietor' (five Liberals, three Conservatives). This was, however, merely the tip of the iceberg, because others, whom we know to have been colliery proprietors, listed themselves either as 'gentleman', or 'mining engineer' (for example, Sir William Thomas Lewis). Others, whose main occupation was listed as 'engineer' or 'contractor', had strong colliery connections as chairmen, shareholders, directors, or close relatives of coalowners, e.g. W. H. Mathias (Ynyshir) and H. Oakden Fisher (Penarth). These account for a further fifteen or so (it is hard at times to distinguish them). Then there were the ironmasters such as W. T. Crawshay, representing Cyfarthfa; and the tinplate manufacturers from West Glamorgan such as R. Cook Jenkins (Aberavon), Rees Harries (Llandilo Talybont), W. Sims (Llansamlet) and David Davies (Morriston). Added to these were the aristocratic industrialists and landowners Sir (Henry) Hussey Vivian, Bt (Tyrdennau) (four years later to become the first Lord Swansea), his brother Mr Arthur P. Vivian (Margam), Sir John Talbot Dillwyn-Llewelyn, Bt (Loughor and Penderry, related both to the Talbots and to the Vivians, and a prominent landowner), and the Earl of Dunraven (Bridgend). The prominent shipowner and coal shipper John Cory (a director of the Barry Docks and Railway Company) represented Barry and Cadoxton. Other industrialists included a substantial quarry-owner (E. Edwards, Llantwit Fardre) and a brick manufacturer (J. Jenkins, Merthyr).

Where the proprietors themselves were not involved, they were often represented by their managers. Thus William Jenkins Ystradfechan, general manager of the Ocean Colliery Company, represented Pentre-Ystrad, E. P. Martin, manager of the Dowlais Steel Works, represented Caeharris, and J. Roberts, manager of the Forest Steel Works (another Crawshay fief) represented Treforest, while colliery agents such as Walter Bell (Merthyr Vale) also took their place on the council. The great mineral and industrial estates, the Plymouth, the Bute, and the Talbot, were represented by their land agents, Robert Forrest (Llandaff), H. Stuart Corbett (Penarth) and W. Hunter (Briton Ferry) respectively. Many of these prominent figures were returned unopposed.

Among the other councillors were several professional men. There were four solicitors (including Walter Morgan), one coroner (R. H. Rhys, listed as 'gentleman'), four surgeons (including Henry Naunton Davies of Porth, who represented the Cymmer district of that town), two nonconformist ministers, and one barrister-at-law (who turns out to have been Oliver H. Jones of Fonmon Castle, the prominent Vale landowner). Cowbridge was represented by its mayor, Thomas Rees.

There were four 'farmers', a title which could disguise a major landowner (e.g. William Morgan Tynewydd, who represented Treherbert); and four grocers. This leaves us with merely a handful of people of other occupations: one schoolmaster, one retired schoolmaster, one builder, one bookseller, one bootmaker and one builder.

All but two of these members stood in either the Liberal or the Conservative/Unionist interest (the two exceptions being 'Labour and Liberal' members, the schoolmaster representing Pentre Ystrad and a solicitor representing Caerphilly). There had been something of a Liberal landslide, 47 Liberal members to 19 Conservative/ Unionists.

William Henry Mathias, who had stood in the Liberal interest, found himself surrounded by old friends and acquaintances. From the YLGB there were Walter Morgan and William Jenkins. Thomas

Griffiths had been a candidate for Cymmer, but had been defeated by Henry Naunton Davies. Then there were Henry Oakden Fisher; William Morgan Tynewydd; Idris Williams (who came onto the Council in a post-aldermanic by-election) and J. Blandy Jenkins, a former railway contractor who had added the 'Jenkins' to 'Blandy' when he had inherited the vast Jenkins estates, which made of him one of the largest landowners in Glamorgan.[27] Idris Williams joined the council in 1892, followed in 1895 by Henry Lewis Tŷ Nant, Mathias's close associate as managing director of the Albion Colliery, who won Cilfynydd unopposed.[28]

At the first formal meeting of the new council, in Pontypridd on 1 April 1889, Sir Hussey Vivian was unanimously elected chairman. W. H. Mathias was appointed to four committees: the Roads and Bridges Committee, on which he was to play a leading role for the next thirty years; the Local Government Committee; the Standing Joint Police Committee (which was to be of considerable importance in the strikes of 1893 and 1898); and the Parliamentary Committee. To his areas of expertise from the YLGB (sanitation, road and bridge building, planning, representation of the council in relation to parliamentary bills etc.), he now added law and order (an interest that became even greater once he became a JP in 1893).

Mathias's attendance at these committees was impeccable. Indeed, he also took on membership of innumerable sub-committees of the Roads and Bridges Committee which dealt with specific local situations. Soon, he had become the most prominent member of that committee, his name a byword for local authority power.

Over the years, the complexion of the GCC was gradually to change. The first signs of this were in the 1892 elections, when the newspapers were surprised to note that seven representatives of labour (mostly under the Lib-Lab flag) had been elected. They include some of the best-known names in the labour history of south Wales: David Morgan ('Dai o'r Nant'), miners' agent for Aberdare, who was returned for the Gadlys division of that town for 'Labour';[29] Isaac Evans, miners' agent, of the Neath, Swansea and Llanelli Miners' Association, (who was to emerge as one of the leading opponents of the sliding scale), returned for Resolven as a 'Lib-Lab'; T. D. Isaac (Labour), one of the miners' representatives on the Sliding Scale Committee, returned for Treorchy; John Thomas

(Liberal), miners' agent, returned for the Garw Valley; Moses Moses (Liberal), a working miner, who gained a surprise victory over his fellow-Liberal Idris Williams at Cymmer by 26 votes (though Idris Williams immediately got onto the council in one of the post-aldermanic by-elections, and Henry Naunton Davies, who had won the seat in 1889, was by now an alderman); Thomas Thomas (Labour), who gained a landslide victory over the Liberal candidate in the Crawshay domain of Cyfarthfa; and Morgan Williams (Liberal), checkweigher at the Standard Collieries Ynyshir, who won Porth and Penygraig from a Conservative candidate.[30]

At this early stage, however, the new recruits were engulfed in the predominant tone of the council, of which Sir Hussey Vivian was again made chairman. It is perhaps significant that about half the councillors had been returned unopposed (including Mathias once more).[31] And there were still major coalowning figures on the council, such as Fred Davis (Ferndale), Evan Evans Bevan (Dulais Valley), Clifford Cory (Ystrad), F. Cory Yeo (Gower), John Newell (Coedffranc), and John Powell (Sketty), and Sir William Thomas Lewis remained an alderman. In other areas, prominent local employers, such as J. C. Meggitt the building entrepreneur (Barry), obtained the local vote. Also, the 'landed' and aristocratic line remained, with the two Vivians, Sir John Dillwyn Llewellyn Bt., Sir John Jones Jenkins, Oliver Jones of Fonmon Castle, and several others.[32] At succeeding elections between then and 1914, further representatives of the industrial and landed classes to be returned included Lord Aberdare, Herbert Homfray of Penllyn Castle, the steel manufacturer Francis Gilbertson, the colliery proprietor John Glasbrook, and many others.

It was not to be until well into the twentieth century that the complexion of the council was to change in any real sense. It is true that in 1895 when, after the death of Lord Swansea (as Sir Hussey Vivian had become), it was necessary to vote in a new chairman, the council rejected his brother Arthur Pendarves Vivian, thus avoiding what looked like becoming a perquisite of the Vivian family. But in his place was chosen J. Blandy Jenkins, a rich and prominent landowner.[33] The old aristocratic choices died hard. For example, a few years earlier, despite the opposition of the small minority of members who were working men, the three representatives chosen for the County Councils Association, which met in London, had been the two Vivians and Sir John Talbot Dillwyn Llewellyn.[34]

Evidence of Mathias's already prominent position on the council is shown by his election to the position of alderman at the first meeting of the new council on 15 March 1893. Aldermen were voted into their position by the council immediately after each election, and served for a period of six years (their councillor's seat meanwhile going through a by-election). Mathias was to remain an alderman for over twenty-five years.

Though the complexion of the GCC changed considerably in the first decade or so of the new century, W. H. Mathias's dominant position upon it does not seem to have diminished until after the First World War. On the Ynyshir ward, he was regularly returned, and just as regularly he was thereafter elected alderman for a period of six years, necessitating each time a by-election for the Ynyshir seat. Up till 1910, the holder of the seat was Thomas Henry Morris, a surgeon who lived at Ashfield House, Tylorstown. After the aldermanic election in 1910, however, the candidate in the subsequent by-election for the Ynyshir seat was Mathias's nephew William James Thomas, the principal employer in the area, who won it unopposed, and who remained a county councillor until 1919.[35]

On the council itself, Mathias's power and influence appear to have continued unabated, right up to the end of the war. Indeed, during the war he seems to have played an even more prominent role than before. On the Roads and Bridges Committee, of which the chairman of the council Blandy Jenkins was chairman, Mathias was the most important other member, sitting on almost every sub-committee and being chosen to represent the council on almost every special commission. Among the other members of that committee one still finds other representatives of the moneyed classes, including John Glasbrook the Swansea coalowner, William Forrest the agent of the Earl of Plymouth, and, from 1910 onwards, William James Thomas.[36]

When Blandy Jenkins died in 1915, Mathias, now aged seventy, was the obvious choice to succeed him as chairman of the Roads and Bridges Committee. For the next four years he not only filled that role with his usual vigour (and sat on almost every sub-committee); he also, by virtue of this chairmanship, became a member of the powerful Finance Committee of the council. He also continued to serve on the Local Government Committee and the Parliamentary Committee.

As the end of the war approached, there was no sign within the council that any of this might change. Alderman Mathias continued with his multiple tasks. In June 1918, for example, he was chosen as one of two representatives of the Parliamentary Committee to go to London in connection with the council's opposition to the Swansea Extension Bill, counsel having been briefed. It looked as though he was likely to continue to serve in his customary position of prominence for years to come.

The political world was changing, however, and local government representation was changing with it. In 1919, a thunderbolt struck. In the council elections of that year, Mathias was challenged for the Ynyshir seat by George Dolling, a leading Labour activist who was a checkweigher at the Standard Collieries. Dolling was, ironically, a former political associate of William James Thomas's (they had been the two people to sign Mabon's election papers at the 1910 election). Dolling was successful in unseating Mathias. The shock must have been enormous. The local newspaper was as always sympathetic to Mathias:

> Most people, even on the Labour side, sympathise with Mr W. H. Mathias. To fail to get returned after 30 years of able continuous service would be a bitter blow to most people. We are living in times, however, when Labour is strongly asserting itself and it is not to be wondered at that a man of Mr Dolling's views and popularity should wrest a seat from one who sits on a board of colliery directors. To the miners it was a matter of principle more than personality – therefore Mr Mathias's great services availed little.[37]

Mathias's *Western Mail* obituary says that the GCC, 'realising how ill they could afford to lose the services of the "grand old man of the county council" ... lost no time in co-opting him as a member'.[38] Yet there is no trace whatsoever of this arrangement in the minutes of the GCC or of the council committees including the Roads and Bridges Committee, from all of which his name remained absent from the time of his defeat in the polls.[39] One can only presume that this was wishful thinking on the newspaper's part.

Yet even to the end Mathias held a powerful position in the public mind. In his lifetime, his virtues as a public man were continually being noted by the press, and at his death, his obituaries went even further. He was described as having given 'great services, possibly unequalled services, upon the Glamorgan County and the Rhondda Urban Councils', and having 'departed this life, like the great patriarch of old, full of years and honours.'[40]

One gets the impression that William Henry Mathias was in his element on the Glamorgan County Council. Not only did he enjoy using his expertise for the public good; one is also tempted to believe, from all accounts, that he enjoyed power and the trappings of power; and that he also enjoyed the use of political wiles for their own sake, in collaboration with so many people who shared his outlook and interests. There is no doubt that he was an extremely effective operator, and that, as on the YLGB/RUDC, like many good operators he also did a certain amount of good for the public.

7

'The history of the undertaking is rather peculiar': The Cowbridge–Aberthaw Railway and the Rhondda Connection, 1886–1892

Alongside the laudable vigour, enthusiasm and skill of the second-generation entrepreneurs in the Valleys, we find certain other characteristics of a different kind: mutual 'back-scratching', and exchange of favours; the use of public position to pursue private interest; insider dealing on a massive scale; the relentless driving of hard bargains once the upper hand had been gained; and ruthless treatment of anyone, however innocent, who stood in one's way. In this and the next chapter, we will be looking at two specific examples of entrepreneurial practice, which reveal a few of the important characteristics of this period and this society. In both these examples, W. H. Mathias plays a leading role. In this first chapter we will be dealing with the tangled series of events which surrounded the creation of the railway line from Cowbridge to Aberthaw in the years 1889–92.

These have always presented something of a historical puzzle. Why was such a line envisaged, when the chances were that it would run at a loss? Why, after years of refusal to consider supporting such a line, did the Taff Vale Railway Company suddenly change its mind in the year 1888? Why did the Cowbridge and Aberthaw Railway Company so speedily fail? Who made anything out of it? Various theories have been put forward over the years. New evidence has now emerged, which links events in the Rhondda with what was happening in the Vale of Glamorgan.

Cowbridge's previous railway experience

The market town of Cowbridge, in the Vale of Glamorgan, had until the mid-nineteenth century been a major staging-post on the main road to Pembrokeshire (as witness the fine coaching inns that are still to be found there). It had been a centre in which most of the local gentry had their town houses, and it had had a flourishing social life. When the railways came, however, the main route of the South Wales Railway (later the Great Western Railway) to the west was routed via Llantrisant, about six miles to the north of Cowbridge. It has been suggested that this was the fault of the burghers of Cowbridge, who supposedly had not wanted the newfangled mode of transport running through their territory; but the truth appears to be that the decision had been made because the route via the Ely valley to Llantrisant, and thence via the Ewenny valley to Bridgend, was very much easier in engineering terms.[1]

Whatever the reason, the decision as to the route looked like making the hitherto prosperous borough of Cowbridge into something of a backwater. The town soon realised how much it suffered from its isolation from the railway, and from 1855 onwards, people had begun to advocate the construction of a branch railway to Cowbridge from Llantrisant station (at Pontyclun, about a mile or so south of Llantrisant). It was at first difficult to get backing for the venture (the South Wales Railway was not interested), and it was not until the Llantrisant and Taff Vale Junction Railway was incorporated in 1861, to build a railway from the TVR main line near Pontypridd to link with the South Wales Railway at Llantrisant, that the way became clear for a Cowbridge Railway, backed by the TVR.[2] The Cowbridge Railway Company that was formed was run by local worthies, and was grossly underfunded. Though the TVR gave a small proportion of the initial funding needed, and agreed to use the line with its own rolling stock, the organisational backing needed for a successful venture was almost completely lacking. As years went by, the line, started in 1863, developed more and more problems owing to false economies in its construction, and at the same time the company was getting deeper and deeper into debt. By 1874, it had not yet paid its contractors, and had paid only three of the 23 landowners over whose land the line ran, so that the landowners were now threatening to repossess their land. The Cowbridge directors, faced by the loss of their line, tried in 1875 to get the TVR to lease their railway for £3,000 a year. The TVR offered half that sum. On this basis, the TVR took over the running of the line in August 1875.[3]

Considerable work needed to be done on the line, which was in a very bad state after years of poor maintenance. One of the main contractors used on this work was Richard Mathias, aided by his son William Henry Mathias. The railway was put in good working order, and the line from Llantrisant to Cowbridge was to remain in use until after the Second World War.

The experience of this line might have been expected to give pause to anyone thinking of other north-south railway ventures in the Vale of Glamorgan, particularly as critics of this earlier venture had pointed out the lack of economic justification for such a line through the Vale. Yet within a very few years of the failure of the Cowbridge Railway, powerful voices were beginning to advocate an extension of the line from Cowbridge to Aberthaw, on the coast.

Aberthaw

Aberthaw was at this time a small harbour at the mouth of the river Thaw, or Daw, almost due south of Cowbridge. It had been prominent in the coastal trade along both shores of the Bristol Channel, but had declined in importance over the years. In the early 1880s a number of coalowners, led by David Davies of Llandinam, had decided to try to find a suitable port as an outlet for their coal to bypass the Marquess of Bute's Cardiff monopoly. As is now history, they eventually decided on Barry. Among the original places they had thought possibly suitable for this purpose, however, was Aberthaw; but 'the engineering and other difficulties concerning sea currents were considered so great that it was decided to abandon the idea of using it, and attention was turned to the Barry Sound, between the Island and the mainland, instead'.[4] In 1884 an Act was passed for the construction of Barry Dock, and for the Barry Railway linking it to the mining valleys. This led to the mushroom growth of Barry, the population growing within a very few years from less than 500 to over 35,000. This appeared the death knell for Aberthaw.

However, at about the same time as the coalowners had been considering Aberthaw as a coal port, a man called Daniel Owen had been perceiving other possibilities for the area. Owen was a powerful self-made man of local origins who lived at Ash Hall, Ystradowen, just north of Cowbridge. He had made a fortune as a timber merchant in Australia, but had now returned to Wales. Here, amid other ventures, he had founded a flourishing printing and publishing business, and then, with Lascelles Carr, editor of the *Western Mail*, had become joint-proprietor of that newspaper in 1869. In 1884, Owen and Carr had combined all these business interests, including the Western Mail, into a company entitled 'Daniel Owen and Company Limited'.[5]

Daniel Owen's flair for the use of natural resources had made him a fortune in the timber business. He now, in the early 1880s, turned his attention to another natural resource, limestone. In this his judgement, as we shall see, turned out to be more faulty. The coast at Aberthaw was rich in lias limestone, both in the cliffs and in an extensive bank of pebbles. The lime itself was not produced, however, at Aberthaw, the stone and pebbles being shipped elsewhere for this purpose, in the small local coasting vessels which traded along the south Wales coastline, and over the Channel to Bristol, Somerset, Devon and Cornwall. A man called Stephen Collier from Bridgend, who had produced a plan for the production of lime at Aberthaw itself, approached Daniel Owen in 1881 for his backing. Later in the same year Owen, Collier, Lascelles Carr and James Hurman, the traffic manager of the TVR, visited Aberthaw, with Owen making the case to Hurman for producing a lime works there, and for a railway to be constructed from Cowbridge to Aberthaw.[6] Such a link would lead, via the Cowbridge Railway and Llantrisant, to the mining valleys, in which limestone was at such a premium for roadbuilding and public works.

James Hurman, as traffic manager of the TVR, was a crucial figure in the company's practical decisions. A good example of the way in which the board followed his advice is the occasion in March 1887, when a deputation of the residents of Llantwit Fardre, Llantrisant and Cowbridge attended the TVR board to ask for the provision of additional trains between Cowbridge and Pontypridd (there were currently four a day), and to ask for a new station to be provided to serve Church Village, on the Pontypridd–Llantrisant route. James Hurman reported to the board on these requests in April, effectively scuppering the idea of additional trains both because of lack of passenger demand and because of operational difficulties. He backed, however, the request for a new station at Church Village, and the directors concurred.[7]

On the question of an Aberthaw line, Hurman does not seem to have been impressed. As a result, the TVR made it clear that they would not give their support to the idea. As Owen must have realised, without a rail link his project would be doomed. He was undeterred, however, and kept up his lobbying of the TVR for the next few years, but still without success. Indeed, as late as 1886, when the station lay-out at Cowbridge was rearranged, that arrangement '[did] not suggest that the TVR was then contemplating an early extension of the Cowbridge branch'.[8] It looked as though there was no chance of a railway to Aberthaw ever being built.

It is surprising to find, therefore, that in January 1888 Owen appeared confident enough to go ahead with his scheme for the lime works, even though at this stage there was 'no indication to suggest that the TVR was prepared to back Owen's proposal'.[9] Yet without a rail link the scheme would not be viable. Did he have inside knowledge of a change of mind by the TVR? At all events, he, Lascelles Carr, Collier, and a local Aberthaw limestone merchant and shipowner called John Thomas, leased the necessary land from Oliver Henry Jones of Fonmon Castle in December 1887, and the 'Aberthaw Pebble Lime Company Ltd' came into existence on 28 January:[10] 'A gigantic limeworks on the famous Aberthaw shore [was] conceived, completed and working within the twelve months of 1888.'[11]

Dramatically, when the works were opened in December 1888, Owen was able to announce that the TVR had reversed its policy, and 'was prepared to assist with the construction of the railway'.[12] What had caused this change of policy on the part of the TVR? As the *South Wales Daily News* commented, in relation to the fact that the swift construction of the lime works had so closely been followed by the decision to build a line, 'the history of the undertaking . . . is rather peculiar'.[13] Various unsatisfactory explanations have been put forward:

Firstly, it has been suggested that the plans for the Vale of Glamorgan Railway (a subsidiary of the Barry Railway), from Bridgend to Barry via Ewenny and Llantwit Major, appeared to the TVR to be an incursion into its territory, and that an extension of the Cowbridge line to a point on the Vale of Glamorgan line like Aberthaw could have been of strategic value. As the Vale of Glamorgan line was, in 1886, not yet a definite proposition (it was not to be started until 1894), this seems a thin reason – particularly as the Vale of Glamorgan hardly seems the TVR's natural 'territory'.

A second, more serious suggestion has been that the TVR, which had failed to get access to Barry Dock from the east via Penarth, might now have had in mind the use of the new railway as a means for accessing Barry from the west. It is, however, unlikely that the TVR had at this stage any such idea of linking with Barry. As Chapman has pointed out, they would have known that such a plan would have got into serious legal difficulties; and there is little evidence of such an idea in the speeches made by TVR representatives at the cutting of the first sod of the line, on 7 February 1890. These speeches were particularly cautious. George Fisher (chief engineer of the TVR Company) warned that 'a great deal would depend upon the inhabitants of the country through which the railway would pass', and the engineer J. H. Brewer suggested that Aberthaw might now become 'a seaport and seaside residence'[14] (presumably on the basis of the popularity of the Leys, an open area of coast nearby – now occupied by a power station – to which many people came from the valleys 'by horse-drawn brakes',[15] before the delights of Barry Island, accessed by the Barry Railway, supplanted it). It is true that, by 1892, Owen himself was putting forward for the first time the idea of an extension of the new line to Barry, no doubt because it was by then becoming clear that the line was already in serious financial difficulties, as was the Aberthaw Pebble Lime Company. But even at that stage 'the attitude of the TVR was less clear' and, in the event, nothing of the kind was ever attempted.[16] And there had never been any chance of the other possible type of access to Barry, for example a link between the two railway companies' lines. At Aberthaw, there was never to be such a link and, when the Vale of Glamorgan line had been built, passengers who wished to change lines had to alight and take a considerable walk between the two stations.

Another argument, put forward by the chairman of the TVR at a critical meeting in May 1889 at which the decision to back the line was challenged by some of the shareholders, was that such a railway was bound to be built by someone, and that it was desirable that the TVR should have the line and protect its interests. This argument smacks of an *ex post facto* justification for the decision taken. It was not at all likely that anyone else would build such a line, given the grave doubts as to the financial viability of such a venture.

The caution of the TVR shareholders was understandable, given some of the warnings they had been given. A prominent TVR shareholder, Major Brickman, who owned land on the proposed route, said that 'the traffic on the projected line would not be enough to pay for the greasing of the wheels of the trains', and that the enterprise was 'foolish in the extreme'.[17] The *Barry and Cadoxton Journal* commented scathingly:

> The question naturally arises in connection with the construction of this railway, 'What is its object?' It is difficult to believe that the Aberthaw Lime Works will ever be of sufficient importance to make the line pay . . . The passenger traffic between Aberthaw and Cowbridge will certainly not be very great.[18]

Feeling among the shareholders was such that the chairman had to tell them to 'trust the directors', which, as the *Barry and Cadoxton Journal* pointed out, was an instruction, 'to shut their eyes and open their mouths and see what would be put in them'.[19] Finally, at a meeting of the TVR in Bristol on 26 August 1890, the directors were forced to accede to a call for the appointment of a committee 'to inquire into and report to shareholders upon the management of the company's undertaking'.[20]

What, then, had caused the TVR to change its mind about a Cowbridge-Aberthaw line? To get some idea of the forces that may have been at work, we will need to look further afield, to Porth in the Rhondda valley.

The Aber Rhondda Coal Company

Siamps Thomas, once his Standard Collieries at Ynyshir had become his major interest, had decided to sub-lease the old Troedyrhiw Colliery (now called Aber Rhondda). A company called the 'Aber Rhondda Colliery Company Ltd' (in which one of the leading figures had been the shipowner John Cory) had leased it in 1882, but had wound itself up in March 1884.[21]

This is where Daniel Owen comes once more upon the scene. He and William Henry Mathias (whose house Green Meadow lay next to the mine, on the Aber Rhondda Road) decided to form a new company to continue the working of the mine. In coalmining terms there was sense in the venture. Mathias and Owen may have had other factors in mind, however, in the forming of the new company.

This is the first sign we have of Owen and Mathias knowing each other (though Owen's daughter had married the son of Mathias's old Porth friend, Dr Henry Naunton Davies). Owen may have chosen to work with Mathias because the latter was the son-in-law of the head leaseholder of the mine. He may also have seen Mathias's proximity to the mine as an advantage, in that he could be (as he turned out to be) an effective 'on-the-spot' director. But there were no doubt other factors which accorded with Owen's preoccupations at this time. Mathias, with his professional roadbuilding interests, and his local government interest in the provision of limestone, was a natural person for Owen to cultivate. Also, Mathias had worked closely with all the main officials of the TVR, and was particularly friendly with James Hurman.[22]

It comes nevertheless as something of a surprise when we find that James Hurman was to be the third main partner in this mining venture. It was on 2 October 1886 that the first activities in relation to the new company, the 'Aber Rhondda Coal Company Ltd' took place. Four men (Daniel Owen, W. H. Mathias and James Hurman, together with a Cardiff accountant, William Bartlett) negotiated on that date a lease of the Aber Rhondda pit from the Troedyrhiw Coal Company (whose active directors were now Siamps Thomas and Matthew Cope); the lease included 'all the unworked portions of the No. 2 Rhondda seam, and the farm and lands called Penrhiw and Troedyrhiw . . . and the pit, and plant, sidings, fixtures' etc.[23]

A month and a half later, on 15 November 1886, the new company was formed. The major shareholders were Owen, Mathias and Hurman. Of the seven people with lesser shareholdings in Aber Rhondda, three more had TVR connections. They were the engineer Henry Oakden Fisher, Richard Wain, proprietor of the Penarth Hotel (which had been built by the TVR in Penarth in 1868) and Richard Mathias, William Henry's father. The four other shareholders were Francis Lock (a contractor), Walter Bartlett and Ivor Roberts (Cardiff accountants), and John Jones, the company's solicitor. The directors were Owen, Mathias, Hurman and Wain, with Owen as chairman.[24]

The Aber Rhondda venture can be counted as having been a success. As a start in the coal industry for W. H. Mathias it was a comparatively modest one, but a remunerative one. It is more difficult to assess the value of the venture for Owen. All may, of course, have been perfectly straightforward. Mathias may have introduced his TVR friends to the scheme as natural partners, and Owen may have gone in with this without other thoughts. On the other hand, Owen may have seen the company as a way of getting these crucial decision-makers 'on his side'. Whichever was the case, this close financial partnership between the major negotiators from both sides of the Aberthaw project was bound to make them more inclined to agree, and to work together. Certainly, the attitude of the TVR in relation to the Cowbridge–Aberthaw line changed by 180 degrees in the period between November 1886 (when the Aber Rhondda Company was formed, and when the signs were still adverse to any TVR approval of any such line) and the end of 1887 (Owen would hardly have gone ahead with building the lime works in January 1888 unless he had had some informal assurance by then that the TVR's attitude would change). It was Henry Oakden Fisher who, in late 1888, undertook a survey of the proposed route (a survey which turned out to be an over-optimistic one, and which was to be the main cause of the company's eventual financial troubles). It is interesting to note, also, that Hurman now became a shareholder in Owen's Aberthaw Pebble Lime Company Ltd.[25]

The Cowbridge-Aberthaw Railway [26]

On 19 August 1889, the first meeting of the directors of the Cowbridge and Aberthaw Railway Company took place in Cardiff. Daniel Owen was appointed chairman, the other two directors being Sir Morgan Morgan, a recent mayor of Cardiff (1887–8), knighted in his period of office, who was to be the unsuccessful Conservative candidate for South Glamorgan in 1892, and his son Colonel John Morgan from Brecon. George Fisher and James Inskip were made directors as representatives of the TVR. As at Treferig, J. H. Brewer was appointed engineer and surveyor. However, at the next meeting, on 26 September, Henry Oakden Fisher was appointed joint engineer with Brewer. The initial shareholders were listed. W. H. Mathias was among them, his 780 shares, of £10 each, being exceeded only by Daniel Owen (1000), Colonel John Morgan (1500), Sir Morgan Morgan (1000), and James Inskip (1000). There were five other shareholders, holding 200 or less: two of them were George Fisher and Henry Oakden Fisher.

Mathias's decision to become a major shareholder in the new venture was typical of his techniques. In this case, he clearly had his eyes on the contract for the line. At a meeting on 23 January 1890, four tenders for the contract were considered. Brewer and Oakden Fisher recommended Mathias's tender, and the board accepted this. [27]

On 7 February 1890 an opening ceremony was held on the site of the new Cowbridge Station. George Fisher, for the company, presented a silver shovel to Mrs Naunton Davies, daughter of Daniel Owen, who cut the first sod. The ubiquitous Revd David Watkin Williams, of Fairfield, Pontypridd (who owned a number of properties in the Cowbridge area) proposed the health of the railway, speaking of 'the great advantage it would confer upon the neighbourhood through which it would pass.' Sir Morgan Morgan spoke confidently of the future; George Fisher and Brewer less confidently, though Fisher insisted that it was the TVR's 'intention that it should be a success'. [28]

W. H. Mathias was accompanied to Cowbridge by his brother Richard James, who assisted him in the contract. They rented a large house called St Quentin's, opposite the castle in Llanblethian, just south of Cowbridge. William Henry spent his time between St Quentin's and Porth, but Richard and his family appear to have settled in Llanblethian for the time being.[29] As his father had done with him, at the time of the Cowbridge Railway work in 1875, W. H. Mathias also involved his young son, James Henry Mathias (aged 24), in the work for this contract.[30]

Throughout the period of the contract (1890–2) W. H. Mathias kept up his regular attendance at the Ystradyfodwg Local Board (rarely missing its fortnightly meetings),[31] at the Glamorgan County Council, which at this time met alternately in Pontypridd and Neath, and at the Roads and Bridges Committee (of which Henry Oakden Fisher also was a member).

Mathias's reputation as a 'character' whose grand ways gave rise to wonderment among the locals is borne out by an anecdote relating to him in this period:

> One afternoon Mr Mathias, the owner of a fast trotting pony and trap, missed the train to Pontypridd. He particularly wished to keep an appointment at his destination and made for Pontyclun at full speed in his trap, arriving there before the train. He completed his journey by train and kept the appointment as arranged.[32]

Work forged ahead on the new railway, though it was discovered that the cuttings had to be made through rock that occasioned far more work than had been expected from Fisher's survey. By August 1892, the line had been completed, and it successfully passed its Board of Trade inspection in September. It was officially opened on 1 October 1892. A special train left Cardiff at 11.15, and took a circuitous route via TVR lines, first to Treforest, then to Llantrisant Junction, and then to Cowbridge, picking up guests at various points along the way. At Cowbridge, they were greeted by Daniel Owen and Sir Morgan Morgan, and the party then proceeded down the line to Aberthaw, where the line was declared open by Mrs Beasley, wife of the chairman of the TVR. There followed a celebratory luncheon at the Bear Hotel, Cowbridge, where some notable speeches were made, particularly a bullish one by Sir Morgan Morgan, who answered those who said the line would not pay by foretelling a magnificent future for Aberthaw as a port, equivalent to the meteoric rise of the port of Barry. 'At the terminus of the new line there was a natural harbour, and already a great number of small vessels visited it.' Among the guests were naturally the two Mathias brothers and their wives. When the toast to 'the Engineers and Contractor' had been drunk, W. H. Mathias, after responding, 'presented Mrs Beasley with a handsome silver salver as a memento of that day's event'.[33]

The line had cost about £120,000 (£7.5 million in modern terms). This had exceeded the authorised capital by about £30,000 (£1.87 million). Mathias's quotation, on which his choice as contractor had supposedly been based, had been a serious underestimate (probably on the basis of the faulty survey). That the venture was getting into financial trouble was soon clear:

> Without the prospect of an extension to Barry, or of the development of a port at Aberthaw, the traffic potential of the new line was limited to the requirements of the lime manufacturing industry at Aberthaw, and the agricultural produce of the lower part of the Vale of Glamorgan served by the railway.[34]

By July 1893, Beasley of the TVR was raising questions in relation to the Cowbridge and Aberthaw Railway's accounts. It soon became clear that the TVR would have to take the Company over. The Bill to accomplish this took some time, but in an Act of 17 August 1894[35] the TVR acquired the company as from 1 January 1895, and on 19 December the last meeting of the directors, presided over as usual by Daniel Owen, took place.[36] Meanwhile, the Aberthaw lime works, which had been the main cause for the construction of this line, had also been getting into financial difficulties. Seven months earlier, on 1 May 1894, the Aberthaw Pebble Lime Company had had to be wound up, and an administrator appointed, because 'the Company cannot, by reason of its liabilities, continue its business'.[37] Daniel Owen's Vale of Glamorgan ventures appeared to have come crashing to the ground. He retained his interest in Daniel Owen and Co. Ltd, but in 1895 he died, and in 1896 that company, too, was wound up.[38]

Though the Cowbridge and Aberthaw Railway Company had done so badly, Mathias had himself done extremely well out of the venture. He had made thousands from the contract, in various tranches (and had also been allotted further shares in the company). In total, the company paid him £76,845 (about £4.78 million in modern terms), most of it in 23 tranches between April 1890 and July 1892, which were paid promptly. His final estimated account for £7,500, which was presented in December 1892, was not however paid,[39] and he was forced to come to the board on 10 February 1894 to call attention to the fact that 'a large amount of money remained due to him upon the final certificate'.' The board, in dire financial straits and with the TVR takeover already in prospect, resolved to allow interest to him on the amount, at 3.5% per annum, backdated to 1 January 1893.[40] When he was finally paid, at the handover to the TVR, the final certificate, with the interest added as from January 1893, had risen to £9,960 7s. 9d.[41] Also, his shares in the Cowbridge and Aberthaw Railway were converted into the equivalent amount of valuable TVR shares.

It is interesting to note that on the Ystradyfodwg Local Government Board, where limestone was regularly purchased in thousands of tons at a time, and where Mathias kept a stern eye on suppliers,[42] the Aberthaw Company was a principal supplier from the opening of the line to the time of the company's demise in May 1894.[43]

The Cowbridge–Aberthaw line continued until 1932, first under the TVR and then under the GWR, but always as a loss-making concern.

When judging cases such as this, it is hard to come to clear-cut conclusions. The involvement of TVR executives in a business venture run by a man with whom they were having to deal on other very delicate matters could conceivably have been innocent; Mathias may just have been pleased to involve his friends from a variety of spheres in what promised to be a remunerative venture, and not have thought about the implications of this down in the Vale of Glamorgan; Owen may have joined the venture, similarly, without afterthoughts. And the TVR change of mind about the Cowbridge–Aberthaw Railway could conceivably have come about perfectly innocently. A more than strong suspicion remains,

---

however, that there was more to it than that. The change of mind was so violent, so sudden, and so out of kilter with the firm opinions of the TVR up to that time; it coincided so closely in time with the setting-up of the Aber Rhondda venture; and it was kept secret until the very last minute. It all seems to add up to a business arrangement of a kind only too common in late nineteenth-century south Wales.

8

Further peculiar undertakings: Windsor Colliery, Abertridwr and the Parc Newydd Estate

From the 1890s onwards, William Henry Mathias had considerable business interests in the Aber valley, just north-west of Caerphilly. These included a directorship of the Windsor Colliery at Abertridwr, ownership of a strategically-placed farm, Parc Newydd, and the development of workers' housing in the area. All in all, these various activities give us some prime examples of Mathias's business methods.

Parc Newydd Farm and the Windsor Colliery

Some time before or in the year 1892 W. H. Mathias and his friend Walter Morgan, the Pontypridd solicitor, jointly bought the 104-acre Parc Newydd Farm, near what was to become Abertridwr.[1] This was to turn out to be a remarkably lucrative investment, as within a few years Insoles, the major mining company which had developed the Cymmer Collieries in Porth, was to sink the Windsor Colliery, Abertridwr, very close to this site. At first sight, the decision to buy a farm in that almost uninhabited area of the Aber valley must have seemed a surprising one, and the resultant profits unexpected. But when we realise that the Insoles engineer entrusted with the sinking of the Windsor Colliery, who was to become its first manager, was Mathias's old friend Thomas Griffiths, we can perhaps guess that Mathias had been benefiting from inside knowledge (as was possibly the case in relation to a number of the other properties he bought which turned out to have mineral potential).

In 1892, Insoles took out a 99-year lease, from Mathias and Morgan, on the minerals under Parc Newydd Farm. The deadrent was £300 per annum, and the royalty one twelfth of the average selling price, for large coal, and one twenty-fourth for small coal.[2] The sinking of the Windsor mine started in 1896. For this purpose a company was formed, the Windsor Steam Coal Company, in which the lease was now vested. Mathias bought a substantial number of shares, 500 in all, in this new company; this was seen by the directors as 'a significant statement of confidence in the Company'.[3] So much so, that when in 1901 a new company was formed, the Windsor Steam Coal Company (1901) Ltd, Mathias was asked to become one of the directors (all the others having been directors of the 1896 company). He also became 'a very large, if not the largest shareholder' of the new company.[4] As in other cases (for example Albion or Cowbridge–Aberthaw) early investment in shares in a company led to his either becoming a director, or having other advantages.

Parc Newydd was extremely well placed in relation to the new venture. Though the mine was to be sunk on land belonging to the Earl of Plymouth (which explains the title 'Windsor Colliery' – the Plymouth family name being Windsor-Clive), Parc Newydd was close enough to warrant substantial mineral royalties for coal extracted from beneath the farm. Added to this, the farm had the advantage of covering the whole area of the narrow valley across which any railway line would have to pass. When the Rhymney Railway Company decided in 1896 to build a line up the valley to serve not only Windsor Colliery, but also the Universal Collieries at Senghenydd at the head of the valley, it was forced to negotiate with Mathias and Morgan, who struck a hard deal, as a letter from the general manager of the railway to the company's solicitors bears witness: 'These people have got an enormous amount of money out of the Company in fact almost as much as the farm cost, and still retaining the minerals there.'[5]

But this was not all. Mathias and Morgan, like so many other entrepreneurs of their time, also became property developers. In the mid-1890s, they developed extensive workers' housing on the Parc Newydd land. In contemporary documents, it is described as 'The Mathias Estate, Senghenydd'[6] (the distinction between Abertridwr and Senghenydd not being common at this time).

It is interesting to note that Walter Morgan's partner in the solicitors Morgan, Bruce and Nicholas, Gerald Bruce, had followed Morgan's example and bought, also in the early 1890s, the neighbouring farm, Gwernymilwr, for the purposes of mineral rights and property speculation. He was later to form a company to run the Gwernymilwr Estate, entitled the 'Gwernymilwr Land Company Ltd', of which one of the main subscribers was Dr George Dawkin, Mathias's son-in-law.[7]

Two sets of documentation relating to the Parc Newydd estate tell us something of Mathias's attitudes when dealing with his properties, and with any threats to his interests. Both sets are to do with water, which was of course a major problem for the new communities being formed in the valleys.

The abortive Rhymney Water Board Bill of 1911

From the proceedings of the Select Committee of the House of Lords dealing with the Rhymney Water Board Bill we learn much about what Mathias had been up to in the Aber valley. We also witness the way in which the close-knit entrepreneurial society of the valleys could marshall its resources to oppose a Bill it saw as a threat.

By an Act of 1898 all the small gas and water undertakings in the Rhymney valley had been amalgamated into the Rhymney and Aber Valleys Gas and Water Company (RAVGWC). Little thought appears, however, to have been given by the local authority responsible, Caerphilly Urban District Council, to the provision of water to the previously isolated Aber valley, much of which was at any rate at a level which the RAVGWC could not reach.[8] In the circumstances, those who were developing property in the Aber valley, at Abertridwr and Senghenydd, set about providing their own supply, in about 1896.[9] The people concerned were W. H. Mathias and Walter Morgan, who built the Parc Newydd Reservoir; Gerald Bruce, who built the Gwernymilwr Reservoir; David Williams, owner of the Cwmbyir Reservoir at Abertridwr;

and William Francis Rowland of Abertridwr House, who owned the Abertridwr Reservoir. The Aber valley was the only area in the district that at present had to rely in this way on what were officially described as 'owners of private and unauthorised supplies'.[10]

By 1911, some of the major local authorities in the area had become impatient with the performance of the RAVGWC, and decided to form a water company of their own, the Rhymney Water Board, financed from the rates, which would take over the water part of the RAVGWC's remit. A Bill was prepared, and was considered by a Select Committee of the House of Lords in July 1911. This Bill was strongly opposed by a large number of bodies, including not only the RAVGWC, but also the major railway companies and a number of the local authorities affected. The main concern appears to have been the effect it would have upon the rates. The local press stressed the disadvantages of the scheme. The *Monmouth Guardian* suggested that 'the two great urban authorities on the Glamorganshire side of the Valley attempted to coerce the smaller Councils on the Monmouthshire side into a compact which would be as ruinous financially to the ratepayers as the benefits would be useless'.[11] The *Bargoed Journal* declared:

> Rates are high enough in Gellygaer to-day but when these wild schemes are carried out we can expect them to reach 10s with a possible 11s in the pound. All property holders will turn aghast at this, enterprise will be crippled, and even cottagers who have taken the trouble to understand the question can see the time when the rents are going up another 1s.[12]

Nevertheless, given that one of the aims of the Bill was to provide a proper water supply to the Aber valley, one might have expected the private owners who had so far had to provide the supply themselves to have welcomed the advent of a new company which would take over their responsibilities; but such was not the case. Prominent among the petitioners against the bill were 'W. H. Mathias and Others', who consisted of Mathias together with Walter Morgan's Executors – his father William Morgan, his widow, and the Rector of Llandogo; Gerald Bruce's 'Gwernymilwr Land Company Ltd'; David Williams; and William Francis Rowland. In other words, the owners of the four reservoirs listed above. The reasons they gave for their opposition was that 'their property, rights and interests will be prejudicially and injuriously affected if the Bill is allowed to pass':

> Both Senghenydd and Abertridwr are colliery villages dependent, in the case of Senghenydd, upon the Universal Colliery, and in the case of Abertridwr upon the Windsor Colliery, and in both villages, which stand at a very high altitude, there is a large number of workmen's dwelling-houses, between 600 and 700 of which are at present supplied with water from the four reservoirs of your Petitioners. Your Petitioners' estates have been rapidly developing, and your Petitioners being unable to obtain water from the Rhymney and Aber Valleys Gas and Water Company (that Company being relieved by their Acts from affording a supply otherwise than by gravitation from its reservoirs) have been compelled themselves to provide water for these villages and have accordingly expended large sums of money in constructing the before-mentioned reservoirs and other works for the purpose of providing a good and efficient supply.[13]

The bill, they asserted, would allow the Rhymney Board to compete with them in supplying water to the said houses, supported by the rates 'to which the Petitioners contribute'. The value of their property would depreciate and there was no provision in the bill for compensation.

As we shall see later, this concern to maintain their own supply did not entirely ring true (and once the bill was safely out of the way, Mathias abandoned this position, trying to off-load his water provision onto the RAVGWC). The question of the rates which would be exerted for the proposed new company (as opposed to the private RAVGWC) seems to have loomed far larger with them. They had built extensive housing, which would be affected adversely by any change in the rates; and added to this the local mines would have to pay the greatest amount of the rates (as Thomas Griffiths was to point out in his evidence). W. H. Mathias, as a very large shareholder in the Windsor Colliery, would hardly have been unconcerned at such considerations.

In fact, Mathias appeared in a number of guises among the various other petitions as well, as did a number of his closest acquaintances and collaborators. As chairman of the Pontypridd and Rhondda Joint Water Board, he was one of the two signatories (alongside Morgan's and Bruce's partner Walter Nicholas, clerk to the board), of its petition, which claimed that the new company's supplies would be taken from Pontypridd and Rhondda's natural source of supply. He was one of the directors of the Treforest Electrical Consumers Company Ltd, which claimed in its petition that the supply of water to Treforest Generating Station would be imperilled by plans for a reservoir from the waters of Taf Fechan; among the signatories to this were Mathias's friends and colleagues Thomas Griffiths and William North Lewis. And of course Mathias's nephew William James Thomas, and his cousin by marriage John Thomas Fernbank, were directors of RAVGWC, one of the leading objectors to the scheme.[14]

Though the Glamorgan County Council was not among the petitioners (presumably because no direct interest could be found), it is interesting to note that its Parliamentary Committee (on which Mathias sat) did consider whether to petition, and in fact expended some money in lawyers' fees before deciding not to.[15]

When the bill came before the Select Committee of the House of Lords in July 1911, the main evidence heard was of course from the major bodies concerned – the railway companies and the local authorities. When it came to the petitions by the four owners of reservoirs in the Aber valley, and by the other bodies with which Mathias was concerned, however, a number of his close friends and colleagues were in evidence at the hearing. His private case as a water-supplier was represented by the barrister Rhys Williams of Miskin Manor, who also represented on Mathias's behalf the Pontypridd and Rhondda Joint Water Board. Williams called in evidence, as his two main witnesses, Thomas Griffiths and Walter Nicholas: Griffiths because of his knowledge of the local situation, as manager of the Windsor Colliery; and Nicholas because he was the solicitor dealing with the affairs of all four private petitioners.

The bill eventually failed, and it was not until 1921 that a Rhymney Water Board was eventually set up. The 1911 House of Lords Select Committee proceedings do, however, give us some fascinating details about Mathias's water undertaking. The promoters of the bill had clearly decided to assert the unsuitability of the supplies provided by the four owners of reservoirs, and it was Mathias whose water came under the closest scrutiny. Early in the proceedings the inspector of nuisances for the Caerphilly Urban District Council gave evidence that, of the whole district in his charge, Senghenydd (which included Abertridwr) and Aber had the 'least satisfactory supply'. Mr Mathias's Parc Newydd estate was supplied, he said, from a small stream by means of 'unsocketed pipes'. In his opinion the source, a small one, was 'unsatisfactory', and ran short in the summer months. At the prompting of one of the promoters' barristers, Mr St John Raikes, this witness now produced a bottle, later described scathingly by Rhys Williams as a 'jampot', in which he had water taken from the tap in one of the houses served by the Parc Newydd supply. The exchange on this matter is illuminating:

RAIKES: What are those black things in it. Can you tell us?

MORGAN: Portions of frogs, I think.

RAIKES: Or tadpoles?

MORGAN: Yes.

CHAIRMAN [The Duke of Northumberland]: Are these live tadpoles or dead?

MORGAN: Dead.

Rhys Williams was however, determined to prove the suitability of the water for human consumption. When an expert witness (Rhys Pendril Jones, Fellow of the Institute of Chemistry and Demonstrator in Bacteriology at King's College London) was produced by the promoters of the bill, Rhys Williams managed to get him to say that he had no objection chemically to Mathias's water, and that he considered it to be of 'fair quality bacteriologically'. On the other hand, Pendril Jones declared Gwernymilwr's supply to be 'unfitted for human consumption' (human excreta and the carcasses of two dogs had been found in the reservoir), and Rowland's supply to be 'quite unfitted for domestic purposes' as *bacillus coli* had been found in it.[16]

Though Williams was counsel for all four of these petitioners, most of his effort was expended upon Mathias's interests. He succeeded in giving the impression that, even though the Mathias supply was not perfect, it was infinitely superior to all the other supplies around it. The final blow was struck when Thomas Griffiths, prompted by Williams, agreed that he himself had drunk the water. Counsel for the promoters of the bill facetiously pounced upon this, but Griffiths remained steadfast:

MR TALBOT: Have you recovered?

GRIFFITHS: I was not ill.

MR TALBOT: But they are not very nice waters, are they?

GRIFFITHS: If they were otherwise, if they were offensive, I do not think I would have drunk them.

Rhys Williams thereupon came back to the charge (interrupted in vain by Talbot):

MR WILLIAMS: You know that there are nearly 3,000 persons supplied by these wells at the present day. Have you ever heard of anybody suffering from an epidemic?

MR TALBOT: If they like to go on being supplied from them they can.

GRIFFITHS: I have not heard of any outbreak.

These exchanges were, of course, only a small part of the extensive proceedings.

The Gwernymilwr Company went into liquidation in December of the same year.[17] The Mathias Estate continued. It has to be said, however, that while Mathias's water appears to have been better than that of the other suppliers in the valley, it was clearly not of what we would nowadays consider good quality. This is surprising, given the searching inquisitions which we have seen him making as a RUDC councillor, into the quality and the supply of the water in the Rhondda valleys.

That Mathias was not as concerned as he claimed to be by the prospect of his water supply being taken over is shown by his attempt, only four years later, to sell it to the RAVGWC. All this makes it likely that, whatever the varied reasons given for his opposition under various hats to the bill, the underlying reason was probably the one adumbrated by Thomas Griffiths on behalf of the Windsor Colliery, and by the *Bargoed Journal*: the prospect of higher council rates to be exerted on the major collieries in the area, and on the landlords of the housing estates.

Negotiations with the Rhymney and Aber Valleys Gas and Water Company Ltd, 1915–1918

These negotiations dealt with what was, for Mathias, a minor amount of money (£120, or about £6,000 in modern terms). They show, however, something of his tenacity in refusing ever to lose on a deal, or to be defeated by others in a negotiation.

The RAVGWC had decided by 1915 to try to expand in the Aber valley. By now, Mathias appears to have been looking for a way for the Parc Newydd supply to be taken off his shoulders. On 8 February 1915, his agent approached the company to enquire if 'they were prepared to negotiate for the purchase of the Mathias Estate water supply.' On 23 March, the company offered £80 for the 850 yards of four-inch main, but declined to offer for the reservoir (which had by now developed a leak). No response was made to this for two years, until 1 May 1917, when Mathias's agent asked for a further offer. The company repeated its 1915 offer of £80. On 30 August the agent asked for an improved offer. The company decided to let the correspondence 'lie on the table.'

This appears to have riled Mathias, who decided on sterner measures. On 30 October 1917, he sent a letter to the company, stating that the Mathias estate intended discontinuing the supply of water to the occupants of the housing, and asking the company to buy the mains 'upon the basis of a reasonable valuation'. This threat had at first no effect. It was resolved, at the meeting that considered this letter, that the company could not 'improve upon their previous offer'. It is worth noting that Mathias's nephew William James Thomas, and his cousin John Thomas, were both prominent members of this board.

Mathias now decided to bring up his big guns. Morgan, Bruce and Nicholas were the solicitors for the Mathias estate at Parc Newydd. The letter they wrote to the RAVGWC purported nevertheless to have been written on behalf of the tenants of the estate. It asked the company to supply water to them, 'as the Landowners had given notice that they would not supply the property with water after the 31st December next'. The letter was received on 3 December. It finally spurred the company into action. They asked their engineer to 'report on the condition of the present mains and the manner in which they are laid.'

The water was cut off on the night of 31 December. The next morning, New Year's Day 1918, at an urgently called meeting, the company resolved that John Thomas Fernbank and the manager should go and see Mr Mathias and 'endeavour to come to some arrangement for taking on the water mains laid down by the Estate'. It is interesting that John Thomas should have been chosen. He was not only a relative by marriage of Mathias's, but he had also been for a number of years a close colleague of his on the RUDC, where they represented the same ward in the same party interest.

Thomas reported back on 26 February. In the interim, we can only presume that the people on the estate were without mains water. Thomas said he had met Mathias, and had arranged with him to buy the water mains and meters on the estate for £200 (modern equivalent about £10,000). Mathias had thus managed to get two and a half times the sum they had originally intended to pay. His strong-arm tactics had worked. Nevertheless, the board, confirming the arrangement, 'thanked Mr Thomas for conducting these negotiations'[18]

All of this gives us some insight into Mathias's methods, but also into his determination never to be defeated. The sums involved were trifling by comparison with the money concerned in most of his major deals, yet he had been prepared to dig his heels in, and cause hardship to his tenants, in order to get his way. In the event, the company flinched, and William Henry Mathias won.

Like so many in south Wales in the late nineteenth century, William Henry Mathias appears to have been almost unaware of what nowadays would be regarded as the norms of business and professional life. Clashes of interest, for example: as a director of the Albion Colliery, and a magistrate, at the time of the 1893 Hauliers' Strike, he was prepared to hear the cases for summonses against the workers from his own colliery, and to issue the summonses.[19] And on the Ystradyfodwg Local Board, he never seems to have declared an interest (even when contracts were being awarded to members of his own family), and he often accepted membership, or chairmanship, of sub-committees that would to a modern eye seem inappropriate (such as where his own companies, or his father-in-law's, were involved), but which may to his fellow-members have seemed appropriate precisely because of his involvement.

The last two chapters have shown further examples of Mathias's methods: the use of inducements to get officials of a railway company to change their mind on a matter they had firmly decided against; the use of insider knowledge in order to purchase what was to be a very valuable piece of land, which then, by the driving of very hard bargains with all concerned, brought in even more money; the use of a wide variety of bodies, in which Mathias and his friends were concerned, in order to back a petition in relation to his own interests; and the ruthless use of innocent tenants in order to put pressure on a Water Company with whom Mathias was having a dispute.

Yet he was not alone in all this. When we look at the practices in local government, and in business, in south Wales in this period, we see that such activities were not so much an exception as the rule. Mathias was no better, and no worse, than most of his contemporaries in the claustrophobic society of the Valleys middle class, where everyone knew everyone, and where 'connections' were all-important.

James ('Siamps') Thomas

William Henry Mathias

Rachel Mathias

Tynycymmer Hall, Cymmer, Porth

Dinas, showing pollution in the Rhondda Fawr river
(by kind permission of Rhondda Cynon Taf Library Service).

Tynewydd Colliery, Porth
(by kind permission of Rhondda Cynon Taf Library Service).
An early photograph, looking up the Rhondda Fach valley.
The house in the background, in the centre of the picture, is
Siamps Thomas's house Mount Pleasant, and the tall chimney in the
right background is the Troedyrhiw (Aber Rhondda) Colliery.

The monument to Siamps Thomas, New Bethel Chapel,
Mynyddislwyn

145

Two Disasters

9

Heroism or negligence? Siamps Thomas and the Tynewydd Disaster, 1877

When one peruses the index to *The Times* for the second half of the nineteenth century, it becomes clear just how common, and how expected, mining accidents were. For each three-month period of the index, there is a major section headed 'Accidents', the greater part of which comes under the sub-heading 'Mining'. Hardly a week went by without, somewhere in the United Kingdom, a mining accident occurring of a magnitude that warranted a report in *The Times*.

In any history relating to the coal trade, then, pit disasters are bound to have a role to play. In this and the next chapter, we will be taking two of the most famous disasters, the Tynewydd Inundation of 1877 and the Albion Disaster of 1894. They will tell us many things. Firstly, we will be shown the constants of the disasters themselves: causes ranging from natural conditions to sheer carelessness to deliberate and reckless corner-cutting by management, and the propensity of juries at inquests and at inquiries to exonerate management, whatever the evidence. Secondly, we learn much about the changing nature of coalmining in the years separating these two disasters. This includes the larger scale of operations; the deeper mines; the volatility of steam coal; the effects of the move to limited liability companies; and the change from an owner-management intimately involved in the day-to-day activity of the mines, to distant directors employing professional managers. Thirdly, we gain insight into the communities in which these disasters took place: the involvement of owners, managers and miners, alongside each other, in the rescue attempts; the solidarity within the community, whether in chapel or in fundraising activities; the reliance on the local *crachach* in relation to the organisation of fundraising; the tendency for such fundraising to lead to major disputes and so on. These disasters, through the newspaper reports of them, provide a unique insight into Valleys life at this time.

Members of the Thomas/Mathias clan were intimately involved in both these disasters, as were a number of the other members of this entrepreneurial society who are familiar to us from the preceding chapters.

The Tynewydd Inundation

In 1877, the Tynewydd pit in Porth was employing about a hundred and fifty men. Siamps Thomas of the Troedyrhiw company, as well as being part-owner, was also the manager (as was often the custom at this stage of the development of the coalfield). The pit had been successfully sunk to the No. 3 Rhondda seam, 'Coffin's coal', at a depth of about 92 yards. The mine was close to the river, the Rhondda Fawr; and just on the other side of the river was the New Cymmer pit (sunk by George Insole, but leased since 1860 to T. C. Hindes of Neath, and now commonly known as 'Hinde's pit'). It too had originally been sunk to the No. 3 seam, but some years back that seam had been exhausted, and so those workings were abandoned, with only the upper seam, the No. 2, being worked. The abandoned No. 3 seam became filled with water. Those workings were, it later became clear, perilously close to the workings, at the same level, in the Tynewydd pit.[1]

On the evening of Wednesday 11 April 1877, five miners who were on the point of leaving the heading in which they had been working at the Tynewydd pit (Thomas Morgan and his two sons Richard and William Morgan, Edward Williams and William Cassia), suddenly heard a rush of water. They immediately turned into a 'rise', a side-cutting which led upwards from the main heading, where they were soon trapped by the rising water. Other men working in the pit also became alarmed at the noise, and retreated ahead of the flood. Most of the workmen managed to get out, but eventually it was realised that fourteen men were missing, including the three Morgans and Williams and Cassia.

The cause of the inundation soon became clear. One of the workmen in the heading, driving in the direction of the old Cymmer workings, must have broken through into them. Rescue operations were soon set in motion for the fourteen trapped men. Siamps Thomas, all accounts agree, was there from the start, directing operations, and was in the pit throughout the night, together with a number of neighbouring coalowners and managers. One of them, Thomas Jones, owner-manager of the Ynyshir colliery, suggested that they should see to pumping the water out of Hinde's pit, but he was informed that there was no water in that pit. Undeterred, he went the next day, with Richard Packer, Siamps Thomas's son-in-law, to the top of Hinde's pit, and dropped a line into it, whereby he found out that there were about 35 yards of water in it. When the two men returned to the Tynewydd mine, they found the assistant inspector of mines, Mr Galloway, examining the maps of the two collieries; from these, and from Jones's report, Galloway realised that Jones's suggestion of pumping out Hinde's pit should have been adopted the night before. It would now take some time for pumps to be made ready at Hinde's pit, but meanwhile a large pump was borrowed from Mr Jones's Ynyshir pit, and taken down the Tynewydd mine itself, to try to lower the water there.[2]

Of the trapped men, the five of the Morgans' party were the easiest to reach. There was a dry level near the one in which they were trapped, separated from it by about twelve yards of coal. Both the trapped men and their rescuers started work, and by Thursday morning four yards had been worked inside, and eight yards outside. A small hole was made through the barrier – and then tragedy occurred. The men had not realised the effect of the flood upon the air pressure in the confined area where they were. William Morgan struck the hole with his pick, and the released air pressure dragged him in, and the hole was plugged by his head. Though his father and brother tried to drag him out, he had been killed outright. The other four men waited until the air pressure had subsided, and then got out, exhausted from cold and hunger.

Two of the other trapped men, Edward Williams (Edward o'r Maendy) and a boy called Robert Rogers, were in another heading, and were heard knocking soon after the inundation. When the rescuers reached that heading, however, they discovered that it was full of water, and as no knocking was now heard, it was feared (which turned out to be the case) that they had been drowned.

This left seven men still in the pit, presumed alive, as knocking was still being heard. It tells us something about the floating nature of social distinctions in the mining community at this time, when we realise that two of these colliers were related to the owner/manager, Siamps Thomas. One was his nephew, George Jenkins, aged 31, son of Siamps's elder sister Ann, and a native of Mynyddislwyn like his uncle. We are told that he had been employed at this mine for the last 22 years, that is since he was nine years old,[3] having started there within three years of the mine being sunk by his uncle in 1852. Another was Moses Powell, who was a brother-in-law of Siamps's son, Thomas James Thomas (the two men having married the sisters Mary and Rachel John, daughters of William John, a boatman from Upper Boat).[4] With them were three other adults (David Jenkins, John Hughes and John Thomas), one adolescent, David Hughes (14), and William Hughes, described merely as 'a lad'. These were men who had been working a good deal further down in the mine, in an area which was now flooded to the roof. 'Morgan's stall', however, in which they had taken refuge, was a short 'rise' from the main heading, and though the water level in the mine as a whole was higher than the highest point of the stall, air pressure was keeping the water at bay for the time being.

There were, however, about 300 yards of roadway filled with water between the rescuers and these men. It was therefore decided to keep on pumping.[5] Despite all efforts, however, hardly any effect seemed to be being made. It was therefore decided to try using divers, and two men were sent by the London firm of Siebe and Gorman.

The divers went down the mine between 2 and 3 pm on Saturday, when the trapped men had already been in the mine for almost three days. 'Morien', the reporter from the *Western Mail*, accompanied the working party that descended, and has described the scene for us. Those who took command were Daniel Thomas,

owner of Brithweunydd colliery, and William Davies, manager of
Coedcae collieries. They were accompanied by Siamps Thomas, and
by a number of other owners and managers from neighbouring
mines, and from further afield.[6]

By Sunday morning, it had become clear that the divers could do
nothing. There were too many obstacles in the water. Later, further
knocking from the trapped men was distinctly heard, and the
frustration of the would-be rescuers was extreme. By evening,
however, Siamps Thomas was able to report that the pumping had
succeeded in lowering the level of the water in the intervening
roadway, enough for it soon to be possible, by about midnight, for
a number of men to start cutting through the forty yards or so of
coal between them and the trapped men.

The cutting commenced, and by Monday evening it was felt that
a breakthrough might well be possible by Wednesday morning.
Concern was expressed at the conditions for the trapped men, who
would not have eaten for almost a week by that time. Thomas
Morgan, however, stated that there were in his stall three pounds of
candles, and people supposed that the men had subsisted on them
and on the water around them.[7]

On the rescuing miners continued, hewing through a wall of
coal. They were in a narrow space, at points less than three feet high,
which sloped downwards at about 4 inches per yard, and every
piece of dislodged coal had to be pulled up behind them. Three
shifts of four men each were employed, supervised severally by
Daniel Thomas, Siamps Thomas, and William Davies of Coedcae,
and working four-hour shifts round the clock.

On Wednesday morning, at 3.15, the voices of the trapped men
were heard. It was realised that the rescuers now had to go very
carefully because there was danger of either drowning or stifling
the men when the breakthrough was made. A boring apparatus was
brought into action, to make a hole to communicate with the men,
and if possible to supply them with food. But as soon as a small
opening was made, there was such a rush of air that the hole had to
be plugged again. Those present described the roar of the air as
being like that of a blast furnace. The plug was once or twice forced
out, and it took enormous effort to replace it.[8] And soon another
danger arose, which set back the rescue considerably when they

were within a few yards of the men. At about noon on Thursday, there was a sudden rush of gas, which extinguished the rescuers' lights, and forced them to escape to the surface. Brattice sheets were put in place to deflect more fresh air into the tunnel to disperse the gas, but though the rescuers returned to continue the work, they had several times to retreat to the shaft.[9] The bravery of the rescuers was remarkable, in that one of the greatest fears of every miner was that of explosions caused by escaping gas. As one of the rescuers put it, 'it would have sent us up the heading like dust'.[10]

In order to protect the trapped miners and the rescuers when a breakthrough occurred, stout air doors were now erected to resist escaping air and gas, and also to help confine any explosion that might occur. After a while, Siamps Thomas pulled out the plug again. He told George Jenkins they would send him some food, but Jenkins called out for him to 'shut the hole, we will be drowned'. The opening of the hole was causing the water level within Morgan's stall to rise again. George Jenkins's later account (translated from the Welsh, which was the language used not only by all the trapped men, but also by their rescuers) is worth quoting at this point, particularly for the words that passed between Siamps Thomas and the men:

> Yesterday [Friday] morning we could hear them outside working towards us, and coming nearer and nearer. They knocked a third time for the last time during the last four yards that they worked. Mr James Thomas, the manager, called out to us that we should be out soon, and that we should have food in a short time. But we were in for a few hours after that. To the knocks that were made outside I made answer, and then I called out to Mr Thomas and asked him how long did he think we should be in there. 'About half an hour', he answered. But it was longer than that, a good bit. [. . .] The last thing I asked Mr Thomas was if they had food, or anything to take, ready for us when we came out of the water. 'Yes, my dear boy', he said, 'sufficient for you.' They were then trying to push through some tubes with food in them, but we had no food until we came out on to the level.[11]

The final breakthrough was perceived as being dangerous both for the rescuers and the trapped men. The men who made the final push were three young miners, Isaac Pride, Abraham Dodd and

Gwilym Thomas. When Isaac Pride (to whom Siamps Thomas had finally said 'Go on and work it out')[12] broke through the final barrier, he was thrown back against the air door by the blast of escaping air, but soon set about enlarging the hole, which he and Dodd then climbed through. The five trapped men, who had for so long been without food and water, and who were huddled together in a small cavity above the water, were almost too weak to move:

> Todd went to the assistance of John Thomas and David Jenkins, who were the weakest of all, and Pride succeeded in making a passage for the boy David Hughes to go out . . . When the poor fellow got up to the hole Pride lay down on his belly in the water, and made a bridge of himself so that Hughes might get safely over the bottom coal without going through water or having to climb.[13]

George Jenkins and Moses Powell were both remarkably strong men, and while the other men were being brought out and taken to the pit mouth, they struggled to the shaft on their own. *The Graphic* described how, when they caught sight of Siamps Thomas, 'who is very popular with the men . . . they pressed forward and embraced him with great fervour'.[14] Later, in the makeshift hospital room to which the men had been taken at the Tynewydd Inn, about sixty yards from the top of the shaft, Siamps Thomas was to be observed sitting at George Jenkins's bedside.[15]

The day after the rescue, a thanksgiving meeting was held at Cymmer Welsh Independent chapel. There was a congregation of about 1,500, consisting mainly of miners and their families. *The Times* described the service thus:

> The service was remarkable for the religious fervour displayed. Aged miners, in homely language, offered up their humble thanks for the deliverance of the captives. After each prayer a hymn was given out and sung by the whole congregation, the prayers and hymns being in the Welsh tongue. The music was of a highly cultivated order, and strangers present declared that it was the best congregational singing they had ever heard.[16]

It was noted that the hymns were obviously so well-known that 'very few appeared to require the assistance of books'.[17] An address was given at this service by Edmund Thomas Llwyncelyn, one of the coalowners who had been involved in the rescue.

The immediate aftermath

The public, not just in south Wales but also in the United Kingdom as a whole, had been following events closely, and with emotion. The newspaper accounts were accompanied, in *The Graphic* and the *Illustrated London News*, by artists' impressions of the scene and of the men involved, and by diagrams of the mine. The plight of the entrapped men was matched, in the public's eyes, by the heroism of the rescuers, of which one observer had commented that it had been 'a spectacle more grand in its sublime and unseen heroism than that great Crimean battle charge which makes one proud to be a Briton'.[18]

The rescuers had included not just the miners whose toil and endurance had been so remarkable, but also the array of mine-owners and managers who had spent their time down the pit, directing operations, and at the same time sharing the dangers, in particular those from gas explosions. All the newspapers listed their names. Among them, *The Times* singled out in particular Siamps Thomas, 'a veteran in coalmining, whose age would have been sufficient excuse for keeping away'.[19] Other prominent coalowners and managers who had taken part included Daniel Thomas Brithweunydd and his brother Edmund Thomas Llwyncelyn; Thomas Jones Ynyshir; William Thomas (Brynawel), currently manager of Resolven; Henry Lewis Tŷ Nant (Siamps Thomas's manager at the Energlyn colliery); William Davies Coedcae; and several others, including the managers of Kilylai, Blaenclydach, Cymmer Level, Llwynypia, and Navigation collieries.

The immediate desire of many was to raise money to look after the widows and dependents of those who had died, to help the men who had gone through this terrible experience, and to reward the heroic rescuers. A committee of Members of Parliament had been formed 'for the purpose of presenting a sum of money to the working parties in recognition of their indomitable pluck and perseverance'.[20] The Lord Mayor of London set up a Mansion House Appeal. The *Daily Telegraph* set up a 'Welsh Miners' Fund'.

And, meanwhile, a local appeal was being organised as well. On the evening of 21 April, the very day of the rescue, a committee was formed at the Rheola Hotel, Porth, 'to receive money for the relief of the sufferers', and at the same time to reward the rescuers with 'some permanent record of their gallantry'; the secretary was Richard Packer, and the treasurer Dr Henry Naunton Davies, who had been the main medical man at the scene of the disaster.[21] And on 25 April, at County Hall, Pontypridd, a public meeting was held, with Judge Gwilym Williams of Miskin Manor in the chair, to open a subscription.[22] These appeals were later to lead to much controversy.

Other storm clouds were gathering. The question of the responsibility for the disaster was being raised, and preparations were being made for the inquest. On 24 April, Mr Wales, Her Majesty's inspector of mines for south Wales, visited Porth and spent a long time with Richard Packer,[23] who had worked as clerk of the work throughout the rescue attempt.[24] The next day, it was reported that 'prior to proceeding with the inquest the local managers will examine the workings, and . . . a survey will be made'.[25]

An editorial in the *Western Mail* on 27 April drew attention to a question that was to be put in the House of Commons, that day, by Alexander Macdonald MP.[26] This question raised serious matters:

> To ask the Secretary of State for the Home Department if, considering the interest manifested in the case of the men entombed in the Tynewydd Colliery, South Wales, he will direct someone to attend the inquest, to be held on the 3rd proximo . . . Further, if he will direct or order that the enquiry may be of the most searching character, to ascertain if the provisions of the Mines Act, 1872, in respect to large bodies of water, were being fully carried out prior to the inundation.

The editorial, noting that this suggested that 'there had been faults which could have been obviated', called for the inquiry 'not to be of that slovenly and perfunctory character which unfortunately is too often associated with matters concerning the lives of miners who have been killed by explosion, or by what are supposed to be unforeseen accidents'.[27]

In answer to Macdonald's question, the Secretary of State said he was prepared to order 'an inquiry of the most searching character' (echoing Macdonald's words), and that directions were being given for a lawyer to attend it on behalf of the Home Department. Macdonald himself, at a council of the Miners' National Union in Leeds on 28 April, arranged for Mr William Pickard, of Wigan, to attend the inquiry on the union's behalf. He declared that 'there were queer and ugly rumours afloat concerning the disaster'.[28]

Questions about the observance or otherwise of the Mines Regulation Act 1872 were now fairly widespread. A letter to the *Western Mail* on 1 May, for example, from 'An Old Miner', said that 'it was generally known that the Cymmer Pit (better known as Hinde's Pit) contained a large accumulation of water.' He continued:

> We are all aware that, according to the Coal Mines Regulation Act, in approaching places likely to contain a large accumulation of water, sufficient bore-holes must be kept in advance of not less than 5 yards in length, also sufficient flank holes in the sides, and the working places are not to exceed 8 ft in width. Now, as Parliament has deemed laws necessary for the protection of our lives, why should not these laws be put into effect? I trust that there will be a fair investigation made into the causes of the late catastrophe, and that the incident will be a warning to other colliery proprietors.

Finally, he declared his hope that there would be 'acting on the jury an impartial set of men, who care more for the lives of their fellow-creatures than personal interests.'[29]

A further letter in the *Western Mail*, on 5 May, gives us some insight into how the management at Tynewydd was reacting to these criticisms. A copy of the Mines Regulation Act had in fact just been put up in the colliery – but in English, which made it hard for many of the workforce to read it. The letter-writer, 'Jenkin Three-Foot', asked what use it was putting it up *after* all that had happened. He suggested that the management was trying to mislead the observers at the inquiry. The letter is worth quoting in full, as its wording gives us some insight into the problems many of the Welsh-speaking miners had with the English language:

Sir, - I do want to put a fair question, as it seems to my mind, through the paper I value of the Western Mail. Perhaps Mr James Thomas, or Mr Packer, or someone in Cardiff, if not the Valley, belonging to the Troedyrhiw Coal Company, will send answer direct immediate. You will excuse me, if you please, but I want to know why the company, or them as do do the work for the company, in authority proper, do put up now a new sheet of Mines Regulation Act on the colliery? It can't do a good deal of good now, I do fancy, after what have happened, though it may blind Mr Pickard and a few more of them as come to Porth in the present time. Whatever, that I do admit, it was good notion to put one up now only this I do ask the same time, why they have him in the English language, not in Cymraeg, as is more like we want, cause Act of Parliament was awful hard always, especially the more in strange language, when we do speak here our native which is proper like it should be, as I am glad. Perhaps they do know at Tynewydd; perhaps they will tell me for cost of one penny in your valuable influence Western Mail. – In hurry obedient, excuse, and remains.

By the Cymmer   Jenkin Three-Foot[30]

The Inquest

The inquest started on 3 May, at the Rheola Inn, Porth. The Government's barrister had not arrived, and an adjournment was asked for, but the coroner, Mr George Overton, impatiently decided to proceed without him. By mid-day on the next day it became clear that they would have to adjourn until 15 May. These initial proceedings had, however, produced some matters of interest. Firstly, after an hour or two in which the witnesses had been Siamps Thomas and Evan Thomas (a haulier who had been one of the first to see the water), both of whom had been speaking in Welsh, Mr Pickard asked if the witnesses could be examined in English. The coroner replied that he would check the translations, 'but he thought it was hard for a witness to be examined in a language the idioms of which he did not understand'. This would presumably cause problems not only for Pickard, but also for the government barrister when he arrived. Secondly, the coroner, though saying at the start that they must take notice of the Mines Regulation Act, later remarked that 'he himself could not understand the rules, and he pitied the poor men who had to understand them'.[31]

The inquest resumed on 15 May. Siamps Thomas was the only one of the proprietors to be present. None of his partners in the Troedyrhiw Company, who by now numbered Matthew Cope (William Cope's son), John Lewis and the 86-year-old Thomas Collingdon (former manager of the Bute Docks, and former secretary to the Marquess of Bute),[32] had turned up at the pit at any point in the rescue operation, and they did not put in an appearance here either.

Various things became clear in the course of the cross-examinations: Siamps Thomas had believed that a known fault continued right to the point where the men were working; such a fault would have been a barrier to prevent water from getting through;[33] he had also believed that Hinde's pit was deeper than Tynewydd, and that consequently water would not come into the latter; a December plan of the workings, that showed that there was at that time only forty-four yards to the boundary between the mines, had been ignored by all concerned; the mining regulations in relation to places where water was likely to be a danger had not been observed.

When the overman, Richard Howells (Siamps Thomas's second-in-command in the colliery) was examined, he made it clear that the regulations had meant little to him, as he 'could not read or write in English, and could not write in Welsh'. He could 'read through the rules, if they gave him time', but was 'not sure he had read them at all.' Mr Thomas had never told him about the forty-four yards, he said, and he knew nothing of a map. It was suggested to him that he was 'going on blindly, in search of a fault, wherever it came.' To this he replied doggedly that he was 'going by his master's directions', and that if he 'had got orders [he] would have applied them'.[34]

It had already been established that the fireman for that part of the colliery, David Rees, could neither read nor write also, and a lengthy discussion ensued, next day, as to whether such knowledge was necessary for these men. Mr Pickard said that in Lancashire it was usual to appoint as overman or fireman people who could read and write. He also pointed out that, to carry out the procedures prescribed by the Act, 'a person of ordinary capacity should have anticipated and provided against [the matter], even the subordinate officers of the works.' If holes had been bored, the presence of the water would have been detected. 'He considered the omission of this principle was culpable neglect. He could come to no other conclusion.' At the suggestion of Mr Leresche, the government barrister, he reworded this as follows: 'It was what any manager or overman ought to have adopted under the circumstances, if he had taken the trouble to think about it at all.'[35] These two outsiders transformed the rather cosy hearing that the coroner seemed to have planned.

Siamps Thomas's counsel now brought out, in Thomas's defence, the question of his past exemplary record. Pickard admitted that there had been only one fatality in the 25 years between the opening of the pit in 1852 and the year of the disaster, and that that spoke well 'for the manner in which it is conducted'. Pickard also admitted that Thomas was 'a good, practical, experienced man', and that 'it would be very wrong of him, when he found a gentleman holding the responsible position of manager of three or four mines, if he did not respect that position as a test of experience'.

Mr Wales, the inspector of mines, under questioning, stated that the mines regulation in question had not been complied with; to that fact he attributed the inundation and the consequent loss of life. Under cross-examination, however, he then gave Siamps Thomas a very good character reference. The exchange is notable for the coroner's intervention in the middle of it, which points to his continued leaning towards Thomas:

Mr Simons: Did not Mr Thomas evince intelligence and skill as a mining engineer?

Mr Wales: I found in Mr Thomas a very practical, intelligent man. He gave me very valuable information. Since the inundation the impression on my mind is that he is a very intelligent man.

Mr Simons: Did you find him skilful, courageous, resolute, and persevering in carrying out the measures for the rescue of the men? –

Mr Wales: I did.

The Coroner: No man could be more active in his exertions.

Mr Simons: Did you find him always ready to find machinery, or outlay, or labour?

Mr Wales: I never heard of any such thing as the sparing of cost on the part of Mr Thomas.

The coroner, in his summing up, could not ignore the comments of Pickard, Leresche and Wales as to culpability; but he made a fighting retreat by seeming to point to the overman rather than to Siamps Thomas:

> He found that the officers of the pit, whose duty they might imagine was to watch matters, were even so ignorant that they could not read or write, and knew nothing whatever of the plans

He now came to the question of the Act, which Pickard, Wales and Leresche had established as the main cause for indictment. He dealt with it entirely straightforwardly:

> Do you consider that was in compliance with the Act? If it was not, I fear you cannot come to any other conclusion than that there has been a violation of the Act, and amounts to culpable neglect or manslaughter.

He nevertheless continued to question whether it was the overman or the manager who was responsible.

The jury retired for three hours. On their return, they said that they had decided that Thomas was guilty of culpable neglect, and returned a verdict against him of manslaughter. He was formally committed for trial at the assizes, and was allowed bail of £200.[36]

Reactions and the fate of the various funds

Many were thunderstruck by this verdict, so different from the bland cover-ups to which people had become accustomed at disaster inquests. People were also amazed that a man with such a reputation for carefulness and safety as Siamps Thomas should have been found guilty of such negligence.

The most remarkable of the reactions to the verdict was, however, that of Thomas's own workmen at Tynewydd. On the Monday after the verdict they held a meeting at the Tynewydd Inn, and unanimously resolved to present an address to Siamps Thomas, which ran as follows:

> Dear and respected sir: - We, the workmen employed at Tynewydd Colliery, desire to express our sympathy with you in your grief and trouble in consequence of the recent disaster at the above-mentioned colliery . . . As you, sir, well know, many of us have worked at the above-mentioned colliery under your management and supervision for upwards of twenty years, and some of us for upwards of thirty years at this and other collieries.
>
> During this time you have, through your unexampled competency, prudence and care, in all cases of danger, been so successful in preventing accidents of any kind as to create amongst your workmen such confidence in your abilities and care to watch against accidents, by either water or gases, that we always felt happy and considered ourselves safe in any place you should think proper to ask us to work.

They went on to describe how, some years ago, when his workings were approaching the Dinas old workings which contained water, he had taken all the usual precautions in such cases (boreholes etc.) to make sure there was no danger to the men or the mine. They then explained why they thought that a quirk of nature had misled him at Tynewydd, and expressed their confidence in him for the future:

> We are of opinion that the recent accident at Tynewydd was the result of a very uncommon occurrence – the sudden running out to nothing of a fault of seven yards in depth, on which we all believe you relied as a barrier between your workings and the boundary, and which we consider would be a sufficient barrier against water and gas.
>
> We therefore desire to assure you that the occurrence – serious as the consequences have been – has not in the least degree diminished or shaken our confidences in your abilities and care as a manager, and we beg, one and all, to assure you that we are now as ready to work under your supervision as we were on the last day before the accident occurred.

Finally, they prayed that God might preserve him, and calm his mind as regards recent events.[37]

Other, more prominent members of society were speaking up for Siamps Thomas, as well. In *The Times*, William Forsyth MP,[38] who had visited the Porth area in the aftermath of the rescue, having praised the brothers Edmund and Daniel Thomas, 'whose services have not been sufficiently known to and appreciated by the public', then spoke of Siamps Thomas: 'I may add that I heard on all sides the strongest testimony in favour of the character and past conduct of the manager of the Tynewydd Pit, Mr James Thomas, against whom the coroner's jury returned an adverse verdict the other day; but it would be wrong to say more on the question of his responsibility, which will be the subject of further judicial inquiry.'[39]

Meanwhile, the administration of the various funds was continuing; and, in an unprecedented move, it was announced that the Queen had changed the requirements for the award of Albert Medals (which had until then been for deeds of heroism at sea), making it possible for them to be awarded for deeds carried out on land.

The London funds, of course, had to rely on local knowledge as to who should be the recipients of their awards, and they had recourse to prominent local individuals. The Lord Mayor's Mansion House Appeal, the largest of them, relied entirely, for the first report on which its London committee would deliberate, on that ever-present figure the Revd David Watkin Williams of Fairfield House.[40] Williams was also one of the three people chosen to give evidence to the Home Secretary as to those entitled to Albert Medals – the other two being Judge Gwilym Williams of Miskin Manor, and Mr Wales, HM inspector of mines for south Wales.[41]

The Daily Telegraph fund relied on four people prominent in local society. The egregious Revd David Williams was one of them, and Dr Henry Naunton Davies another. The other two were R. Williams (manager of the West of England Bank in Pontypridd); and William Henry Mathias, Siamps Thomas's son-in-law.[42] (This is one of the first glimpses we get of the prominence which Mathias, now aged 32, was already achieving in local society.)

The Telegraph awards were the first to be announced, on 9 June. There was £1,200 in the fund. After benefactions to the rescued miners and the widows and dependents of those who had died, £550 was left over, of which most was given to the miners who had been rescuers, though silver tankards were given to some of the mineowners and other people involved, including Siamps Thomas, the three brothers Isaiah, Edmund and Daniel Thomas, and William Henry Mathias.[43]

The result of the inquest does not seem to have deterred the givers of these awards from putting Siamps Thomas prominently on their list. In other quarters, however, there was some embarrassment. The list of the recipients of the Albert Medal which appeared in the *London Gazette* on 7 August included four First Class medallists (including Isaac Pride and Daniel Thomas), and twenty-two Second Class, including Siamps Thomas. On 10 August a correction, dated 8 August, appeared in the same journal: 'In the list of persons on whom the Queen has been graciously pleased to confer the Albert Medal, published in the London Gazette of Tuesday last, 7th inst., the name of "James Thomas" was inserted in error.'[44]

The Mansion House fund raised the enormous sum of almost £5,000 pounds[45] (equivalent to at least £450,000 in modern terms). This sum, collected almost entirely from English sources, and unmatched by any other disaster funds in the period, showed the enormous interest that had been taken in the events of Tynewydd by a public who had followed the harrowing accounts of the trapped men and of the attempted rescue day by day in their newspapers, illustrated in many cases by dramatic drawings of the scene, the characters and the events. The distribution of this money, and that of the local fund, were both to cause considerable controversy. There had already been some ill-feeling by mid-June,[46] caused by the Daily Telegraph awards. By the time the Revd David Watkin Williams gave his first proposals for distribution of the Mansion House fund, on 12 July,[47] the stage was set for major conflict.

On 17 July, a letter of protest at Williams's list from a number of prominent owner/managers, which had been sent to the Lord Mayor of London, was published in *The Times* and the *Western Mail*. In it, they claimed that Williams's report and recommendations were 'grossly incorrect'. They said that if the list remained as it was, they would decline to accept the awards they had been given. Accounts in the newspapers differed as to the names signing this letter, with Siamps Thomas's name being among them in some cases, and not in others. The evidence appears, however, to point to his having been one of the signatories. The others were Daniel Thomas, Edmund Thomas, William Davies (Coedcae), David Davies (Pontypridd), David Jones (Cymmer Level) and Thomas Jones (Ynyshir).[48]

The Lord Mayor's response to the protest, addressed to 'Mr James Thomas, Tynewydd Colliery, and others', was prompt. He had been intending to visit Pontypridd to preside at the distribution of the awards, but he had now decided not to. He made some trenchant points with regard to the intentions of the fund, and, calling their bluff, accepted their declining of their awards:

> The vote was adopted by the whole committee, and while I, personally, held (and still hold) that no part of the fund collected by me at the Mansion House was subscribed by the public with the view or for the purpose of rewarding gentlemen in your position of life, yet it was thought that pieces of plate of considerable value with appropriate inscriptions might be acceptable to you in recognition of the meritorious services you rendered. I am sorry you think it right to decline a memento of such an event, but I fully accept as final your determination in that respect.[49]

Local opinion was jubilant. A placard was posted throughout the district, rejoicing that 'the Mansion House Committee have determined to take them at their word and NOT GIVE THEM ANYTHING'.[50]

South Wales opinion in general appears to have been shocked by these men's actions. As the *Central Glamorgan Gazette* put it:

> The bloom which rested upon the noble deeds performed at the Tynewydd Colliery has been rudely, pettishly, and selfishly disturbed. This has not been done by the working colliers – the real heroes of the transaction – but by their masters, the *gentlemen* actors in the drama, who could not brook to subjugate their merits to other men's decision, or place any other value on their acts beyond a money consideration. They have . . . lost both honour and reward, both renown and the grace of their acts.[51]

Siamps Thomas's trial was scheduled to start on Monday, 6 August. By a quirk of fate, the Lord Mayor of London (who had decided to come after all) came to Pontypridd two days before that, on 4 August, to distribute the Mansion House fund and to celebrate the Albert Medals. The occasion was a magnificent one. After a procession through the town, the proceedings started with Mr Talbot, the Lord Lieutenant, distributing the silver tankards given to the owners, managers, etc., by the Daily Telegraph fund. Then the House of Commons prizes were given to the worker rescuers; and the climax of the proceedings was the distribution of the Mansion House awards.

After the subsequent naming of the Albert medallists, Judge Gwilym Williams made a speech, in which he drew attention to what was clearly, in his view, a heartwarming statistic: that among the Albert medallists were four colliery proprietors and seven managing agents of collieries. He then touched on the delicate question of Siamps Thomas:

> Others there were, and many, who so distinguished themselves, although they did not fall within the cases contemplated by the Royal Warrant. Indeed in one instance, that of Mr James Thomas, manager of the Tynewydd Colliery, I am permitted to say that he was recommended for a medal of the second class, but that his case, for reasons which you will readily imagine, has been reserved for future consideration.[52]

After all the presentations and speeches, luncheon took place in Market House, 'served by Mr Chalk, of the Cardiff and County Club'. This splendid meal, for more than 350 people, was given by the Revd David Watkin Williams of Fairfield, who was toasted at the end of the meal by Lord Aberdare.[53]

It is fascinating to note, in Matthew Cope's later memoirs, that he, as a partner in the Troedyrhiw company which owned Tynewydd mine, was amazed not to have been invited to these celebrations:

> Here comes a curious fact that will be read with surprise, I am sure. I cannot speak of this memorable event from knowledge. I was not present because – I was not invited! I was a principal proprietor of

the colliery, but I was not invited to be one of this great gathering. I do not know why. I never knew why. There is the fact, and I simply record it as a curiosity.[54]

This shows a singular lack of insight. One of Cope's partners, the manager of Tynewydd, was about to face trial for manslaughter. The authorities of the Tynewydd mine were therefore all under a cloud. Yet Cope (who did not turn up to any of the legal proceedings, not even the inquest) appeared to think that he himself was entirely detached from all this, and was affronted at not having been invited to the celebrations of the rescue. This shows how little he felt himself, as a Cardiff docksman, to have any direct responsibility for the mines of which he was part-owner. This attitude of his, we shall see, was to be even more pronounced at the time of the Albion disaster (where he was chairman of the directors) in the 1890s.

Two days after this splendid event, Siamps Thomas entered the dock at the Glamorganshire Assizes in Swansea, charged with manslaughter.

The Trial

The proceedings in Swansea (6-7 August), before Baron Cleasby, started with the presentation of the prosecution case by Mr Bowen, QC. He rehearsed the stipulations of the Mines Regulation Act with regard to the measures to be taken when approaching water, saying that he 'would show the jury that not only did the prisoner neglect to carry out the directions of the Act of Parliament, but he did not take such precautions as any prudent man would have taken supposing the Act . . . was not in existence'. He also pointed out that in December it had been calculated that there were forty-four yards to go to the boundary with the other mine. As the progress in that area was from six to seven yards a fortnight, 'it was merely a matter of calculation to find when they were getting into close proximity with the boundary.' The prisoner had believed that there was a fault, which would be a sufficient barrier to keep out water:

If, however, that fault had existed at all, it should have been come to sixteen yards in advance of the place where the heading had been driven on the 14th of December. That must have convinced the prisoner that no fault existed. It would be proved that there was no fault.

No instructions had been given to the foreman (that is, the overman) by the prisoner, nor was the foreman told that the precautions ought to taken. The prosecuting counsel ended by musing on the reasons for Thomas's negligence:

> The colliery had been worked with great success until this occurrence, and that might have accounted, although it could not have justified, the defendant's negligence

The evidence of Thomas's subordinates turned out to be fairly damning. Charles Oatridge, who had been the man who had broken through to the old workings, said that on the day of the accident he had drawn attention to the damp state of the coal. Richard Howells, the overman, according to Oatridge, 'said there was a fault near, and that there was no danger from water'. Asked about the role of Siamps Thomas, Oatridge said: 'I had not seen Mr Thomas (the prisoner) in the pit for about two months before the incident.' Richard Howells could recall Oatridge's comment about the damp coal. He declared, however, that he did not know they were getting near the boundary. He had seen a plan at the office, but he had not understood it. Siamps Thomas had told him, six months before, that there was a fault, but had not told him how far Oatridge was to work. 'If I saw anything wrong it was my duty as overman to report it to Mr Thomas. I did not know what I saw on the 11th was dangerous, and did not, therefore, report to Mr Thomas.' He stated that the last time he saw Mr Thomas in the heading was 'some time previous to the occurrence.' When counsel, bearing in mind Oatridge's comment about Thomas's absence from the mine, questioned him further about this, Howells backtracked, however, saying that 'Mr Thomas goes through every part of the mine in his turns'.

Earlier in the proceedings, Dr Henry Naunton Davies, called to give medical evidence as to the deaths, had used this as an opportunity to praise Thomas's record:

I know the colliery, and have known Mr Thomas as a careful manager for twenty years. He has always shown himself very anxious for the safety of the men, who have presented him with a testimonial. Up to the time of the accident, and now, he is held in the highest esteem. He was assiduous in his efforts to relieve the men.

The defence counsel, Mr McIntyre, in his summing-up, stressed that given Thomas's record, what had happened was a mere 'error of judgement' rather than culpable negligence. He stressed also Thomas's heroism in the rescue, and painted a terrible picture of the fate that awaited him if he were convicted:

> Now they were doing their utmost to make him a felon. For the rest of his life he would, if convicted, be branded as a felon. As far as the punishment was concerned his lordship had power to send him to penal servitude for life. Was that the sort of crime of which Mr Thomas ought to be convicted?

Various character witnesses were now brought in. Judge Gwilym Williams said he had known Thomas for twelve or thirteen years. He described him as a most careful manager, greatly respected in the district for his high integrity. The Revd David Watkin Williams said he had known Thomas for twenty-seven to twenty-eight years, 'ever since he came to Glamorganshire to live', and that Thomas had 'a high reputation' as 'one of the most skilful managers'. And a very powerful gun was brought into play when Mr William Thomas Lewis (the Marquess of Bute's agent, and a powerful figure in the valleys) said: 'I have known the prisoner for 21 years. I have always found him a thoroughly practical man, and very careful of those employed under him. He has a high character for integrity and respectability.'

Despite all this, the judge's summing-up was distinctly adverse. He asked the jury to consider 'whether the prisoner was justified in not putting into effect the regulations prescribed by the Act of Parliament.' They must also consider his attitude to the question of whether there was water in the other mine or not:

> Was it not negligence to suppose merely that there was no water? The prisoner could have gone to the other mine, and have inquired, and

if he was told there was no water then he would not be responsible. Ought he not to have made it certain for the purpose of safety?

And then there was the question of the distance to the boundary. 'If he had given attention to the matter', the prisoner must have known that just before the accident they were very near the boundary. 'He need not tell them that if the prisoner had not given his attention to the fact he was guilty of negligence.' Given the fact that the fault had not been met with where expected, 'was the prisoner at the bar justified, as a reasonable and prudent manager, in proceeding to the point he did without taking the prescribed precautions?' The jury's choice was this:

> If they thought there was a sufficient justification for the prisoner to act as he did in approaching pent up water which was dangerous, to act upon a conclusion more or less uncertain that the fault would be a protection, then they would return a verdict accordingly . . . If they came to the conclusion that he was not justified in believing, as a reasonable man and manager, that there was no water in the mine, and if they also thought that he had no justification in coming to the conclusion he did after working close to the boundary without taking the precautions of the Act of Parliament, then he would be guilty of culpable negligence.

Things must have looked pretty black for Thomas at this point. The jury retired, but after about 45 minutes returned to say they could not agree. Two hours later, they returned once more, and the foreman said that they were about equally divided, and that there was no chance of their agreeing, even if they were locked up all night. Siamps Thomas was therefore discharged, and bound over for a sum of £200, to appear for a retrial at the next assizes 'if called upon on the part of the Crown'.[55]

A further controversy

Ironically, the day after the trial the *Western Mail*, in error, printed the name of 'James Thomas' among the list of those who had received an Albert Medal.[56] Such mistakes can only have added to the distress of the Thomas family, as they awaited the possibility of a further trial some time in the future. As the *Pontypridd Herald* was later to say, 'The owner was set at liberty on bail, in the painful position of a man who would in all likelihood be called upon to answer the same charge on a future occasion.'[57] The fact that this was not a certain outcome, given the phrase 'if called upon' in the Swansea judgment, can only have added an element of uncertainty which was possibly more painful than an inevitable return to the courts.

The mixed views of so many of the local inhabitants of the Rhondda, with regard to Thomas's current position, can best be seen in yet another controversy – this time with regard to the local Pontypridd fund for the victims and rescuers. On 20 October and 8 November, two letters from the Revd Bickerton A. Edwards, vicar of Llanwonno, were printed in the *Western Mail*, in which he criticised the sub-committee charged with the distribution of the funds as having come to 'one-sided, incongruous conclusions'.[58] Six of the owners and managers who were foremost in planning the rescue of the five miners were to be presented with illuminated addresses on vellum; but why had Siamps Thomas been left out?

> It cannot be denied by anyone who has a regard for the truth that Mr James Thomas did more from first to last towards the rescue of the entombed men, both by the work he did and by the risk he incurred, than any other of the managers and colliery proprietors. I think I may say so without offence. His very strong claim was rejected simply on grounds of prejudice. In fact, a man who has not been convicted by a judge of assize, and a jury who had patiently weighed all the facts of the case, is branded as 'guilty' by the arbitrary opinion of a local sub-committee. Instead of dealing with facts bearing on the rescue of the miners after the inundation, the sub-committee went out of their way to give an arbitrary opinion as to the cause of the accident, and to pass sentence accordingly. Is not this one-sided and partial dealing?[59]

At a meeting at the Porth Hotel on 5 November, the report of the sub-committee (which consisted of six men,[60] including John Calvert, the mining pioneer, and Idris Williams) was presented. It was opposed by Edwards, who reiterated his criticisms, and proposed that Thomas should be added to the list of managers who were to receive illuminated addresses. Idris Williams, who had originally gone along with the decision not to do anything about Thomas 'until after the trial', now felt that the committee, by not agreeing to present Thomas with an address, 'were thus in a manner judging him, after the charge against him had not been proved at the assizes'. He hoped Thomas would now be added to the list. A motion was put to that effect, which was agreed.[61]

The controversy rumbled on in the press. But on 1 December the distribution was finally made, with Thomas included. What had become clear was that, for some people, the Swansea trial had shown that the charges against Siamps Thomas had not stood up. For others, the judicial process was still incomplete. Which was true?

The Second Trial

That question was answered, when Siamps Thomas was once more brought to court, in Cardiff before Mr Justice Mellor, on Tuesday 9 April 1878. That the whole question had been in doubt right up to the last moment was shown by the judge's comment, in his eventual summing-up, that, though the trial was in the calendar, he had not been aware, right up to the night before, that it would actually be taking place.[62] In other words he, like many, could not believe that the Government would go through with it. Why had they decided to do so? As the *Pontypridd Herald* put it:

> For a man to find himself in peril of his liberty on so serious a charge as that of manslaughter is a serious position indeed. But to place him in the position of a criminal a second time, after an interval of six months and on the same charge, is a hardship that only very exceptional circumstances can justify.[63]

What were the special circumstances in this case? The prosecuting counsel, in his introductory speech, gave some account of them:

> Mr Bowen dwelt upon the importance of the inquiry as affecting such a large number of miners employed in the district, and remarked

that they must not allow what the defendant had done after the accident to warp their judgment in deciding whether it was by the manager's culpable negligence that the accident happened.[64]

In other words, the government saw this as a test case (a rare opportunity, given the verdict of the coroner's court), in which the carelessness of many mining managers with regard to the safety of their men could be highlighted, and a message sent for the future. Yet the specifics of this case did not, in fact, lend themselves to this aim. Thomas had been shown, unlike many managers, to have a past record of care for his men's safety (as the judge was to point out in his summing-up). And the prosecution in fact seems to have been conducted, in this second trial (by the same barrister who had been so trenchant in the first trial), in a fairly lacklustre manner. Indeed, the defence counsel, Mr McIntyre, drew attention to Bowen's attitude, forced into prosecuting by a decision taken elsewhere:

> He was afraid, looking at the prosecution, that there was a greater power behind the throne, which compelled Mr Bowen to take up this case, which he seemed to do with apparent dislike.[65]

Bowen did not even bring on the witnesses who had been so damning to Thomas in the previous trial. The *Pontypridd District Herald* asked whether 'the arrangements for the prosecution [were] purposely devised to allow the jury an opportunity of giving the venerable-looking accused an honourable acquittal'.[66] These arrangements, and the evident sympathy of the judge for Thomas, clearly did not meet the Government's intentions.

The defence counsel, in his summing-up, made great play upon the absence of the crucial witnesses, claiming that he had been unable to cross-examine them. He also stressed Thomas's previous record: he had 'managed the mine so well that the Government inspectors did not think it necessary to examine it, and that there had not been an accident for 21 years'. The evidence of a number of people, including Judge Gwilym Williams, was tendered, 'to speak to the high character, care, and skill always displayed by the defendant'.

Bowen, summing up for the prosecution, concurred in 'the previous high character borne by Mr Thomas', but urged that 'if he had been guilty of culpable neglect this previous good character must not shield him'. He stressed that 'this present case was brought forward, not so much against the defendant Thomas, but for the protection of thousands of colliers in the district and elsewhere – and he believed the number amounted to a million in the United Kingdom – whose lives were dependent upon the care of the manager'.[67]

In the judge's summing up, 'the tendency of his remarks seemed generally in favour of the defendant' – so much so, that there were 'frequent attempts made to cheer the remarks of the learned judge', though they were at once suppressed. He started, while praising the Act, by making a distinction between those at whom it had been directed, and those who 'desired to look after the safety of their men.' He hoped that by his remarks he might 'mitigate any supposed feeling on the part of the prosecution or the jury.' While he 'exhorted [the jury] not to be led away by too much sympathy with the defendant', he also asked them 'not to take too much into account the circumstances of the accident, which caused the death of several persons.' He then went on to draw a contrast between 'gross neglect' and 'ignorance, or an error of judgment', and to point to the dangers of *ex post facto* judgements:

> The regulations of the Act of Parliament were intended for the preservation of human life, and these regulations the manager was bound to observe. It might have been the wisest course for the defendant to have adopted those precautionary regulations, and to have bored to ascertain if there was water ahead, but the jury would have to decide whether by his not having done so, there was any culpable neglect on his part, seeing that he expected to come to a fault. Of course, since the accident they had a lot of information supplied, but they must take Mr Thomas's position as he stood before the accident occurred. He strongly pointed out that a man might, with the most honest intentions, commit an error of judgment.

After condemning 'the manner in which the prosecution had been conducted on the part of the Treasury', the judge told the jury that if they felt the defendant was 'only guilty of an error of judgment, the law was not so absolute that they must find him guilty'. He then slated the reasons for which the case appeared to have been brought:

He thought the Act of Parliament was a magnificent one, but it should be closely watched, and proceedings taken under it for the public good should be taken with fairness and impartiality, and the case taken upon its merits and not because there were millions of colliers or millions of masters – if there were so many – affected thereby, which was immaterial to the question.[68]

The jury retired, and returned within five minutes to declare an unanimous verdict of 'not guilty'. Siamps Thomas was discharged, 'and left the court with a numerous body of friends'.[69]

This was a serious setback for the Government in its attempts to ensure the safety of miners by bringing to justice those who were responsible for the many mining accidents that occurred year on year. Many of these accidents were the direct result of 'corner-cutting' by mineowners more intent on profit than on safety; yet most inquests and inquiries tended to exonerate those in charge, even in the face of compelling evidence. The Tynewydd case had, by its dramatic nature and the heroism of the rescuers, struck the imagination of the general public throughout the country. That public, and the Government, had been primed to seek in this instance for an 'inquiry of the most searching character', which would 'not be of that slovenly and perfunctory character which unfortunately is too often associated with matters concerning the lives of miners who have been killed.' For this purpose not only a government barrister, but also a prominent representative of the miners' union, had been sent to the inquest. That inquest, partly because of these observers, had produced the unusual result of a verdict of manslaughter. The resultant trial had been marked by strong evidence as to negligence, and by a judge's summing-up that had been adverse to the defendant. The jury's inability to come to a unanimous decision must have seemed perverse in the extreme. It is no wonder that the Government should have decided to proceed to another trial.

Yet in this they had miscalculated. From the first trial it had become clear that Siamps Thomas, by his actions (or lack of them), had been responsible for the accident, and the deaths. But the delay, and the picture of a man having such a matter hanging over him for so long a time, had aroused considerable public sympathy for him; and the general opinion as to his previous care for the safety of his men, and his previous clean record with regard to accidents, as vouched for not only by the experts, but also by his men, also seems to have carried a great deal of weight. Added to that, his unstinting efforts to save the men, referred to by so many witnesses, were bound to have an effect, despite all the legal warnings that this must not be taken into account. The lacklustre performance of the prosecution at the second trial seems to have reflected these considerations. Furthermore, the judge appears to have been incensed at the idea that a man, according to the prosecution's own statements, was being tried as an example, for the benefit of thousands of miners elsewhere, rather than being tried on the merits of the individual case. One must also bear in mind that the court appeared to be filled with vociferous supporters of the defendant, and that the whole atmosphere appeared here, as opposed to in Swansea, to be entirely in his favour. The scenes at the acquittal seem to have been almost triumphal, and one wonders the extent to which fellow coalowners and managers were there, and saw the outcome as a deliverance from a general threat, in that the government might well hesitate before undertaking such lengthy and costly proceedings again. And, indeed, the situation with regard to inquests and inquiries appears to have remained, from then on, much as it had been before.

The jury had decided that Siamps Thomas had committed an 'error of judgment' rather than 'culpable negligence'. What caused this 'error of judgment' on the part of a man reputed as a 'hands-on' manager who was careful about matters of safety? If one takes into account the fact that, at the time of the accident, his new venture at Ynyshir appeared to be reaching the moment of striking steam coal, one must presume that his mind was not sufficiently on the job, and that he must have left more to subordinates than was wise (certainly much of the evidence gave the impression that he not been seen much at the mine recently). Combined with this, there appears also to have been some pig-headedness on his part in relation to his theories about the fault that would protect his mine from any water at Cymmer, and also his entrenched belief that at any rate there was no danger from such water, which had either been pumped out or had been at a lower level than Tynewydd's No. 3 seam. But no-one seems to have raised the point that, by having appointed to key positions the subordinates that he had, he bore ultimate responsibility for their shortcomings, their ignorance and illiteracy, and for the fact that they were also apparently incapable of coming to any independent judgment without referring to their manager. The management structures at Tynewydd appear to have been slack and informal, which may well have worked in the very earliest stages of mining exploration, but which were inadequate in a working mine of about 150 men, and in the new situation created by the Mines Regulation Acts. They were also centred on a manager who took all the decisions, and did not delegate happily; this could be particularly dangerous when, for any reason, the manager's mind was elsewhere, or he himself was absent for any length of time.

Be that as it may, Siamps Thomas could now go free. The next few years were to be devoted to the development of his successful new mine, the Standard Collieries at Ynyshir, which was to be the basis for his vast fortune.

10

The Albion Disaster, 1894

On 23 June 1894, the Albion colliery was to be the scene of one of the greatest disasters that had taken place in the south Wales coalfield up to that time. As with the 1877 Tynewydd disaster, the Thomas/Mathias family was closely connected with events. A marked difference had taken place, however, within this period of twenty years, not only in the nature of mining enterprises, but also in the relationship between owners and the mines under their control.

Compared with the Tynewydd colliery, the Albion was a vast enterprise. Where, in 1877, the Tynewydd had employed about 150 men, and had been sunk to the No. 3 seam to a depth of 92 yards, the Albion employed in 1894 more than 1,700 men, and had two shafts that had been sunk to the Four-Foot seam of steam coal to a depth of 646 yards. One must not, of course, exaggerate the change for the coalfield as a whole. Even by 1877, the Tynewydd (sunk in 1852) had been smaller than most of its neighbouring mines. Steam coal mines were sunk to far greater depths than bituminous coal mines. As early as the mid-Seventies 'the average depth of the shafts in the eastern part of the coalfield had increased to 200 yards, while the deepest sinkings . . . had a depth of over 400 yards'.[1] Even so, the new venture in the 1890s in the Taff valley, the Albion, was a culmination of the trend to larger and deeper mines with larger workforces, which had been going on for the past forty years. The Albion was also an example of the change in managing practices that had been going on during the same period. In the 1870s, many of the owners had been managers in their own pits, with a hands-on approach to their work, and an intimate knowledge of the men working under them. There had, however, been a growing tendency for mining enterprises to become limited liability companies. This had not at first made much difference to the practices of the small group of men who continued to dominate the coal companies in the area; but, 'as time passed and the firms grew the nature of the involvement [of the owners] changed, usually becoming more remote and strategic as more managerial functions were delegated to professionals'.[2] The Albion colliery illustrates this change admirably. Though its managing director, Henry Lewis Tŷ Nant, was an experienced mining engineer, it became clear from the inquiry into the Albion disaster that he had had little direct input into the running of the mine. The other directors had had even less. Matthew Cope, the chairman, remained even more firmly a Cardiff docksman than his father had been. All the other directors, apart from William Henry Mathias, were based either in Cardiff docks or in London, while the list of seven initial 'subscribers' included two ship-owners, two coal exporters and a banker.[3] The newest director, W. H. Mathias, however, though his involvement appears on the surface to have been as purely financial as theirs, lived in the Valleys, and did in fact have experience of mines (as was shown by his participation in the Tynewydd rescue, and by his involvement in the Aber Rhondda Coal Company). The Albion disaster shows him to have been more in the tradition of the old mine-owners than might have been expected. The day-to-day running of the Albion mine was left to its professional manager, Philip Jones.

One thing had not changed in the mining areas, however. As the Albion disaster was to show, the tendency was still for local magistrates and juries to exonerate examples of managerial negligence at inquests and inquiries.

Mining was as perilous as it had always been. With the exploitation of steam coal, however, one danger had taken on particular significance: that of explosions. The Four-Foot seam '[gave] off immense quantities of gas at very great pressure'.[4] By the mid-1880s accidents from explosion were among the two greatest causes of mining deaths (the other being 'cave-in or fall'). South

Wales suffered particularly from deaths by explosion: its figure was fifty per cent higher than the industry as a whole.[5] The causes of the explosions were a matter of dispute; but in 1880, William Galloway, inspector of mines, propounded the view, which soon became fairly widely accepted, that dry coal dust could transmit flame throughout a mine and create a massive explosion.[6] Among the methods used to try to counteract this, the main ones were those of spraying water in the roadways, and of providing mechanical means of ventilation (particularly necessary at the depths the mines now reached).

The Albion was already well-known as a 'dry and dusty' mine, and the Four-Foot Seam there 'produced a considerable quantity of fire-damp'.[7] It was classified as a 'fiery colliery'. All the more reason for great care to be taken with regard to safety. The mine was ventilated by a Schiele fan, and water was supposed to be sprayed continually throughout the mine.[8] As we shall see, however, there were various shortcomings in these safety measures at the time of the disaster.

The Disaster [9]

At 2 p.m. on Saturday 23 June 1894, the 'night shift' – a cleaning and repair shift that worked in the mine from 2 p.m. to 8 p.m. on Saturdays, when no coal was produced – went down the Albion mine. There were about 290 of them. The *Times* report as to what happened shortly thereafter is a very graphic one:

> About a quarter to four o'clock a loud report was heard, followed almost immediately by another, and the mouth of the pit was immediately enveloped in thick black smoke, through which tongues of flame shot into the air. The concussion on the surface was tremendous, and the force of the blast was so great that the top of the pit was completely blown to pieces, and large baulks of timber were hurled about in almost every direction.[10]

Amazingly, the Schiele fan continued to work. Philip Jones, the manager, arranged for temporary repairs to be made to the fan covering. He then, at about 5 p.m., went down the pit, together with his son William Jones, who was acting under-manager, and a number of the workmen. They were met by a scene of desolation. Conditions were so bad that they returned to the surface at 7.15 p.m.

Nobody knew how many men were in the mine when the explosion occurred. The first estimate was about 262, but at the eventual inquest it was declared that 'as far as could be ascertained' there were 295. Many of the miners concerned were not known personally either to the manager or to the under-manager, or even to the fireman.[11] By this time, it was not just the owners who were distant from the men; within the mine itself the management was far more distant and impersonal than had been the case in former years.

As for the board of directors, some of the most important of them were, at this time, distant in space as well as in spirit. The chairman, Matthew Cope, and the managing director, Henry Lewis, were on a yachting holiday with their wives, heading for Norway. They received the news when in harbour at Antwerp, and immediately decided to head for home, reaching Cilfynydd on Tuesday, the 26th.[12]

One of the directors, William Henry Mathias, was however close at hand, at his home in Porth. He was at the mine within a very short time of the explosion. The Welsh newspapers were unanimous in praising his contribution to attempts at rescue. According to the *Western Mail* 'Alderman W. H. Mathias JP, the only director of the company who was present, worked hard during Saturday night and Sunday taking charge of the operations on the surface'.[13] The *Pontypridd Chronicle* declared that his 'indefatigable and untiring services in directing operations are deserving of the best admiration'.[14] The *Pontypridd District Herald* said that he 'took in charge the whole of the surface arrangements, and was untiring in looking after those who were brought up and who needed assistance'.[15] The *Cardiff Times*, too, praised his superintendence of operations.[16]

Meanwhile, 'colliery managers and mining officials had arrived from all parts of the Rhondda, Aberdare, and Merthyr valleys, and parties of exploration were at once formed'.[17] They were headed by Thomas Griffiths of Cymmer collieries. From the Standard collieries came the manager John Thomas Fernbank. And there were many others. Apart from Mathias, the only representative of the Albion company was its secretary, Mr D. Ellis.

Rescue parties went down throughout the evening. The hay-loft of the extensive stables at the mine was at first used for treating the wounded, but soon it had become a temporary mortuary. 'Most of the victims were badly mutilated, confirming the already growing suspicion of the rescuers that the explosive force had been much greater than originally believed.'[18] The bodies were laid out, and throughout the night relatives came looking, by the light of lanterns, for their loved ones. In many cases it was impossible to identify the bodies, and sometimes ones that had been taken had to be returned to the loft owing to false identification.

By midday on Sunday, the 24th, 103 bodies had been recovered, but many more were to be brought out as the hours went by. Vast crowds surrounded the mine. Given the ghoulish activities, in our own time, of passers-by in relation to accidents on the motorway, we should not perhaps be surprised that many sightseers came from far and wide. What does surprise, however, is that the TVR should have put on special trains to bring those sightseers to the area, and that drayloads of beer should have been brought to Cilfynydd to replenish the pubs in order to slake the thirst of these masses.[19] On the other hand, no services were held in the places of worship in Cilfynydd that Sunday, 'it being felt by ministers that it would be useless to do so, seeing that the calamity had spread such widespread grief, and there was so much public excitement'.[20]

Two things now concerned those who were having to deal with the consequences of the disaster: the means of coming to the aid of the dependents of the dead, and (more urgently) the logistics of dealing with the dead bodies. In both of these issues, Mathias found himself closely involved.

Evan Owen, general secretary of the South Wales Miners' Permanent Provident Society, arrived at Cilfynydd late on the night of the 23rd to record details of the bereaved and to organise payments. As the scale of the disaster became clear, Owen estimated that the sum needed from the fund would be about £60,000 to £70,000.[21] On Monday, the 25th, Sir William Thomas Lewis, chairman of the Provident Society, hastened from London. A special Taff Vale train brought him the last lap from Cardiff. On arrival, he immediately had an earnest consultation with three men: Alderman W. H. Mathias, Evan Owen, and Mr George Campbell, of the

Central Association for dealing with distress in mining centres. Sir William told them that 'he would wait upon the Lord Mayor of London and the Mayor of Cardiff upon the subject of opening relief lists.'[22] Within days the Lord Mayor started an appeal, and a local relief fund was set up as well.

A far more urgent task was that of disposing of the bodies. Here the two representatives of the Albion company who were at hand – David Ellis and W. H. Mathias – took a major part. On the morning of Sunday, the 24th, David Ellis sent telegrams to three Pontypridd undertakers, and to one from Cardiff, 'asking for 250 coffins to be made of "the finest elm", the expense to be borne by the Albion Company'.[23] By the morning of Tuesday, the 26th, the organisation of the funeral arrangements was in progress. In one office, Evan Owen was paying £5 each to the relatives of the deceased, to help with funeral expenses; in another, David Ellis was issuing vouchers for the bereaved to draw coffins from the store. Meanwhile Mathias, realising that the churchyard at Glyntaff, Pontypridd, would not be able to cope with the number of interments involved, sent a number of men over the steep hill behind Cilfynydd to the little country churchyard of Llanfabon, where his father, Richard Mathias, had been churchwarden until his death in 1890. A new graveyard had recently been opened in the field opposite the old churchyard. Only a few interments had taken place there up till now. On Tuesday and Wednesday, fifty of Mathias's men dug graves in that new graveyard.[24]

Glyntaff was a multi-denominational cemetery, with separate sections of ground for burials of each denomination. On Wednesday, twenty-seven were buried in the nonconformist section, three in the Roman Catholic ground, and eleven in the Church of England section.[25] 'Nearly all the ministers and clergy in the town and district took part in performing the sad funeral rites.'[26] Meanwhile other bodies were being carried by mourners and friends over the steep hill to Llanfabon churchyard:

> The task of carrying the dead was an exceedingly laborious one, as the rays of the sun were simply scorching, whilst the arid dust which continually rose from the road made the lot of the processionists somewhat uncomfortable . . . The scene presented by the mournful

cortege as it wended its way slowly over the road leading to the top of the hill was unique and unprecedented, and one which is not likely to be soon forgotten by those who witnessed it. At the graveyard itself the scene was an extraordinary one, many of those who had joined in the sad cortege dropping on the grass simply exhausted by the walk and the heat of the sun.[27]

They were met at the gates of the churchyard by the Revd Daniel Leigh, vicar of the parish, and his curate and another clergyman from Treharris. There was an attendance of some thousands.[28]

The press noted that 'as the cemetery is Church property, these three clergymen officiated throughout',[29] because 'nonconformist ministers had no status in this churchyard'.[30] This appears extraordinary, as the Burial Laws Amendment Act 1880 had specifically given nonconformist ministers the right to conduct funerals in the churchyards of the Established Church. But it is known that many clergy, particularly Tractarians, still ignored the requirements of the Act, to the extent that 'the conflict and dissent over burial rights and privileges did not evaporate until well into the twentieth century.' And, though the nonconformists had the law on their side, 'people do not like rows at funerals', and, despite certain well-publicised cases of conflict, the reaction of most people who were burying their dead was to put up with what the clergy demanded.[31] Even taking account of this, it seems remarkable that the Revd Daniel Leigh and his two colleagues should have insisted on what they evidently still perceived to be their rights (which were no longer legal rights) in the face of a tragedy of this magnitude – and that the newspapers should clearly have been unaware of the actual legal situation.

The next day, Thursday, more funerals took place both at both Glyntaff and Llanfabon. Given the exceedingly hot weather, many of the corpses were showing signs of decomposition. 'By now the conditions in the hayloft were almost beyond description, and Superintendent Jones ordered that the eleven bodies still not identified be buried in Llanfabon',[32] together with eleven other bodies. But 'notwithstanding the objectionable odour which rose from the quickly decomposing corpses within the coffins there was no scarcity of mourners, the dead being carried on the strong shoulders of miners, many of whom were comrades of the departed at the Albion Colliery'.[33] A crowd of over five hundred mourners attended at Llanfabon churchyard.

The authorities found that they had to disinfect a number of the houses in which the corpses had lain. Conditions in the village were appalling. Nevertheless, it was reported that W. H. Mathias (despite the fact that his fellow-directors Cope and Lewis had finally arrived on Tuesday) 'was again in attendance' throughout Thursday.[34] There is no mention of the presence of the other directors, who were presumably keeping a low profile. A week later, too, on Friday 6 July, Mathias assisted Evan Owen and J. S. Cullen (accountant of the Permanent Relief Fund) in the payment of the second instalment of funeral allowances, and sums in relief of the widows and children.[35]

So far, the main concerns had been practical ones of the moment; but soon minds turned to the causes of the accident.

Before the Inquest

Within two days of the disaster, on Monday 25 June, an inquest was opened at the New Inn Hotel, Pontypridd. There were two coroners, as the mine stretched under the river Taff, and the accident therefore fell between two jurisdictions. The Albion Colliery Company was represented by a Cardiff solicitor who expressed regret that 'Mr Henry Lewis, Tynant' was out of the country, and asked for the inquiry to be adjourned for a month. This was agreed (even though Henry Lewis would arrive the next day, the 26th).[36]

The inquest was to resume on Monday, 16 July. In the meantime, of course, opinions were expressed freely about the causes of the disaster. The south Wales newspapers concentrated on the record of good management by the company. The *Western Mail*, for example, stated that the mine 'stands in the very forefront for the manner in which it has been sunk and the level driven, together with the enlightened policy which has marked its management'.[37] The *Pontypridd Chronicle*, commenting on the fact that 'peace and prosperity [had] reigned over the rapidly-increasing district of Cilfynydd since the colliery was opened', described the mine as 'one of the largest and best regulated pits in the south Wales coalfield'.[38] The *Pontypridd District Herald* went even further, stressing the care given by the company to safety measures:

> The colliery was a fiery one, but the provisions made by the proprietors, regardless of expense, shows the absolute impotency of man's controlling agency, should the pent-up forces of nature under this restraint find a weak spot through which it can revel in destruction and slaughter ... The opinion of experienced mining engineers is unanimous in favour of the fact that the condition of the mine in the hands of those responsible, left little or nothing to be desired.[39]

Despite such pre-emptive strikes in favour of the management, other voices were being raised. Doubts, for example, were being voiced as to the composition of the jury for the inquest. The workmen of the Cambrian colliery passed a resolution 'strongly protesting at the selection of the jury empanelled to investigate the cause of the explosion, and appealing to Members of Parliament to legislate in the matter, so as to secure the rights of the working community to appoint two-thirds of the jurymen on fatal accidents in coal mines'.[40] The concerns of these workmen were not unjustified, as the record of previous inquiries shows us. The general nature of such inquiries is described by Morris and Williams thus:

> The legal measures to punish owners or managers guilty of negligence and to provide the compensation for those affected by accidents remained only partially effective. Juries still showed unwillingness to return verdicts of manslaughter against the powerful coal-owners of their own neighbourhood, and on the rare occasions when officials were committed to the assizes on this charge they were invariably acquitted.[41]

Nevertheless, the general opinion in the press seemed to be that the Albion Colliery Company had done what it could to deal with the problems of a particularly fiery mine. In the newspapers, there were extensive quotations from the report of Henry Hall, HM inspector of mines for the Liverpool district, to the Royal Commission on Explosions from Coal-dust in Mines, which had recently appeared. In it he had said:

Of the whole of the dusts tested, that from the Albion Colliery, Glamorgan (Aberdare or Merthyr Four-Foot Seam, or Upper Four-Foot) excelled all others in violence and sensitiveness to explosion, and this seam has the worst history of any in the kingdom, upwards of 1,600 persons having been killed in it by explosions since the year 1845.

The view of the *Western Mail*, in relation to this, was firmly in favour of the company:

In view of this opinion, it speaks well for the management of the Albion Colliery that, notwithstanding the character of its dust, the present is the first disaster that has occurred there during the six years and a half which have elapsed since coal was first raised there.[42]

Most of these opinions were, of course, based on conjecture. It would take the inquest to reveal the true evidence, even if the inquest would in no way resolve the matter.

The Inquest [43]

The inquest resumed on Monday 16 July, at the New Inn Hotel. Observing on behalf of the Home Office was a barrister called John Roskill, and Abel Thomas QC MP[44] appeared on behalf of the company. Samuel T. Evans MP[45] acted on behalf of the Cambrian Miners' Association, for the relatives of the deceased. Those present connected with the Albion colliery included Henry Lewis (managing director), W. Lewis (agent), D. Ellis (secretary), Philip Jones (manager), and the commercial manager and surveyor. There was a jury of seventeen people. The inquest was to be a remarkably long one, taking place from the 16th to the 20th, and from the 24th to the 27th.

The jury was made up almost entirely of people unconnected with mining: it included a number of local shopkeepers, two innkeepers, a schoolmaster, a waterworks manager, and the clerk to the Llanwonno School Board. One of the innkeepers, John Thomas of the Bunch of Grapes Inn, objected to the proposed chairman, Hopkin Davies, an accountant, on the basis that he was 'not conversant with mining'. But he was overruled.[46]

John Roskill (1860–1940) was to play a major part both in the inquest and in the subsequent trial.[47] Born in Manchester in 1860, he had joined the London Bar at the relatively late age of 28, becoming in 1888 a pupil of H. H. Asquith, of whom he remained a close friend throughout his life.[48] Asquith was of course Home Secretary in 1894, so this perhaps explains the sending to Pontypridd of Roskill, whose sense of responsibility to the Home Office for the conduct of affairs in the Albion case appears to have been great. Added to this, he was a passionate man. After he had taken silk in 1903, and developed a big commercial practice, his annoyance at a fairly minor matter in a railway amalgamation case in 1908 led to fisticuffs between Roskill and the opposing counsel, Edmund Vesey Knox. This led to the former losing almost his entire practice (though, through Asquith's influence, he received a minor consolation prize by becoming Judge of the Salford Hundred Court of Records, a county court). It should be added that Roskill, after reading mathematics in Oxford, had also become a B.Sc. of the University of Manchester and an Associate of the Institution of Civil Engineers.[49]

On the first day of the inquest, the main evidence was that of Philip Jones, the manager. Much of the questioning of him related to the subject of 'shot-firing' which, it was alleged, had been taking place in the mine at the time of the explosion. This was the process whereby explosives were used to remove timbers which were no longer serving their purpose. Though not widespread, the practice was not illegal (even though the mining inspectors had been campaigning for its abolition)[50] so long as the correct procedures were followed. Shot-firing should only be done between shifts, when few men were down the mine; all precautions should be made to make sure that no-one was in the vicinity of it; and special watering arrangements needed to be made, to ensure the damping-down of any coal-dust which might cause an explosion. Jones explained that his practice was in accord with these measures:

There were written instructions [which he produced] for firemen and shotmen. He relied upon the regulation of the Coal Mines Act and his own written instructions – 'No shot-firing between shifts.' The shotmen would examine a place before firing and water the place in accordance with the rules.

In the proceedings on the next day, Tuesday, Jones was already developing the theory that the company was from now on to use: that the accident had been caused by a vast release of gas subsequent to a roof fall, in a completely different part of the colliery from where it was contended that blasting had taken place. He could not avoid, however, considerable cross-examination still related to blasting. Roskill pointed out that on that Saturday there was no gap between the shifts. Jones declared ignorance of this:

> Are you aware that on this particular Saturday the repairing shift went down at the very moment the day shift was coming up? – No, I am not aware of that.
>
> In fact they crossed each other, without any interval? – I can't say. If the shot-firing was going on before the day shift came up it would be against the rules? – It would be against our custom. Our blasting is all between shifts.
>
> And if there is no interval between the shifts, what then? – Well, we can't blast.

Jones also declared that watering was routinely done in such cases. But, under cross-examination, he was forced to admit that 'he never on any occasion went to see whether the regulations he had given to firemen were properly carried out. He did not know it was his duty to do it, never having received any complaints. The method of watering he had explained was not within his personal knowledge, as he had never seen timber blasted in this colliery.' It gradually became clear that neither the manager nor the under-manager had ever been present when shots were fired in timber, and that they supervised neither the blasting nor the watering arrangements.

Even more importantly, Jones admitted under close cross-examination that he believed that charges *had* been blasted on that day, though he now insisted that this had been at two o'clock. 'No shots were fired after two o'clock', he said.[51]

The next day, Wednesday, Philip Jones was recalled again. Roskill had worked out the reason why there had been no gap between shifts: there once had been a gap, but that had recently been changed. Getting information from Jones was, however, like drawing teeth:

Didn't three o'clock used to be the time for the afternoon shift to go down on Saturdays? – Yes.

How long ago was it altered? – About two months.

There was then an interval between the shifts? – Oh, yes.

What was the reason for the change? – A deputation from the men and miners' agents came and asked to be allowed to start sooner and finish an hour earlier in the night, and permission was given.

On Thursday, the 19th, other witnesses were now called from among those in lesser positions of authority, who backed up the picture of a well-ordered mine. William Garnett, night-fireman, assured that precautions were taken before firing to see that the place was well-watered and free from dust. Now that the shift system had changed, with no gap between shifts, firing always took place on Saturday nights, after the night shift had gone. 'They had never fired shots when men were at the bottom of the pit.' Gwilym Rees, day overman, while confident in his assertions, nevertheless gave cause for doubt, as he stated that there was time between the shifts to fire shots, despite the fact that the timescale had been changed:

> He gave instructions for the shotholes to be prepared about half-past one . . . They would be fired off between the day and evening shift on Saturday. The day shift ended at two o'clock, and the evening shift were supposed to go down about that time, but he reckoned that there was time between the shifts to fire them. If there would be no time then they would be fired at the end of the night shift.

It was not until Wednesday 25 July, however, that a dramatic change in the picture came. New evidence came, which contradicted most of the evidence from the manager and from senior employees. It also reinforced the picture already given by Jones's evidence, that senior management was, to put it mildly, semi-detached from the working practices in the mine.

A new cause for concern was that one of the men, Anstes, had had a store of about 25 lb of explosive down the mine. William Lewis, agent of the colliery, declared lack of knowledge and lack of responsibility:

William Lewis . . . said there were no special instructions as to the firing of shots between shifts. He did not know that it was anyone's special duty to look after Anstice [*sic*] and see that he did not take more than 5 lb of explosives into the mine. The storekeeper would not give him more than that at a time.

The Foreman: Still, we have the fact that he had as much as 25 lb in the mine.

Witness: He might have taken it down at 5 lb at a time.

All this reinforced concerns about the laxity of governance at the colliery; but it was the evidence which came next, from other workmen, which showed how much the evidence heard so far had been hiding the real truth, and how lax procedures actually had been. It also painted a picture of an atmosphere of fear down the mine.

William Rowlands, fireman, spoke of accumulations of gas. It was his duty to report the discovery of such accumulations to the overman, but the report was not entered upon a book:

> Mr Roskill: Did you never report the matter to anyone but John Evans? – No.
> Why was that? – Because if I made a complaint I might as well go away.
> Do you mean you were afraid of being dismissed? – Yes, exactly.
> Did you not think it was your duty to yourself and other workmen to make this public? – No doubt it was my duty ...

Rowlands then spoke about shot-firing. He had been working in the colliery for five years. He described how it was regularly undertaken when the shifts were down the mine:

> He had spoken of it to John Evans [the night overman], and said, 'Do you think it right and safe to blast this timber?' Evans replied, 'Well, indeed, boy, what shall I do?' Witness proceeded to speak of firing timbers on the inside double parting of Grover's about two months before the explosion, on a Saturday, between three and four o'clock, when the night shift men were down.

James Davies, ripper, declared that he had seen shot-firing done without proper safety:

He did not think he could report the matter to the workmen's committee with safety, for there were talebearers, and he was afraid. He was certain that the shot-firing took place when the men were in the workings during the shifts . . . He was afraid of complaining to the manager, and had heard of men being dismissed for making complaints . . . He worked in fear in the colliery, and was obliged to do so because he had a large family.

Thomas Owen, rock ripper, said that he had worked at the pit since its beginnings. 'Shots were fired almost every Saturday. That was the usual practice – when all the men were in.'

The questioning now turned to the watering of the mine before shot-firing. Owen had not seen any watering ever take place before firing. The only time he had seen it take place was if a life was lost by a fall. The Coroner was puzzled by this: what possible reason could there be for watering at such a time? The answer was that it must be because the management knew that after a fatality an inspector would be coming to the mine. On the question of shot-firing, Owen had never dared report the matter:

The Coroner: Have you ever yourself drawn the attention of anyone to the dangers of blasting timber? – No, sir: if I opened my mouth to anyone about it I should not be wanted there afterwards (Laughter).

Mr Roskill: And during the five years you were at the colliery you never thought it right to make a formal complaint? – I was afraid.

Have you ever kept away from the mine because of this shot-firing? – No; but I have been afraid many times.

Other workers confirmed the way in which the rules had been flouted. John Evans, rock ripper, said 'he had never noticed watering done on the levels when shots were fired. He had seen timber blasted several times without watering.' Edward Lewis, day ripper, gave evidence of shot-firing on two occasions during shifts. On one of these, he said, 'there was no watering before the shot was fired, though the place was dry'. David Romary, collier, 'never noticed watering done in the pit.' He gave evidence that 'shot-firing was carried on in the mine when men were at work in the pit.'

The most disastrous moment of the day for the colliery company was reached when, in the afternoon, Henry Lewis Tŷ Nant, the managing director, himself came to give evidence. He took what was by now the management line, that the explosion had been caused by secreted gas in another part of the mine, which had escaped in large quantities, occasioned by a rockfall. It was when he was asked about the change in the timing of shifts, for which he had given the permission, that his evidence came unstuck. He admitted that there was not sufficient time between shifts, and stated that he had completely overlooked this aspect of his decision. On the question of shot-firing 'he was aware that explosives were kept in the mine, but he delegated their control to others'.

All the evidence given on this day had been so explosive that on the next day, Thursday 26 July, the hall was crowded with people 'all eager and anxious, and who manifested more than ordinary interest in the proceedings, and often gave vent to their feelings as witness after witness gave evidence which they believed were likely to have shielded the management.' On this day a series of witnesses attempted to reinforce the management's theory about gas released by a rockfall, and no doubt this was what aggravated the spectators. Be that as it may, the spectators must have been satisfied when the experts, the mining inspectors, came down firmly on the side of an explosion caused by an accumulation of coal dust throughout the whole mine, unaffected by watering, and stated that the immediate cause had been shot-firing in these conditions. Henry Hall, HM Inspector of Mines for the Liverpool District, put it all graphically:

> He held that the agent which caused the explosion to devastate the whole mine was the coal dust, which was elevated in immense quantities in spite of attempts at watering. The mine, with the exception of one spot, was dry . . . He found coked coal dust an inch thick on some of the timbers near the shaft and in other parts of the mine. All the phenomena of the explosion were easily explicable if they took dust into account. The dust existed in all the intakes, and added to the force of the explosion, been [*sic*] taken up and increased as it advanced, with the wind behind it, like a prairie fire.

An explosion caused by 'firedamp' (methane gas) could not, in his view, have had such a spectacular effect, over three or four miles of unusually large roadway, unless there had been 'an immense accumulation of gas'; and 'further force in this case would be outward, whereas the evidences were quite the reverse.' He pointed to the clear evidence that the explosion had been caused by shot-firing:

> As to the point where the explosion occurred, it seemed to him that the coincidence of orders having been given to remove certain timbers from the pump dip by blasting, and the fact that the bodies of the persons who used to do this blasting were found, as if sheltering from a shot, he pointed this out as the starting place [*sic*] . . . It was probably the flame from the shots ignited some accumulation of gas over the timbers, and this in turn ignited the dust . . . Blasting was the cause of the Albion disaster.

His final comment was an acerbic one: 'The damping at this colliery was of no earthly use.'

J.G. Robson, Chief Inspector of Mines for South Wales and Monmouthshire, reinforced this view. He had not, he said, been aware that blasting in timber was carried out in this mine. 'He disapproved of it entirely', and if he had known of it he would have tried to stop it. In law, he could not prosecute them for it, but he would have strongly advised the manager to discontinue the practice. It was particularly inadvisable in steam coal pits:

> Blasting anywhere was dangerous even in a house-coal pit, but the danger in a dry and dusty colliery far exceeded that, and blasting in a colliery should be minimised as far as possible.

Like Hall, he 'condemned the system of watering the mine, which he considered very inadequate'. He also entirely discounted the 'gas' theory: 'In his opinion, the pit had been very free from gas.'

The evidence given on these last two days of the inquest would seem to have clearly justified a conclusion adverse to the company, in that it pointed to the disaster having been caused by imprudent shot-firing, and by carelessness in relation to the measures supposed to be taken (cleaning of dust, watering, making sure no shift was down the mine). The evidence of laxity in the management of the mine, too, appeared damning.

Despite the evidence of the Inspectors, the two coroners, in their summings-up, both failed to take sides in relation to the two theories as to the cause of the disaster that had been propounded. And one of them (referring no doubt to the evident excitement of the audience on the final day) went further by hoping that the jury 'would not be led away by the magnitude of the disaster, nor take any vindictive view of the matter'.

The stage seemed to be set for the usual whitewash of management. And though a majority of the jurors (eleven of the seventeen) believed the evidence of the mining inspectors, the remaining six strongly supported the 'roof fall' theory of the company's representatives. This disagreement became clear shortly after they had retired at 5.45 p.m. to consider their verdict, and the coroners were called in. They informed the jury that 'if they failed to agree the inquiry would have to be re-opened and conducted at the next assizes before one of the justices'.[52] Four hours later, they had still not come to agreement. But finally, at 10.20 p.m., they came to a verdict by which 'another inquiry [was] obviated'. The declaration as to the cause of the disaster was, however, necessarily an ambiguous one:

> The jury find that the deceased lost their lives through an explosion of gas that took place at the Albion Colliery on June 23, 1894, which explosion was accelerated and extended by coal dust, but the jury disagree as to the exact place at which the explosion had its origin.

The majority of the jury nevertheless appear to have succeeded in including in the judgement a criticism of the working practices that had been revealed:

> [The jury] are unanimously of opinion that shot-firing was practised in the colliery when the men were at work without sufficient precautions being taken as to their safety and contrary to rules. The jury are also of opinion that the under-manager neglected his duty in not seeing that his subordinates in the night shift performed their duties in accordance with the rules; that the firemen were negligent in not reporting gas when found, and that there is not a proper system of watering in this mine. The jury beg to make the following recommendations: – (1) That shot-firing in timber shall be absolutely

prohibited; (2) that all old workings shall be properly stowed or gobbed; (3) that a record shall be kept of the number of men in the mine at all hours; (4) that thorough inspections shall be more frequently made by her Majesty's inspectors, because we consider the present examinations by the workmen's representatives are worthless.

Though the disagreement about the cause of the disaster, and about the geographical position at which it had started, meant that no blame could be apportioned for the accident itself, the heavy criticisms of the management of the mine meant that the debate remained open.

Reactions

The *Cardiff Times* pointed out in an editorial the implications of the verdict:

Those of the experts and their friends that were interested [i.e. 'had an interest'] in the matter located the explosion at a point where, if it occurred there, no culpability could be attached to the officials in consequence; whereas, those of them who were disinterested located the explosion at a point where, if it took place there, would bring [*sic*] culpable negligence upon the heads of some of those in authority, and the company, in consequence, would be held liable for the disaster.

It went on to point out that if those on the employers' side had been right, the consequences for the coal industry as a whole would be immense, because an accident caused by such an unusual natural event (a vast release of gas caused by a fall) could presumably be repeated elsewhere, and 'the working of collieries will be left surrounded with such terrible probabilities that would be too appalling to contemplate'. If, on the other hand, HM inspectors had been right, then 'the whole disaster was the inevitable result of preventable causes'. The *Cardiff Times* therefore called on the Home Secretary to institute an inquiry.[53]

The Albion Steam Coal Company had meanwhile set up its own investigation into the causes of the disaster. The team that had been chosen, under the mining engineer Herbert Kirkhouse, produced its report on 30 July. Hardly surprisingly, this report exonerated the management, and supported the theory of gas released by a rockfall, specifically contradicting the idea that shot-firing might have been the cause. The six signatories of the report included Alfred Lester Lewis (Cope's agent for the Troedyrhiw Coal Company) and Ithel Treharne Rees (described merely as a former HM Inspector of Mines, though his connection with Albion was close; he had been the main negotiator on the company's side in a dispute with the workforce in September 1888).[54] Of the other four, two were colliery agents, and the other two were simply described as 'mining engineers'. Their rejection of the findings of the inspectors was emphatic:

> We are unanimously of opinion that the disaster was caused by a sudden outburst of fire-damp accompanied by a large fall of rock roof … Such an occurrence was extraordinary, and could not possibly have been anticipated by the management and we, therefore, have *the greatest satisfaction in stating that no blame in the matter can be attributed to any of your officials or employees.* The theory that this explosion originated by shot firing on the Grover side of the shaft is in our judgment inconsistent with the force indications observed by us.[55]

The moment this report was received, David Ellis, secretary of the company, sent it, with a covering letter, to all directors and shareholders.[56] Meanwhile, other friends of the management were riding to the rescue, with further theories as to the cause of the disaster. In the *Western Mail* of 31 July, the views of Mr T. Pascoe Jenkins JP of Tonypandy were reported. He raised the old canard about explosions caused by irresponsible workmen – an argument that had been produced time and again, over the years, in such circumstances:

> Mr Jenkins pointed out that more blame was often attached to the collier for his recklessness than to the manager. 'You know very well', said he, 'how often we are obliged to sentence men to various terms of imprisonment for breaches of the Mines Regulation Acts. In the majority of cases the men are charged for carrying with them to the pits matches, pipes and tobacco; but it is my firm belief that the colliers' clothes and pockets are not properly examined by the

managers, and that a great deal more of this practice is carried on than
is brought to light . . . And the temptation for a collier to indulge in
a smoke underground during what leisure time he has is great, and the
practice is much too often indulged in, at the risk of endangering his
own life and the lives of hundreds of his fellow-workmen.[57]

Though the explanation of irresponsible action by the workmen
had not figured so far on either side, or in either of the reports on
the disaster, it obviously caught the fancy of Matthew Cope,
chairman of the Albion company, so much so that over thirty years
later he was to produce, as indisputable fact, a similar act of
irresponsibility for which no evidence had been adduced at the time:

> It is worth while recalling that this awful disaster, involving the death
> of nearly 300 poor fellows and of 200 horses, was directly caused by
> a dishonest and careless – or too clever – workman. We had missed a
> cartridge, and though we had made every effort to trace it we had
> failed to do so. It might have been mislaid, and we could not accuse
> anybody. We simply could not trace it. But one of the men who
> worked in the pit had got hold of it. He thought he knew better than
> anybody else. He thought he would save himself a bit of trouble. He
> thought he would explode the cartridge and save himself some
> labour with the pick. He did explode it, and with air travelling at the
> rate of 2,000 ft. a minute the inevitable happened. That poor fellow
> paid the penalty for his folly, but the ghastly tragedy of it was that 300
> of his workmates were killed with him. This disaster had nothing to
> do with gases or coal dust. It was caused simply by the concussion
> from the explosion of the cartridge.[58]

Meanwhile, what of the Albion workmen? Early after the disaster,
on 2 July, they had got together with the management to discuss
how the clearing of the mine could best be achieved. It was agreed
that, because of the conditions, shifts would be of only four hours
in length, with no person working more than one shift in any
24-hour period. In places where the air was good this could be
extended to shifts of six hours.[59] On the evening of Sunday 22 July,
however, Philip Jones unilaterally changed this arrangement, putting
up a notice which read: 'The six hours shift will not continue after
to-night. The ordinary ten hours shift will continue on Monday

morning.'[60] Immediately all workmen, after a meeting to discuss the matter, 'unanimously resolved to adhere for the present to the four or six hour shifts', and a deputation called on Jones to communicate this result. On their return, the deputation reported that they had 'failed to come to any arrangement with the manager'. In consequence the men decided to go on strike 'pending a settlement of the dispute'.[61]

The result of the inquest inflamed things still further, and at a meeting held on 31 July at the Cilfynydd Workmen's Institute, under the auspices of Mabon, to attempt to resolve the dispute, a very close vote to go back to work was achieved only on the presumption that 'the Government would grant their request . . . to hold an inquiry to investigate the cause of the disaster.' During the meeting Mabon, while proposing resumption of work, had nevertheless 'declared, amid cheers, that he was dissatisfied with the verdict of the jury, and was of opinion that a Government inquiry should be made into the cause of the explosion'. In the event, the decision to resume work was narrowly passed by 233 votes to 219.[62] On Friday 3 August, work resumed at the mine.

The Albion colliers, in their call for an official inquiry, were merely reflecting the view of the labour movement in south Wales as a whole. The day before their meeting, the monthly meeting of the Rhondda miners at Ton, for example, had unanimously carried a resolution requesting the Home Secretary to 'utilise the power given to him under the 45th clause of the Mines Regulation Act, to institute a special inquiry', and instructing Mabon 'to solicit the aid of his colleagues in Parliament in bringing about this inquiry'.[63]

Roskill's Report

John Roskill produced his report to the Home Secretary on 5 September 1894.[64] In it, his judgments upon the evidence were trenchantly expressed, particularly in relation to the evidence given by the people he held responsible. On the question of blasting while the night shift was down the mine, he bluntly stated, 'I am of opinion that the evidence of the manager, and of those who confirmed him upon this point, cannot be relied on'. Of Anstes's evidence, he said: 'His explanation is very unsatisfactory, and from his demeanour, and the way he gave his evidence, I am not inclined to believe it.'

The facts seemed to him to be clear. On blasting during the night shift, he said: 'The matter was simply overlooked, and there is abundant evidence that blasting on Saturdays took place during the night shift.' On watering he commented: 'The conclusion I have come to . . . is, that although the alleged precautions as to watering may have been taken occasionally, they were not adopted regularly as, in a matter involving such risk, they might and should have been; and further, that there was insufficient control and superintendence over those who had charge of the shot-firing.' Furthermore, 'with regard to the custody and control of the explosives there was great carelessness'. On the question of the storage of explosives below ground, and the ignorance of the manager and agent with regard to it, he commented that these facts 'show, it is submitted, deplorable recklessness on the part of the chargeman, and insufficient control by the management'.

In a lengthy section he outlined the arguments with regard to the causes of the explosion, and stated that he had been led to the firm conclusion that 'the theory of the owners, upon the evidence examined above, cannot be accepted as correct'. He and the inspectors had therefore been surprised by the jury's verdict:

> I am satisfied that all the evidence available or relevant, in connection with questions of *fact*, was tendered and heard at this inquiry, and nevertheless the jury were unable to agree where to place the source of the explosion, the majority, however, it is stated, accepting the views of the inspectors.

The reason for the apparently wayward judgment of a minority of the jury was, he believed, because they were not experts, and were incapable of interpreting what they heard: 'The matter is indeed entirely one of *inference* from the evidence, and is really for experts.' For this reason, and because any acceptance of the company's view as to the cause would necessarily lead to a complete change in safety precautions (on the basis that such an unprecedented cause could recur again elsewhere in the coalfield), he now suggested that 'scientific men familiar with the subject' should be asked to look at the evidence produced at the inquiry, and pronounce upon it.

His aim in this was quite clear. If this group of experts decided, as he expected, that 'the theory of the owners cannot possibly be justified', then he would feel justified in advising that there should be a prosecution for manslaughter. He proceeded, starkly, to list those he considered responsible:

> Those who took part in the blasting during the shift on that afternoon are dead. Those who permitted it, and might and ought to have prevented it, are, in my opinion, the managing director, the agent, and the manager.

As far as Henry Lewis, the managing director, was concerned, there was, however, a problem. The Albion was a limited liability company, and directors who had no personal knowledge of, or participation in, the actual running of the colliery would not be personally liable, civilly or criminally. Roskill therefore recommended that prosecutions should be instituted against the Albion company itself, and individually against Philip Jones the manager, William Lewis the agent, and William Anstes the chargeman.

He accepted, of course, that in the absence of 'an opinion from experts of high authority', the situation remained the same as in the immediate aftermath of the jury's decision; in other words, a case for manslaughter could not be undertaken. And in the event, as he had feared, his advice was not taken. There was no attempt to gain the expert evidence he had asked for, and therefore no possibility of a charge of manslaughter. Nor was there any move made to hold a public enquiry such as Mabon and others had been requesting. A case was brought; but the charges eventually brought against the Company, Philip Jones, William Lewis, William Anstes and William Jones (the under-manager), were merely the criminal charges of disregarding the provisions of the Mines Regulation Act.

The Magistrates' Court [65]

The proceedings started before the Pontypridd magistrates on 17 October 1894. Roskill conducted the prosecution; Abel Thomas

QC MP the defence. The magistrates were J. Ignatius Williams (the stipendiary) and seven others, including T. Pascoe Jenkins JP, whose views on the culpability of the workforce had already been rehearsed in the pages of the *Western Mail*.

Since 1872, it had become unlawful for 'any owner, agent, or manager of a mine (or his father, son or brother) to adjudicate summarily on any offence committed under the mining code'.[66] William Henry Mathias, though a member of the Pontypridd bench, was therefore unable to sit as a magistrate on this case; but he turned up in the courtroom, and certainly made his presence felt.[67]

The Albion Steam Coal Colliery Company, William Lewis, and Philip Jones were charged with 'allowing a shot to be fired in a dry and dusty place, all workers not having been removed'. Philip Jones was further charged with 'storing or permitting to be stored in the mine a quantity of explosive substance'. William Jones, the acting under-manager, was charged with 'failing to see that every officer under you and every other person employed at the colliery understood and fulfilled his duty'. Anstes was charged with storing explosive substances in the mine.

Early in the prosecution case, Roskill homed in on the evidence given at the inquest by Henry Lewis about the change in shifts – 'that he had overlooked the matter of blasting under these circumstances'. This now occasioned the first hiccup for the prosecution. The defence challenged this quotation, suggesting that Lewis had not said it. Lewis then appeared as a witness, but (clearly regretting his lapse at the inquest) said that his counsel had told him not to reply on this question. Roskill then said he would prove from the shorthand notes that Lewis had said what he said, and that he proposed to put the shorthand writer in the box. This was objected to by the defence counsel on the basis that 'this was a limited liability company, and no statement made by one member of a liability company could be evidence against the company itself'. It was also pointed out that the shorthand account might be mistaken. Roskill thereupon applied for a subpoena on Henry Lewis, who 'being a director of the company, made an admission which was clearly evidence against himself', even though the Act precluded proceedings against him, the word 'owner' being a body corporate. The stipendiary 'said by admitting Mr Henry Lewis's evidence they would not only be admitting it against Mr Lewis, but also against the Company. He must decide that it was inadmissible.' Defeated, Roskill asked for his contention to be placed on the record.

When it came to the specific charge against the company of 'allowing a shot to be fired', the magistrates decided (despite the evidence at the inquest of this having happened) that they did not have enough evidence to prove that shot-firing had taken place. The stipendiary said 'there was, no doubt, some suspicion'; but that was not enough. Countering this, Roskill pointed out that not only was there 'grave suspicion that the timbers had been blasted', but that 'there was an admission on the part of Philip Jones that they had been blasted.' He put the shorthand writer in the box, who 'read portions of his notes, showing that Mr Jones admitted at the inquest that shot-firing had taken place on the day of the explosion'.

James Davies, ripper, was now called, and asked to repeat the evidence he had given at the inquest about previous examples of shot-firing in the mine. The stipendiary would not admit this question, saying that 'it would not be fair to prove that blasting had been carried on before just for the sake of bringing an inference that the offence was committed on the day of the explosion.' The resultant exchange between Roskill and the bench is revealing, particularly because of a humorous interjection by Abel Thomas QC, which caused those in court to laugh at Roskill's expense:

> Mr Roskill: Do you rule against me about blasting before the 23rd of June?
> The Stipendiary: Certainly.
> Mr Roskill then asked that the bench would disallow any questions bearing upon that point in cross-examination, but Mr Thomas jocularly objected amid laughter.

This was not the only point in the proceedings when we get the impression that Roskill had been cast adrift amidst a Welsh community that was not only closing ranks, but also sharing a sense of togetherness in which an intruder from London was out of place.

Some of the workmen who now appeared (who, as we have seen, had been fearful of the consequences of speaking up) were asked questions by Abel Thomas which Roskill perceived as being threatening. When Abel Thomas managed to elicit from one of them praise for Philip Jones's carefulness and observance of rules, Roskill objected that the question that had been asked was 'like a threat'. What would happen, he asked, if the witness did not return a complimentary answer? The bench nevertheless allowed the question.

As the first case against Philip Jones ('allowing shot to be fired') came to an end, the stipendiary declared that the bench was of the opinion that 'there was no evidence to convict in this case.' Roskill, conceding defeat, said that in that case he would withdraw the prosecution with regard to the agent.

When, the next morning, the case against William Anstes was heard, all was much simpler. This workman warranted no effort, and finding him guilty would not affect the fate of the company. It was found that he had indeed illegally hoarded explosives and he was fined £2.

Philip Jones was then tried on his second count – that of allowing explosives to be stored. Roskill made the point that, given the large box for explosives used by Anstes, it was incredible that it could have existed without the manager knowing. Jones was *responsible* for *allowing* this. There was no suggestion that he actually *knew* of it; but he *ought to have known*. In other words, his not knowing constituted negligence. Despite this, the magistrates, who could not deny Jones's ultimate responsibility, now found Jones guilty of '*inadvertently* doing less than the law required', and fined him ten pounds.

They were now left with the case of Philip's son, William Jones, the acting under-manager. Roskill made the case against him on the basis of what had been heard at the inquest, that 'he committed the continuing offence of not having been down the mine at certain times', and particularly during the night shift. The stipendiary (by now appearing to take on the role of the defence counsel) countered by making great play with the fact that Jones was the 'acting' under-manager. The dialogue between Roskill and Ignatius Williams is almost unbelievable:

> Mr Roskill said he thought the man's admission that he was acting as under-manager was sufficient. It was for his friend [i.e. Abel Thomas] to prove that he was not under-manager.

The Stipendiary: It is no good going into a charge of neglect of duty if there was no duty imposed on him.

Mr Roskill remarked that all through the evidence Mr William Jones referred to himself as under-manager.

The Stipendiary said that a man might believe he was under-manager, but that did not make him so . . .

Mr Roskill contended that the Act was not intended simply to apply to a person appointed by Act of Parliament. If a man acted as under-manager he was under-manager, although not appointed under the statute.

The Stipendiary was of a different opinion.

By now Roskill was clearly exasperated. He referred to the interests of the Home Office, to whom this was 'a matter of some importance'. This was no doubt an error of judgement on his part. Nothing was more likely to cause a local court to dig its heels in than the invocation of 'Home Office interests'. Roskill asked 'for a case'[68] if the point was decided against him. In other words, he was asking for the matter to be referred to a higher court. Ignatius Williams, with a fine disdain for what the Home Office found important, remarked that 'the point was too trivial to grant a case on.' He added that Roskill 'could get a mandamus[69] if he wished'; he was here, obviously, calling what he believed to be Roskill's bluff about intervention by a higher authority. In Williams's view, 'there was only a scintilla of evidence to prove that William Jones was under-manager, because the shorthand writer fancied he heard him say he was so'.

Doggedly, Roskill now 'respectfully' asked for a case, declaring that it was of great importance to the Home Office. Williams went on as though he had not heard this, bringing in his judgment in the following words: 'If that is all the evidence, we find he was not appointed under-manager, and if the man was not appointed under-manager, he was not responsible.'

Roskill again asked for a case, 'but the learned Stipendiary intimated that, as they had come to a decision on the evidence, they could not grant it'. Thus ended the proceedings.

The proceedings in Pontypridd were the end of the matter. There could be no further trial, unless of course a mandamus were brought into play (which it was not). The company was free to continue to produce evidence from its own 'experts' that 'no blame in the matter can be attributed to any of your officials or employees'; the chairman, Matthew Cope, could even continue to claim that it was all the fault of one of the workmen; the managing director Henry Lewis could within a year represent Cilfynydd (unopposed) on the county council, and within a couple of years become chairman of the Monmouthshire and South Wales Coalowners' Association. All was back in order.

The picture given, during the course of the evidence, about the atmosphere of fear down the mine, shows a great contrast with what we have seen of the management style of Siamps Thomas in his mines. The management, here, appears to have been not only detached from the workforce, but also careless about safety, and positively antagonistic to any criticism by the workforce that might bring its methods into question. The decision to water the mine after an accident, when the only purpose of so doing was to give the impression to the inspectors who would be arriving that this practice was regularly being carried out, shows that the absence of such practices in the normal run of events was a calculating neglect of measures that the management knew to be considered necessary by the experts.

One by-product of the Albion disaster was that two years later, in 1896, a new Mines Regulation Act gave the Secretary of State power to prohibit the use of any explosive in any mine, or class of mines, if it was considered to be dangerous. This did not, however, put an end to the various management practices that caused deaths by explosion. Nineteen years after Albion, in 1913, the greatest disaster in the history of the south Wales coalfield took place at the Universal Colliery, Senghenydd. A vast explosion caused 439 deaths. This had been caused by 'the laxity of the management towards the problem of dust, and its flagrant disregard of certain legal requirements'. Many felt the management to be entirely responsible for the deaths. Nevertheless, the courts dismissed all charges against the colliery owners, and all but a few minor ones against the manager. There was almost universal dismay at this indication, yet again, that 'the law favoured the colliery owners against the miner and the mining communities'.[70] Nothing appeared to have changed.

Two Strikes

11

The 1893 Hauliers' Strike

The early 1890s were a time of considerable unrest in the coalfields. In August 1893, a strike hit south Wales, the like of which had not been seen for almost twenty years. The experiences of the Albion colliery, of W. H. Mathias himself, and of Siamps Thomas's Standard Collieries, are illustrative of the coalfield as a whole in this period.

The strike took place because of the steady decline in miners' wages over the past three years.[1] This was as a direct result of the system known as the 'sliding scale', whereby wages were set according to the average selling price of coal. From high levels of pay in 1890, this system had led to a drop of about thirty per cent in three years.

The workforce, while united in its concern at the level of wages, was divided as to whether the sliding scale should be abandoned or not. The system had been set up in 1875, at a time of disarray among the workers after the collapse of a strike of that year and the resultant dissolution of the Amalgamated Association of Miners. It was run by a joint-committee containing representatives of the coalowners and the workers. The system, which was primarily of benefit to the coalowners, had been sold to the workers as fair, and while prices of coal were going up, it did indeed appear to be of considerable advantage to them. The downside, however, was that the system prevented strikes from occurring every time there was a wage dispute, because the workers were bound by legal agreements freely entered into. 'The coalowners thus largely eliminated strikes and lock-outs, while still leaving themselves free to introduce short-term working as in fact happened in 1879 and 1886.'[2]

Prices could go down as well as up. As William Brace the miners' leader was to point out, the system depended on rising prices, if the workers were not to suffer. 'You will find', he said, 'in the history of labour, that if you have three years of prosperity, you will be sure to have three years of poor trade.'[3] The years 1890–3 were indeed poor ones. By 1893, the situation of many of the workers was desperate. Families were often at the verge of starvation. As Morgan Thomas, the Pentre hauliers' leader, put it, the sliding scale was a 'Starving Scale which draws the South Wales miners down to the verge of pauperism'.[4] In this situation, they and their representatives were clear that something had to be done. The only problem was, that they were divided as to what the course of action should be. Though a conference of the south Wales unions decided, in 1892, that the sliding scale agreement should terminate as from 31 December, some felt that this should be merely in order to negotiate a new agreement, while others were in favour of abolishing the system entirely. The two main miners' leaders were at loggerheads on this.

On the one hand there was William Abraham MP (Mabon) of the Cambrian Miners' Association, who was vice-chairman of the Joint Sliding Scale Committee (Sir William Thomas Lewis being the chairman). Mabon, who had been leader of his association since 1877, and Liberal MP for the Rhondda since 1885, had always taken the line that 'It is better to seek peaceful settlement, to go and meet the owners and endeavour to make the best of a bad situation together, rather than fight separately to the end.'[5] Mabon, and a number of the other older miners' leaders, wanted the sliding scale principle to be maintained.

On the other hand there was William Brace of Risca, a much younger man who was the south Wales district agent of the Miners' Federation of Great Britain, a more militant body. Together with such leaders as Morgan Thomas of Pentre, and Isaac Evans of the Neath, Swansea and Llanelli Miners' Association, he was determined that the sliding scale should be abolished.[6]

The start of the Hauliers' Strike

On 24 July 1893, a meeting in Cardiff of Brace's south Wales branch of the Miners' Federation of Great Britain asked for a 20 per cent increase in wages, which was refused. The immediate cause of the strike that broke out on 1 August, however, was the breakdown in trust that had taken place between workers and owners. By the Sliding Scale Agreement, the Joint Committee was supposed to produce its audit by 29 July. When the audit failed to appear on that date, the hauliers, whose wages were lower than the colliers', and who had been inflamed not only by their situation, but also by their militant leaders such as Morgan Thomas, decided to come out on strike. On 1 August the hauliers at the Wyndham pit, Ogmore Vale, stopped work. By the next day the strike had reached the Rhondda, with the hauliers at Parc and Dare collieries. On 4 August a mass meeting of hauliers was held on Morgan Thomas's territory at Pentre, at which it was decided to extend the strike.[7]

Though many of the colliers wanted to remain at work, many others were in sympathy with the hauliers, and wished to support the strike. Whichever view was held in any particular colliery, however, the hauliers were able to force closures, unless – as in some cases – colliers were prepared to take over the hauliers' work. In some places, there was open hostility between the two types of worker, which enabled the employers (and the government)[8] to depict the conflict as being not between employers and workmen, but between two factions among the workmen. On the other hand, despite Mabon's claim that the strike had merely been caused by 'a handful of reckless hauliers', there was a lot of support for the strike among the colliers, particularly in the Rhondda.[9]

Soon most of the collieries in the Rhondda valleys were standing idle. 'Marching gangs' spread the strike into other areas, including the valleys of west Monmouthshire. By 7 August, 40,000 were out of work owing to the strike. Meantime, mining officials had been pressing the owners' association to take out summonses against the strikers for their 'illegal' stoppage – illegal, because under the terms of the Sliding Scale Agreement they had to give notice of their intention to stop work. While this was a common tactic by employers' associations throughout the United Kingdom,[10] it was, as the Keens have pointed out, hardly a conciliatory move.[11] However, by 8 August, at a meeting of the Monmouthshire and South Wales Coalowners' Association at the Angel Hotel, Cardiff, it was decided to 'pursue the campaign of prosecuting the strikers'.[12]

It is important to realise that not all south Wales coalowners belonged to this association. Among prominent coalowners who did not, were Siamps Thomas of the Standard Collieries Ynyshir and the Troedyrhiw Company, and Insoles (and their manager Thomas Griffiths) of the Cymmer Collieries, Porth.[13] We shall see that Siamps Thomas's tactics differed markedly from the association's during this strike, but that the Albion Steam Coal Company (whose managing director, Henry Lewis, was a keen member of the association, and was to be its chairman during the later strike of 1898) carried out the association's policies with the utmost vigour.

The workers at Albion colliery are a very good example of the mixed feelings among the workers at this stage. In a ballot just before the start of the strike, they had voted by a majority of 474 to join the Federation of Great Britain and leave the Cambrian Association.[14] Yet most of the colliers seem to have wanted to continue work, and to persuade the hauliers not to prevent them from doing so. At a mass meeting at the colliery on 7 August, they were addressed by a Mr D. Jones, who, speaking 'in his native tongue',[15] received an enthusiastic reception. He urged them 'to have nothing to do with the Federation but stand to the Sliding Scale'.[16] The Albion hauliers had declared their intention to join the hauliers of the Rhondda valley in their strike. All the colliers and hauliers were present at this meeting, and 'the former impressed upon the latter the folly of dislocating trade at the present moment.' Nevertheless, the hauliers met again on the afternoon of the 7th, and resolved not to return to work on the following day.[17] By the evening of the 8th, the Albion colliery was at a standstill. The Albion management immediately decided to implement the association's policy of prosecuting the hauliers, and on the 9th it applied to the Pontypridd police court for 'the issue of about 170 summonses against two sets of hauliers who had absented themselves from work'. One of the three magistrates who heard this case was Alderman W. H. Mathias – a director of Albion!

The others were the stipendiary (J. Ignatius Williams) and Mr D. Llewellyn. Needless to say, the summonses were issued.[18]

Many of the colliery proprietors were also magistrates, and the blurring of the two functions was at times to be important in this strike, as it was elsewhere in the United Kingdom.[19] But there can not have been many cases of someone hearing a specific application from a company of which he was a director and held a significant number of shares, without leaving the bench or at least declaring an interest. On the other hand, it is clear from the newspaper report of the magistrates' meeting that the 'running' was made almost entirely by J. Ignatius Williams, the stipendiary magistrate, and that the other two magistrates present do not appear to have played a major part in the proceedings.[20]

The Albion cases were heard on the 16th at Pontypridd, with Ignatius Williams again presiding (Mathias was not, on this occasion, one of the magistrates concerned). A total of 130 men were fined one pound each with costs.[21] This, despite the fact that at Ystrad Court on Tuesday, the 15th, Judge Gwilym Williams (who had a record of moderation in such matters) had announced that because of the strike he would adjourn all cases against colliery workmen until 10 October.[22]

Mabon had meanwhile been travelling around the collieries, exhorting the miners to resist the strike, and warning them of their liability for prosecution for breach of contract. At Pentre, one of the centres of disaffection, on 11 August, he told the men they were in the wrong, and should 'return to work and settle their grievances in the proper way between coalowners and miners' representatives'; he was mobbed and prevented from speaking further.[23] On the same day, however, he visited the Albion colliery, where he was 'enthusiastically received'.[24] The Albion miners were either fickle, however, or else different workers attended different meetings. The day after Mabon's visit, Brace followed him to Cifynydd. He advocated that the sliding scale should be abolished, and that the owners should be made to give the men a rise of forty per cent. 'He pointed out that he did not think it right that some people should make fortunes while others were buried in a pauper's grave.' The employers and the workmen could never be on friendly terms, because the employers were organised 'so as to get as much work as possible for the least possible money'. This speech received a 'most cordial' reception from the workers present.[25]

Meanwhile, the situation continued to deteriorate. The owners were beginning to be concerned at the effect of the strike upon their trade, and the advantages that their competitors could take. The south Wales press, from the *Western Mail* to the local papers, began to take the owners' side, as was predictable. A leader in the *Pontypridd District Herald* of 12 August is a typical example. While making a show of concern for the miners, conceding that 'the wages of some of the colliers in the Rhondda are almost starvation wages', the leader-writer nevertheless pointed to market forces, and qualified the aims of the 'Federalists' as absurd, and the hauliers as having an 'insane determination' which was not justified. He predicted an industrial catastrophe, with ships driven from south Wales ports, and the orders going elsewhere. It was all a question of supply and demand:

> One cannot help sympathizing to a certain extent with the Federation body which aims at maintaining a rate of wages which enables life to be endurable. But can this be done? At this point we come into conflict with the immutable laws of supply and demand. These laws are sterner than those of the Medes and the Persians, for the latter could be evaded while the former cannot be thrown aside. The difficulty in south Wales seems to be that in the coal market the masters have to meet with unrelenting competition, with continental coal proprietors who pay much less wages for which they receive longer hours of labour. In this case the Welsh master is compelled to adjust his price to compete with his continental rivals or be beaten out of the market, with the result that he would have to close his pits and the workmen would have no employment. The contention of the Federalists is therefore absurd when they insist upon the wage rate being maintained no matter what the state of the market may be. In the Midlands the strike now in operation at the instigation of the Federation leaders must inevitably be an obstinate one, and also a disastrous one, and hundreds of thousands of families will feel its dire effects, as a brutal weapon to reconcile conflicting economical [*sic*] interests. The hauliers in the Rhondda have at, it is said, a similar instigation refused to go down the pits. What the object of this insane determination may be, few seem to have an intelligent knowledge.[26]

Calling in the military

The employers were by now beginning to feel that stronger measures were needed to bring the strike to an end; and some of the activities of the strikers appeared to be playing into their hands. 'As the strike continued so the attitudes polarized and strikers were forced to resort to intimidation to get the non-strikers to join them'.[27] This made it easier for the owners to 'have troops and extra police drafted into the district, for they could, with some justification, claim that they had loyal workers who needed protection.'[28] The way in which such army protection was eventually brought in, however, raises questions as to fairness and legality.

On 18 August, the Monmouthshire and South Wales Coalowners' Association held a meeting at the Angel Hotel, Cardiff. A meeting of the Sliding Scale Committee had been scheduled for 10 a.m., but as some of the workers' representatives were unable to attend at that hour, the association held a meeting of its own instead. This impromptu meeting speedily built up a head of steam. As a *Times* reporter said, there was 'clear evidence that the employers were preparing for a stubborn defence of the position they have taken up'. First, they decided that today, pay-day, the hauliers' wages should be withheld. Then they resolved that a deduction should be made from the colliers' wages equal to the value of the tools they had in their possession. These measures were to be taken despite the certainty that they would lead to 'serious complications' in the colliery districts. Having so acted as to produce these 'serious complications', the coalowners next decided how they would deal with them. They drafted a communication to the Home Office asking for increased police supervision and the assistance of the military; they also invited the chief constable of Glamorganshire, Captain Lindsay, to attend their meeting; and they held consultations with the chief constable of Monmouthshire, and with Colonel Maclean, the officer in command of the 41st Regimental Depot in Cardiff.[29]

Of course, such a request could not, strictly speaking, be made by interested parties. Properly, it had to be made by the magistracy. As we have already seen, however, a large number of magistrates in south Wales were in fact coalowners, so the meeting entered into communication with 'the presiding magistrates of the districts affected'.[30] As the matter was so urgent, however, the chairman of the association, Sir William Thomas Lewis, 'in his capacity as a magistrate, himself signed the requisition for troops', which stated that 'bands of men in thousands are traversing the districts and are indulging in riotous conduct and unless there be instant action by an adequate force being supplied tonight, the consequences will be calamitous'.[31] Next, the committee contacted the rail authorities, and shortly thereafter the district superintendents of the Great Western Railway and the Taff Vale Railway joined the meeting, to make the necessary travel arrangements for the military reinforcements.

All this took from 10 a.m. to 2 p.m. Only then were the waiting workers' representatives called in for the meeting of the Joint Sliding Scale Committee. At that meeting the chairman, Sir William Thomas Lewis (emboldened no doubt by the decisions that had been taken) told the workers' representatives that 'all the employers in the South Wales Coalowners' Association were determined to require the workmen, as long as they are in their employ, to fulfil the portion of the contract entered into after much deliberation for the continuance of the Sliding Scale in February last'. The workers' representatives meekly produced a manifesto to the workers, asking them to abide by the agreement.[32]

The arrangements in relation to the troops were put into effect very quickly. *The Western Mail* reported that 'a strong military force' was ordered to Cardiff on the evening of 18 August, within hours of the coalowners' meeting, and that within twenty-four hours a squadron of cavalry and two battalions of infantry would be in the neighbourhood.[33] By the evening of Sunday 20th the soldiers were in Pontypridd,[34] and in the words of *The Times* 'South Wales may almost be considered under martial law'.[35]

The newspapers seem to have had a variety of views about who had deployed the troops. While some referred to the fact that it was 'the *magistracy* in the part of the county most affected' who had 'deemed it desirable in the interests of peace' to send for the troops, others merely referred in general terms to 'the promptitude displayed by *the authorities*'.[36] Others guilelessly congratulated the coalowners for bringing the troops in, with such phrases as 'At the request of the South Wales *coalowners*, 1,100 troops and a large number of police have been distributed over the coalfield of the district',[37] or (in *The Times* itself), 'The prompt measures taken by the *Emergency Committee of the South Wales coalowners* to protect the men willing to work.'[38]

Neither the coalowners nor the military appear to have been at all concerned about appearances of being in collusion. At a meeting at the Angel Hotel on Monday 21 August, for example, which was attended by General Sir Richard Harrison, the coalowners congratulated him publicly on his prompt action,[39] and in return General Harrison promised to provide additional troops for them. Furthermore, when the general was making a round of inspection of troops, he was accompanied by Mr James Williams, a representative of the Coalowners' Association.[40]

These facts gave rise to questions in the House of Commons, raised by Keir Hardie, Independent Labour MP for West Ham South. He particularly questioned the coalowners' involvement, and the role of the magistrates. The Home Office replies stressed that this was not a Home Office matter, as the procedure was for magistrates' requests to be made direct to the military.[41]

Meanwhile, in the areas where the military had arrived, meetings of local people were held which condemned those who had sent for them,[42] claiming that this had been unnecessary, given the isolated nature of any examples of violence; indeed, it was claimed that the presence of the military was likely to 'irritate rather than soothe' the people among whom they had been sent.[43] The military had, of course, been sent for mainly in order to break the strike, and that endeavour was quickly successful. By the end of the month the strike was over (the miners' fate having been sealed not only by the presence of the soldiers, but also by the lack of a 'fighting fund', and the absence of any financial help from the Miners' Federation of Great Britain).[44]

The Albion colliery, and W. H. Mathias and some of his friends, were intimately involved in various aspects of this situation. It appears that Mathias, as a magistrate, had been singled out by the local population in Porth for blame for the bringing in of the troops. On 21 August a protest meeting was held in Porth, which appointed a delegation to call on him to 'ascertain for what purpose the military were brought to the district'.[45]

219

When the military had arrived in Pontypridd, most of the men were quartered in the town hall,[46] but the officers, under Colonel Kinder, were quartered in Mrs Miles's New Inn. 'Their bright uniforms, seen through the front windows on the first floor, commanded a great deal of scrutiny from without.' A detachment had been sent to Porth, and it was felt that others should go to Cilfynydd 'in case of emergency'. In fact, a troop of the 14th Hussars were sent to Cilfynydd, where Mathias on behalf of the other directors of the Albion Colliery Company had arranged for their horses to be stalled in the colliery's stables.[47]

The lack of sympathy for the strikers in the south Wales press is vividly shown by a number of stories carried at this time. One, specifically, referred to the cavalry and to Albion colliery, which was still at a standstill. Both the *Western Mail* and the *Glamorgan Free Press* recounted it in detail, the Western Mail's article bearing the title: 'A Hasty Retreat at Cilfynydd'. Apparently, on the morning of 19 August, a large group of strikers collected together in the pit yard, 'with the intention of preventing the firemen and officials from carrying on the pumping operations' that were essential for the maintenance of the mine. Philip Jones, the Albion's manager, tried to address the crowd. 'My dear fellows, it would be much better . . .', he started, but was interrupted by a collier who had been acting as look-out, who shouted: 'Sawgwrn myn jawl'. Immediately they all looked towards Pontypridd, where they saw a cloud of dust which turned out to be the 'sawgwrs' galloping towards them 'in all their pomp and splendour'. 'Duw dad, mae ar ben 'nawr, boys', shouted another striker, and 'in less than 10 seconds, the 2,000 men who surrounded the colliery manager had scampered as fast as their legs could carry them up the mountainside'.[48]

The end of the strike

As the strike began to fail, the press in its relief became more and more triumphant, and used any tactics to scorn the miners' efforts. Thus, the description of a march that had been planned was headed, in the *Pontypridd Chronicle*, 'Amusing Incidents'. The journalist reported that it had been planned that a force of 100,000 strong should march on Ebbw Vale. Though a very large crowd had seen the march off at Cymmer bridge, Porth, by the time it reached Pontypridd Post Office it consisted of only 201 men:

> Thousands had been expected to join at the Pontypridd old bridge, but some rain fell at the time and the reinforcements said they preferred going home to bed. The lads, however, continued their way up to Cilfynydd . . . So ridiculous indeed was the whole affair that the military officers who were at the New Inn front window had a hearty laugh at the whole affair.[49]

And so the strike petered out, foiled by lack of money and by military intervention. As Lord Swansea wrote to Asquith, sending a list of the mines that had returned to work, 'It is very satisfactory'.[50] It had been rumoured that some mines would have had to close because of the strike; but it had in fact hardly affected them. As a statement by Siamps Thomas about his Standard collieries at Ynyshir said on 22 August, a report had gained currency that the pit was to be closed for two years, but nothing of the sort was in fact contemplated, and the pit had 'only been stopped until the present crisis is ended'.[51]

It is interesting to note that, while the Albion Colliery Company's directors, like the majority of the coalowners, had clearly followed the Coalowners' Association's line on refusing to pay the hauliers their wages, and on taking out summonses against those who had ceased work, Siamps Thomas, at Standard collieries, had taken a far more emollient line: 'The hauliers at this colliery were paid all the wages coming to them in due course at the commencement of the strike, and none of them were summoned for breach of contract.'[52]

The workers of the Albion colliery, Cilfynydd, and the Standard collieries Ynyshir, both decided, on 1 and 2 September respectively, to go back to work on the 5th. The only difference was that the Standard colliery workmen, as an act of goodwill, went in on the 4th to light up the boilers, and the night shift went in that evening.[53]

During the Welsh strike, there had also been a major lock-out in the English mining industry. Here, too, the local magistrates had been eager to bring in the military.[54] A major incident at Featherstone in Yorkshire, when two men were shot dead and another eleven to fourteen hit by bullets and injured, 'brought home forcibly to the government the danger of using troops in this kind of situation',[55] and made them realise that the procedures for bringing in the military in such circumstances needed to be examined. The Home Secretary set up an Interdepartmental Committee on Riots to look into the question. When it reported in May 1894, the committee, while stressing that troops should only be used as the last resort, nevertheless appears to have done little to change the status quo with regard to how they should be called out, except to strengthen in some respects the position of the chief constable.[56] Indeed, it made more explicit the absence of responsibility of the Home Office. The results of this were to be felt in the next major strike in south Wales, in 1898.

12

The 1898 Strike

The miners' strike of 1898[1] marked, in the words of John Williams, 'a watershed in the development of industrial relations in south Wales'.[2] The intransigence of the employers, leading to the almost total capitulation of the strikers within six months, made of it the most bitter dispute in the south Wales coalfield in the whole of the nineteenth century. After it, even the moderates who had believed in co-operation rather than confrontation (including Mabon himself) were forced to realise that the old ways no longer worked. The formation of the South Wales Miners' Federation ('The Fed'), affiliated to the Miners' Federation of Great Britain, in October 1898, was a direct result of the strike.[3]

As with the 1893 strike, the experience of the Albion colliery and its directors, and of the Standard collieries, gives some further insights into the issues and activities involved. William Henry Mathias, in particular (a director both of the Albion colliery and of the Aber Rhondda colliery) appears at one stage to have had a role as go-between between the workers under Mabon and the employers. And a number of figures we have seen already, in the 1893 strike and in the controversy surrounding the 1894 Albion disaster (for example, J. Ignatius Williams, T. Pascoe Jenkins, Judge Gwilym Williams, Henry Lewis Tŷ Nant, Sir William Thomas Lewis, Captain Lindsay, etc.) take their place once more upon the stage, in most cases fulfilling what we had already grown to expect of them.

The role of the magistrates in the introduction of the military was to prove an even more contentious issue than in 1893, despite the government inquiry that had intervened. In Pontypridd, where W. H. Mathias was on the bench of magistrates, this role was to be particularly marked.

The start of the strike

The main cause of the strike was twofold: a further decline in wages (even in relation to the low reached in 1893), which led the workers to seek a revision of the sliding scale; and, on the other hand, a substantial rise in costs, which meant, as far as the owners were concerned, that a number of companies were reporting much reduced profits or even losses. Wages formed a major proportion of total costs. This meant that, while the workers were pressing for a change in the sliding scale in their favour, the employers were convinced, either that the terms should remain the same, or that they should be revised in the employers' favour.

The immediate trigger for the strike was the decision by the workforce to give, on 30 September 1897, the statutory six months' notice to end the current sliding scale agreement. Their aim at this stage was, not to do away with the sliding scale, but to improve its provisions. The employers appear to have done little to resolve the issue during the available six months; the first meeting to discuss the matter took place on 12 February 1898, and nothing was decided at it. It was as though the employers were spoiling for a fight; and, indeed, there were other issues, including the reintroduction of 'discharge notes' (certificates that employees had to have from their last colliery in order to be employed at another colliery – a sure deterrent for strikers), that the employers wished to resolve, and for which an unsuccessful strike might give them the opportunity. The employers caused problems for the workers' delegates, too, by insisting that the delegates should have 'plenary powers' to negotiate; this caused suspicion among the miners, that their delegates might be under the sway of the employers. The arguments over this took up much of the time of the people involved, and were a block to constructive discussion. And, to crown it all, at the beginning of March the employers announced that the normal audit of selling prices (to fix the level of wages) would not take place (as prices were marginally rising, such an audit would probably have benefited the workers); and at the same time they gave a month's notice to end the individual workmen's contracts. This notice expired on 31 March; the owners then postponed the notices for nine days, ending on 9 April. It is significant that they made no move to hold negotiations during this period.[4]

Many workmen decided to stop work at the beginning of April, even before the nine days' extension had run out. Mabon remonstrated with them, describing their policy as suicidal.[5] By 2 April, however, sixty thousand men were idle, including the workers of the Albion colliery and of the Standard collieries,[6] both of which had confidently been expected to work.[7] By the 4th it was estimated that about a hundred thousand men were idle.

The chairman of the M&SWCA was now the hardline Henry Lewis Tŷ Nant of Albion colliery. On Tuesday 12 April, under his chairmanship, 'one of the largest meetings of the Monmouthshire and South Wales Coalowners' Association held for some years took place at Cardiff, practically the whole of the colliery companies in the association being represented by their principals'.[8] Sir William Thomas Lewis, chairman of the employers' Emergency Committee, was to be the employers' main negotiator. One of their most immediate concerns was to make sure that the chinks in their armour, which had existed during the 1893 strike, should as far as possible be closed. A major chink had been those mining companies, such as Siamps Thomas's Standard collieries Ynyshir, Thomas's and Cope's Troedyrhiw company, and Insole's Cymmer collieries, which had not belonged to the association, and which had therefore been able to take a different and more accommodating line. As early as 16 April it was reported in the *Merthyr Express* that 'communications are now in progress between the Coalowners' Association and several large outside owners, which, it is hoped, will result in the outside owners joining the association, or, in the alternative, co-operating with them in the adoption of a line of general policy'.[9] Another meeting of the association was held on 16 April, at which it was reported that the following companies had, as a result of these negotiations, 'indicated their intention of entirely supporting the policy of the association' and been admitted as members: Insoles Ltd (Cymmer collieries): the Ynyshir Standard Colliery Company; and the Universal Colliery Company. It was also reported that the Troedyrhiw Coal Company had 'declared their adhesion to the policy laid down by the associated owners'.[10] It is worth noting, however, that D. A. Thomas's Cambrian collieries still remained outside the association, as did a number of smaller collieries, including W. H. Mathias's Aber Rhondda colliery (though in the case of Mathias, as we shall see, non-association did not necessarily denote a softer line in negotiations).

Siamps Thomas's departure from the Rhondda to run his farm in Llanedarne seems to have meant that, though he remained owner of Standard and part-owner of the Troedyrhiw company, the policy decisions made by those actually running the companies could now be radically different from what they had been in his time. In 1893, his attitude had been significantly more moderate than that of the coalowners' association. Now his companies were signing up to a line that was far more bellicose than anything had been in 1893. Some of the language used at the meeting of the coalowners' association on 16 April gives the flavour: members asked for 'the fullest resistance to the workers' demands', which were described as 'extortionate'.[11]

It is significant that the two sides held no joint meetings between then and the end of May. The positions had been taken up; it seemed that both sides had decided that there were no grounds for compromise. Indeed, within a week the workmen's Provisional Committee had decided to move from Cardiff (where they would have been in proximity to the M&SWCA and its Emergency Committee) to Pontypridd.[12]

Within weeks the strike was causing hardship. As early as 23 April, the Merthyr Board of Guardians was noting the 'enormous increase in the number of applications for outdoor relief by reason of the strike in the coal trade', and was considering the opening of labour yards to provide the employment (stone-breaking for road surfaces) which was a necessary concomitant of the provision of relief for able-bodied men. By the 26th, it had been resolved to provide such labour yards 'throughout the Union'.[13]

Lindsay, the magistrates, and the recourse to the military

Captain Lionel Lindsay, who was chief constable of Glamorgan from 1891 to 1936, was a militaristic and autocratic figure. He was highly connected, being a nephew of Lord Tredegar and a descendant of Scottish and Irish nobility (the Earls of Crawford, the Earls of Balcarres, and the Earls of Arran).[14] His father, Henry Gore Lindsay of Glasnevin House, County Dublin (who had married the second Lord Tredegar's sister), had been his predecessor as chief constable of Glamorgan, after service in the Kaffir war, the Crimean campaign and the Indian Mutiny. Lindsay himself had served in the Egyptian gendarmerie before following his father in the Glamorgan post. His appointment is a typical example of the trend whereby county magnates appointed as chief constable 'county men, usually with military backgrounds, men who had a social outlook similar to their own'.[15] Jane Morgan, in a fine article on Lindsay, describes him as taking 'a severe view of the population of the mining valleys whom he compared with the population of his native Ireland'. He intensified, in her view, 'the atmosphere of confrontation between labour and the authorities'[16] during his period of office. R. Page Arnot ascribes his attitudes not just to his Irish background, but to his training in Egypt:

> Captain Lindsay began his career as part of the British Army of Occupation in Egypt . . . His training had been in the Egyptian gendarmerie, a force raised to deal with any disturbance amongst the townspeople or amongst the toiling fellaheen of the Nile Valley . . . and it may be that he never quite disabused himself of the notion that he was part of a Coalmasters' Army of Occupation in south Wales.[17]

Though Morgan's article concentrates mainly on the period from 1910 (Tonypandy) to 1936, her comments on Lindsay's methods could just as easily have referred to the 1890s. She assesses his main impact on policing policy as having been in 'the frequent and almost casual recourse to troops', and 'a much more aggressive response in dealing with picketing and disorder associated with strikes'.[18]

In the 1893 strike, Lindsay had acted promptly when the coalowners, using their position as magistrates, had decided to send for the military. In this 1898 strike, he was himself active in persuading the magistracy of the need for military intervention. This more proactive role on his part was partly a result of the Report of the Interdepartmental Committee on Riots, which had reported in November 1894. While it had stressed that 'the calling out of the military to aid in the suppression of rioting should never be resorted to except as a last expedient', it did little to change the situation whereby the local magistrates and chief constable were responsible for calling out the military, without needing any recourse to the Home Office. Indeed, it strengthened and formalised the role of the chief constable. If the chief constable considered it 'likely that military assistance will be required', he should 'acquaint the chairman of the Petty Sessional Division concerned'. When a county magistrate had come to the conclusion, from information provided by the police or another reliable source, that a military force should be sent for, 'he should cause a requisition to be made to the officer commanding the district through the Chief Constable.' The chief constable should then 'forward the requisition to the proper military authorities, stating the number and composition of the troops which are required'.[19]

Lindsay appears to have had no hesitation in using these powers, while ignoring the important 'last resort' proviso of the report. As Jane Morgan has noted, the report had produced little change in the behaviour either of magistrates or of chief constables:

> Magistrates, many of whom were owners of mines, factories, or other industrial concerns, still had power under the common law to requisition troops, who in turn were bound to obey. Chief constables themselves often preferred to use troops rather than police. The former were felt to be better adapted to riot control.[20]

For about the first month of the strike all was quiet. Captain Lindsay reported to the Joint Standing Committee of the GCC on 10 June that though on 5 May eight men had been convicted and heavily fined for assaulting a workman in the vicinity of the Abercanaid pit, just south of Merthyr; he was forced to admit that despite his apprehension of further disturbances in that area, nothing further had occurred until the 26th.[21]

It is fair to say that the disturbances which then occurred on the 26th were of a very localised kind, and only tenuously connected with the strike. A mass meeting at the Plymouth collieries on that day had taken place without incident, and it was only in the evening that things had begun to go sour in central Merthyr and Dowlais. The main cause of disruption appears to have been resentment at the activities of Jewish landlords and rent collectors in Merthyr and Dowlais, with the reasons for which the *Merthyr Express*, while deploring the violence, nevertheless sympathised, talking of 'unscrupulous advantage being taken of unfortunate workmen', who had been suffering 'unmitigated extortion'. Recent advantage being taken of the striking workmen had, the paper continued, merely been the final straw: 'A single act of oppression would never have produced such an outbreak; it was the letting loose of the smouldering resentment of years.'[22] Over two or three days, the only actual violence, which mainly took place in the late evening, was reserved for the property of (mainly Jewish) landlords and rent collectors.[23]

Despite the fact that the causes for riot appeared so localised, and that the police had so quickly got it under control, Captain Lindsay clearly thought it important to obtain reinforcements in the form of troops; and on Whit Sunday, 29 May, he came from Cardiff to Merthyr to have a special meeting with the Merthyr magistrates, who decided to send for the military.[24] The next day, a detachment of South Wales Borderers (4 officers, 115 NCOs and men) arrived. The officer commanding, Major Morgan, in a report to the Home Office, made it clear that he did not think their services had actually been required, as yet:

Merthyr Tydfil, 30 May 1898 – As far as I can ascertain, the recent disturbances have been caused by a section of people and have been directed against certain owners of small properties who have distrained on their tenants. These owners' shops have been wrecked between the hours of dusk and midnight . . . Troops will be kept out of sight until their aid is actually required.[25]

A Home Office note on this file stated: 'It was apprehended that disturbance might arise on Tuesday night and the soldiers were in readiness but it does not appear that they have been needed.'

A week or so later, there were several days of considerable unrest in the Merthyr Vale and Treharris area (which Lindsay, however, described himself as having 'dispersed without force', and in which the *Merthyr Express* described the crowd as having been 'very respectful to the police and other officers of the law').[26] Nevertheless, on 9 June Lindsay met the Merthyr magistrates at Merthyr station, and persuaded them to ask for 100 further soldiers for Merthyr Vale and 100 for Treharris.

It was now that Pontypridd began to take centre stage. On 10 June, Lindsay put pressure on the Pontypridd magistrates (whose area had so far had no problems) to follow the example of their Merthyr colleagues. After calling on Judge Gwilym Williams in the morning, he later telephoned the magistrates at their meeting to advise that 100 cavalry should be stationed at Pontypridd.[27] The magistrates took his advice, after some discussion (with a minority disagreement). Major Morgan, reporting that it was expected that the magistrates would apply for troops, gave the real reason why cavalry would be useful at Pontypridd: 'Pontypridd would be a good centre for cavalry as three valleys converge there.'[28] Lindsay himself was convinced of the superiority of cavalry in such situations: 'The appearance of [cavalry] in a disturbed district . . . has never failed to have a most beneficial effect. Their mobility enables them to cover such a large area of ground, while the fact of their being mounted enables them to take most effective action.'[29]

The decision of the Pontypridd magistrates on the 10th, under Lindsay's influence, was therefore contrary to the spirit of the 1894 Report. The military were being sent for, not because there was such a situation in Pontypridd that the police could not cope, but because Pontypridd was a useful place to have military if they were to be needed elsewhere. This decision was to cause considerable controversy. Among the Pontypridd magistrates were Lewis Gordon Lenox, of the famous chainmaking company Brown Lenox (in the Chair), William Jenkins Ystradfechan, William Henry Mathias, Thomas Pascoe Jenkins, Thomas Jones Ynyshir, David Llewellyn, William Morgan and Theophilus Hamlen-Williams. Not all the magistrates were in agreement with the decision taken. Some felt that the services of the military were unnecessary, as the district had been so tranquil, and that 'their presence will have a tendency to attract a large number of persons from the outlying districts into the town'. Others, clearly under the influence of Lindsay, believed that 'prevention is better than cure'.[30] Sadly, we do not know which magistrates took which view. After their discussion, the clerk to the magistrates, Henry Porcher, went to Cardiff to see Stipendiary J. Ignatius Williams, and as a result the following (misleading) telegram was sent by the latter: 'Riot expected. Send soldiers; cavalry preferred.'[31]

On the following day, 11 June, 109 officers and men of the dragoon guards (the carabineers) arrived in Pontypridd from Aldershot. Some of the men were billeted in the town (the officers staying, as in 1893, at the New Inn Hotel). It had been decided that a number of the dragoons, at the directors' invitation, should be billeted at the Albion colliery, as the hussars had been in 1893.[32] Considerable objections were, this time, raised to this. The enginemen and stokers of the colliery (on whom its maintenance depended), convinced that the dragoons were there to 'protect the supposed blackleg labour', held a meeting on Monday 13th, at which they resolved that they would not work that night unless the cavalry were immediately sent away from the colliery. We are told that this 'caused some surprise to the authorities'; nevertheless, in order to avoid disturbances, and damage to the colliery, the cavalry left Cilfynydd that afternoon, to go to Pontypridd. The authorities later let it be known that they had done this not because of the action of the workmen, but because the accommodation was unsuitable.[33] That afternoon Captain Lindsay urgently came to Pontypridd by train, in order to discuss, with Stipendiary J. Ignatius Williams and with Richard Packer, arrangements to accommodate 50 cavalrymen in the Pontypridd area.[34]

Objections to the presence of the military were not confined to the miners. At a meeting of Pontypridd District Council on Tuesday 14th, strong protests were made, and a resolution passed which was forwarded to the Home Office and to the local MPs. It read:

> That the Council enter an emphatic protest against the action of the Magistracy in calling for the importation of the Soldiery to the town, believing that their presence is altogether unnecessary and unjustifiable, and calculated to irritate the feelings of the inhabitants generally, and further express their satisfaction that the District has during the present strike enjoyed an immunity from disturbances of any kind, and that the Council seeing no reason for apprehending any change in the prevailing peaceful conditions respectfully ask the Home Secretary to immediately order the removal of the Soldiery.[35]

The proposer of the resolution said that he 'was afraid that the magistrates' decision 'would make it seem to the outside world that the district was in an uproar', whereas 'the district was free from any kind of disturbance, and no industrial war of recent years had been so free of disturbance as this one'. The seconder spoke more forcibly. He felt that the magistrates 'had been misled', and he called for the stipendiary to be asked to convene a special meeting of the magistrates to order the withdrawal of the troops (this to loud cries of 'Hear, hear'). It was resolved that the stipendiary should be asked to do so.[36]

From what we have seen of Stipendiary J. Ignatius Williams (both at the Albion disaster hearing in 1894, and when considering summonses against the hauliers in 1893) it seems hardly likely that he, or the majority of his magistrates, would have acceded to such a request. Indeed, the very next day, Wednesday 15th, something occurred that made the role of the military, and the magistracy, even more threatening. We are told that J. Ignatius Williams received a letter from 'the authorities', commanding him 'to instruct the military if necessary to charge the crowd and use the bayonets, and also to fire with ball cartridges.' He informed a reporter, however, that 'he earnestly hoped he would have no occasion to do so'.[37]   Who were 'the authorities'? As the Home Office took no part in such matters, it must have been either the magistrates or the chief constable.

Meanwhile, in Parliament, questions were being asked. Samuel Evans MP gave notice of a question asking not only at whose request the military had been sent, but also (referring to the points made in the first paragraph of the 1894 report) 'whether there has been any difficulty in the maintenance of peace and order by the police'. He asked what the facts were that had induced the Home Secretary to send the troops in. The Home Office civil servants noted on the file the fact that this had been none of the Home Office's business: 'The Secretary of State's sanction is not required. The procedure as adopted on the recommendation of the 1894 Committee is for the local authorities to apply to the *military* authorities and for the military authorities to make the necessary arrangements.' They had no knowledge of who had requested the military. Reports made to the War Office, they said, had made it clear that no difficulties had been encountered by the police of a kind that would have justified such intervention. In other words, the Home Office washed its hands of the whole matter.[38]

A request by Alfred Thomas MP, for the Home Secretary to consider the desirability of withdrawing the troops from the districts in which no disturbance had occurred, was met with the same response, in a note on the file: 'This presumably should go to the War Office to answer. The Home Office has nothing to do with it – beyond forwarding applications for military aid from the responsible local authorities to the War Office, and pointing out to local authorities the procedure they should pursue.'[39]

The Home Office at this point asked Lindsay for a report of what had been going on, with an explanation of why the military had been brought in. In a report dated 18 June, Lindsay stressed that 'the introduction of the military has been entirely the action of the Justices, and . . . the Coal Owners have had no part in it'. This was surely disingenuous, given the number of coalowners on the various benches of magistrates. It also makes no mention of his own role in spurring the magistrates into action. Lindsay stressed that, though he had at his disposal almost five hundred foot and twelve mounted constables, it had 'been found that the presence of a military force gives a greater feeling of security to the law abiding part of the population and impresses the would-be lawbreakers with the futility of defying the lawful authority'.[40]

In the House on 24 June, Brynmor Jones and Samuel Evans spoke tellingly against what had happened, describing the law-abiding character of the majority of the miners in the area, and the wrong signals that had been sent by bringing in the military. The actions of the justices, said Jones, had been 'about the most ill-advised step that could be taken'. For Evans the presence of the military, in a locality where there had been no rioting or disturbance, posed the real threat to peace and good order. 'The belief', he said, 'was spreading among the men that the object was to terrorise the colliers into subjection'.[41]

Meanwhile, the Mountain Ash Council, in the Aberdare valley, had protested to its local MP, D. A. Thomas, in similar terms to those of the Pontypridd Council. D. A. Thomas replied saying that he was 'in entire sympathy' with their sentiments, and stated that the Home Secretary himself had admitted to him [Thomas] 'that there had been no riotous conduct of any kind among the inhabitants of any part of the Aberdare Valley'. In his view, 'the action of the authorities in asking for the importation of the military is ... quite uncalled for and a reflection upon the peaceful character of the district'.[42]

On the GCC, a stormy scene took place between the veteran miners' leader Alderman David Morgan ('Dai o'r Nant') and the chairman of the council, J. Blandy Jenkins. Dai o'r Nant must have been aware that Alderman William Henry Mathias was one of the Pontypridd magistrates, and that Blandy Jenkins, too, was a leading magistrate. He appears to have chosen with care the person to whom to put his question, 'Whether there was any cause for the introduction of the military into South Wales?' He addressed it to the Chairman of the Local Government Committee. Now, there is no way in which such matters could be within the remit of that committee; but the chairman of it was Mathias's close Pontypridd colleague Walter Morgan, and Mathias and William Morgan (another local magistrate, and Walter Morgan's father) were both prominent members of Walter Morgan's committee. The chairman of the Council, Blandy Jenkins, responded to the question, quite properly, that 'the committee had nothing to do with it', and that the military had been called by the magistrates. This was the opportunity for Alderman David Morgan to inveigh against those responsible:

In reference to the magistrates bringing the soldiers into the district, it was a positive disgrace. They could not get at who had done it. The magistrates were ashamed to show their faces and say who were responsible. There were no deeds which he was ashamed to place before the world, for whatever he did he did conscientiously, but there were some magistrates who dared not show what they had done in this business.

At this point the chairman said that Alderman Morgan was overstepping the limits. Morgan responded by attacking him, as a magistrate, also: 'You would not allow the Chairman of the Local Government Committee to answer my question. You and others have done the business, and you ought to be called to account. (Order, order).'[43]

The military were to remain in the Valleys until the strike was over. When, in early September, it was decided to withdraw them, the press noted that though they had been in Pontypridd for over four months, 'they had no work to do during that period as far as disturbances are concerned, for the miners throughout the Valleys conducted themselves – with just a few exceptions – in a most orderly manner'.[44]

Negotiations, and hardship

There is little doubt that the military had been brought in in order to strengthen the hands of the employers in the dispute. And the employers had taken a hard line, in order to break the men and to make further changes in work procedures that went far beyond the issues on which the strike had been declared. As *The Times* put it in mid-June:

> What has really happened is that the employers, who were by no means satisfied upon all the details of the system of work and payment preceding the strike, have used the strike as an occasion for remodelling the whole relation between themselves and the workmen.[45]

The employers' attitudes towards the various attempts that were made for conciliation are evidence of this resolve. Interventions by Lord Dunraven, and by the president of the Board of Trade (who sent Sir Edward Fry as a mediator) were spurned by Sir W.T. Lewis's Emergency Committee, which said that it could not 'entertain any suggestion placing the settlement . . . into the hand of third parties',[46] and that 'they were prepared to meet the men's representatives only'.[47] The battle-lines remained the same, and soon the employers were to proclaim that there could be no variation in their terms.

The workers' Provisional Committee, based in Pontypridd, had meanwhile been attempting to institute negotiations with individual collieries, in particular those that were not associated with the Coalowners' Association. Most of these negotiations were in respect of a demand for an increase of ten per cent in wages, which some owners, including D. A. Thomas of the Cambrian Collieries, had been prepared to concede.[48] Indeed, when the Clydach Vale miners' representatives had 'waited upon' D. A. Thomas in late June, the latter had conceded a further ten per cent, making twenty per cent in all.[49]

In early July the Provisional Committee met in Pontypridd to discuss the extent to which the demand for an increase of ten per cent had been conceded by individual collieries.[50] As a result of this, on 4 July, a deputation of Aber Rhondda workmen, accompanied by the miners' agent William Evans, 'waited upon Alderman W. H. Mathias JP, and asked for the advance of ten per cent'.[51] The application was refused, and it was decided to place the matter before the Provisional Committee on the 6th.

On the face of it, this would hardly have made Mathias seem a suitable go-between between the Provisional Committee and the other employers; yet, on 12 July, after a meeting of the Provisional Committee had authorised him to do so, Mabon himself went to 'wait upon Alderman W. H. Mathias of the Aber Rhondda Coal Company' in order to arrange a meeting with the 'owners of the collieries concerned in the Cambrian miners' district'. The request was successful, and a meeting was fixed for Saturday 16 July, at the Angel Hotel, Cardiff.[52] That meeting, like all others at this stage of the strike, was unsuccessful.[53]

What had caused Mabon to choose Mathias as a go-between to arrange that meeting? Can it have been that, even though he had refused the ten per cent request, he had expressed to those who had 'waited upon' him a moderate view of the strike? Or may it just have been that Mathias was now one of the few coalowners to have remained living in the Valleys, and was therefore more easily contactable by the Provisional Committee, based as it was in Pontypridd?

Another possibility is that Mabon chose Mathias because he, Mabon, was on very good personal terms with Siamps Thomas and his family,[54] and therefore saw Mathias as a useful contact. Mabon often worked in this way. A very similar situation is described in one of his biographies:

> Today it is difficult to conceive of a dispute being settled by the means often employed by Mabon. On one occasion, for example, he met a young coalowner to consider a dispute which had arisen at his collieries, but after saying a short prayer he made no attempt to discuss the matter. Mabon merely told the employer that he was a close friend of his father, expressed the hope that they, too, would be good friends, and left to tell the miners that the question was settled.[55]

Whatever the cause, Mathias was here given a more prominent role than might have been expected for such a recent recruit to the ranks of the coalowners.

While all attempts at discussion and arbitration appeared to be failing, the workers and their families were in considerable distress. The strike had been undertaken with virtually no funds, and many were now close to starvation. The local Boards of Guardians had done their best, by taking families into the workhouse and by employing the able-bodied men in the stone yards. But by mid-July the Merthyr board was overdrawn by £10,213, and the bank was baulking at authorising cheques.[56] At about the same time, the Powell Duffryn Steam Coal Company, the Merthyr Chamber of Trade, the Hills Plymouth Company, the Rhymney Iron Company and others were putting pressure on the Guardians, threatening them with legal proceedings and a surcharge on individual Guardians, claiming that 'as the large majority of men now receiving parish relief were in a position if they thought fit to resume work', they should be encouraged to return to the mines, as relief payments to them were illegal.[57]

On 30 July, one of the Merthyr Guardians moved the closing of the labour yards in a week's time, on 7 August . This was passed by 26 votes to 12.[58] This was no doubt in part caused by the pressure from the coalowners, though as early as 21 June, before these interventions, the Guardians had already been considering closing the yards. They had been greatly divided on this issue, and eventually, in June, the decision had been staved off by an amendment to defer the matter 'for further consideration', which was passed by only 15 votes to 13.[59] However, now in late July the financial plight of the Board of Guardians, coupled with the pressure from the employers, meant that those who opposed the move had become a minority. The attitude of the chairman of the Board, Thomas Jenkins JP, when speaking to applicants for relief, shows that some at least of the Guardians shared the views of the coalowners. To an applicant who asked whether the Board was not obliged to have care of himself, his wife and family if they were obliged to come into the workhouse, Jenkins replied: 'We shall be able to deal with your wife and children. The pits are open to you, and it does not apply to you.[60]

The closing of the labour yards was the final nail in the coffin of the strike. As Chief Constable Lindsay unfeelingly noted: 'The Guardians are stopping the relief hitherto granted to the strikers. The latter are heavily in debt both to the tradesmen and also to their landlords, and show no disposition to pay or to try to obtain work.'[61]

The strike was now almost at an end. The strikers had lost, through lack of organisation and lack of resources. When, after the delegates had reluctantly signed up to all the employers' demands on 27 August, these were brought to a meeting on the 31st, they were voted through by 61,912 votes to 37,077 (with 8,800 abstentions).[62] They asked their representatives to go back, however, to ask for one concession. One of the added demands that the employers had put forward was that 'Mabon's Day', the monthly holiday on a Monday that Mabon had negotiated some years back, was to be abolished. The men asked for some concession on this. No concession was, however, forthcoming. The employers had decided to rub the men's noses into the dirt.

Mabon's reactions showed just what the employers had achieved; the alienation of even those who had formerly worked closely with them. He asked for 'some tangible concession to go back to the men', and plaintively cried: 'Surely our services to the community and to the coal trade deserve some better treatment at your hands than that which you now offer us.' If the employers persisted in their refusal, 'enduring peace will be impossible'.[63]

Mabon was right. From now on, the old cosy relationships were no longer possible. Also, the lessons of disunity among the miners' leaders had been learned. The strike had been lost because of disorganisation and lack of resources. In October 1898, the new South Wales Miners' Federation was formed, with Mabon as president and his arch-rival William Brace as vice-president. In January 1899, the 'Fed' was admitted to membership of the Miners' Federation of Great Britain. From now on, the south Wales miners became a dominant force in industrial relations, and the industrial scene became the stormy one that the twentieth century was to become used to. The Monmouthshire and South Wales Coalowners' Association had created a powerful enemy of its own devising.

Sir William James Thomas and the New Century

13

'One of the greatest of the Welsh coalowners': William James Thomas's business interests, 1900–1925

William James Thomas's life, after his inheritance of his grandfather Siamps Thomas's wealth and mining interests in 1901, divides neatly into two parts. In the first part, he remained in the Valleys at Brynawel until he was almost 50, and was seen by all as very much a Valleys *notable* on the model of his uncle W. H. Mathias; in the second, after the war he joined with the many other capitalists who had made money in the Valleys and who moved to the coastal towns. He left the coal trade and proceeded to live on the proceeds, becoming a member of the Cardiff *crachach*.[1] The first years were devoted, on the one hand to the amassing of even greater wealth than he had inherited, through the development of wide-ranging colliery ventures; on the other hand, to the giving away of that wealth on a grand scale, above all to medical institutions. In the second phase, while continuing his charitable works, he also basked in the fame all this had brought him, including first a knighthood and then a baronetcy.

When Willie Thomas took over his grandfather's coalowning commitments, he was not entirely unprepared. He had for some years been groomed for this task and continuity had been assured by Siamps's employment of his nephew, John Thomas Fernbank, as manager of Standard. John, born in 1856, was only eleven years older that Willie, but was already a manager of great experience. In the last years of Siamps's life, he worked in close collaboration with his heir and was to continue to do so thereafter. Even after

W. J. Thomas and John Thomas left the coal trade, they were to continue to collaborate in other fields.

Shortly after his succession to his grandfather's estate, William James Thomas was honoured with a presentation from the workmen of the Standard collieries, which took place at a ceremony at Saron chapel. One of course has to beware of placing too much interpretation on such ceremonies, which could only too often be 'set-up' pieces for public consumption. There was one unusual thing about this celebration, however: the person who read out the address in his honour was not the kind of 'place-man' usually used on such occasions, but a representative of Labour on the county council (since 1892), the Lib–Lab alderman Morgan Williams, secretary to the Ynyshir Lodge and a checkweigher at the Standard collieries. Nevertheless, the other tributes to the new owner were so fulsome and ingratiating as to strike an unreal note. The chairman of the presentation committee said that they were honouring him 'not only as a master, but as a friend as well'. Another speaker, after thanking 'the Brynawel people for their kindness towards them as workmen in the past', stressed W. J. Thomas's participation in local life, and in local worship: 'Mr Thomas was always ready and willing to assist any good thing that might be got up in the neighbourhood, and was a very faithful member of Saron.' Finally, the treasurer, Thomas Lewis, one of the oldest workmen in the colliery, praised the Thomas family as a whole:

> During the forty-four years he had been in the employ of the Brynawel people, he had always found them just and kind to their workmen. He did not think there was anybody present who had worked for so many years for the late Mr Thomas as he had. Mr Willie Thomas was also a very good man, and if he followed in the footsteps of his father and grandfather they need not wish for anything more.[2]

Consolidation and enhancement of current holdings

In collaboration with John Thomas, the new owner started by rationalising and consolidating his holdings. In 1902, the Tynewydd mine, which had by now exhausted its main seams, was closed.

On the other hand, the Aber Rhondda colliery, on which W. H. Mathias's Aber Rhondda Coal Company had had a lease, was now taken over by Thomas's Ynyshir Steam Coal Company,[3] as there was clearly life left in its No. 2 seam, and at the same time Thomas acquired from Thomas Jones the old Ynyshir colliery, which was similarly restricted to the No. 2 seam.[4] In other words, W. J. Thomas still saw a place for house coal in his output.

The main source of income, however, dwarfing these minor changes, was the outstanding steam coal from the Standard collieries, Ynyshir (owned entirely by himself) and from the Ynysfeio colliery, Treherbert (owned jointly by himself and Matthew Cope, as the remaining partners in the Troedyrhiw Colliery Company). Matthew Cope, reminiscing a number of years later, described how, once William James Thomas took over, new life was breathed into the Ynysfeio venture, where they both invested in sinking new shafts to even deeper seams of steam coal.[5]

More important even than this, Thomas was soon to be a prime mover in a new, highly successful colliery venture, the sinking of the Navigation pits at Bedwas, in the Rhymney valley near Caerphilly.

The Bedwas Navigation Colliery and Trethomas

The Rhymney valley was to be W. J. Thomas's centre of colliery activity for the period up to 1920. Much like his uncle, W. H. Mathias, he seems to have believed in preparing the ground for his entrepreneurial activities, if possible by purchasing the land on which mining ventures were about to take place. In the first years after coming into his inheritance, he bought considerable property in the vicinity of Bedwas, in the Rhymney valley just east of Caerphilly. Then, in December 1908, he and three others registered a company, the Bedwas Navigation Colliery Company Ltd, to sink a steam coal mine in that area. In the original document, his interest was declared:

> Mr W. J. Thomas, one of the proposed Directors, is the owner of certain property at Bedwas of which the Company proposes to take a lease.[6]

The lease was for 1,475 acres of Thomas's land, on the coal extracted from which he would receive the usual royalties. His land was, of course, also available for housing.

His three main partners in the company were Edmund Hann, the renowned mining engineer from the Aberdare valley, who had been general manager of the Powell Duffryn Steam Coal Company since 1883 and was by now the tenth largest shareholder in that company;[7] Joseph Shaw, a London-based barrister of south Wales origins, who had been chairman of the Powell Duffryn Company since 1897;[8] and John Glasbrook, a successful colliery proprietor from Swansea, who had partnered the Cory Brothers and Thomas Yeo in their Penrikyber National Colliery, Aberdare, in the 1870s.[9] It is interesting to see W. J. Thomas, whose attitude to the workforce had always been so accommodating, now collaborating with Hann and Shaw, under whose aegis the Powell Duffryn management had a very different reputation.[10] When the first list of subscribers to Bedwas Navigation was published in January 1909, Thomas was the most substantial individual shareholder, holding 3,970 £5 shares. Glasbrook held 1,970, Shaw 1,970 and Hann 1,170. The rest of the issue of 24,550 shares was on the whole held in much smaller quantities by individual shareholders. However, John Thomas Fernbank, manager of Standard Collieries (who witnessed W. J. Thomas's signature on the original document) held 800.[11]

W. J. Thomas became the chairman, and Hann the managing director, of the new company. Two pits were sunk just north-east of Bedwas, in the course of the next couple of years. In order to accommodate the large workforce that would be employed in the new mine, Thomas planned, and built, a complete new town on part of the land he owned. This was in many senses a model town, built on a grid system. Even today, one can note the solid construction of the housing, built on the same model throughout, though with houses of differing sizes in the different streets. The township was originally called 'Thomastown', but eventually the name 'Trethomas' (the Welsh version of the same name) was adopted. Apart from the street leading to the mine ('Navigation Street'), most of the other streets were named after members of the Thomas family: James Street (after his grandfather), Thomas Street (after his father), William Street (after himself), and Mary Street (presumably after his grandfather's housekeeper). Another row of houses was named 'Standard Villas', after the Ynyshir colliery.

The Bedwas Navigation colliery was highly successful. It started production in the year 1913, when the output of coal from the south Wales coalfield peaked. William James Thomas's career in the coal trade seemed assured; he had gone far beyond even the exploits of his grandfather. As an article in the *Western Mail* put it in 1914, his mining interests had made of him 'one of the greatest of the Welsh coalowners.' His 'business acumen and soundness of judgement' were praised. Proof of his business skill was, it was said, shown by the fact that 'in thirteen years the number of employees at his collieries has doubled.'[12] It is interesting to note that, in that very year, Thomas started divesting himself of his mining interests.

The Rhymney and Aber Valleys Gas and Water Company (RAVGWC)

Thomas and Hann had already become involved in the substructure of the area around Bedwas, by the time the sinking of the mine started. In early 1905, they had both become directors of the Rhymney and Aber Valleys Gas and Water Co., into which by an Act of 1898 all the small gas and water undertakings in the Rhymney valley had been amalgamated. The original board of directors, in 1898, shows us clearly how the mineowners in the area felt it important to be involved in this undertaking. Of the seven directors, two were also directors of the Windsor colliery, which was just being sunk at Abertridwr in the Aber valley: Robert Forrest (Chairman), and Ithel Treharne Rees. The other directors were Henry Oakden Fisher, Herbert Kirkhouse (the mining engineer who had produced, with Ithel Treharne Rees, the management's report on the Albion colliery disaster), and three members from Bargoed in the Rhymney valley.

In 1903, Forrest relinquished the chair, to be succeeded by Henry Oakden Fisher. In 1905, Hann and W. J. Thomas were appointed directors to replace Kirkhouse and Treharne Rees. They were both assiduous members of the board. Eventually, in 1914, they were joined by John Thomas Fernbank. John Thomas and W. J. Thomas were to remain directors until 1935.[13] The company was a reasonably successful one, though it had difficulty in fulfilling all its responsibilities, particularly on the water side. It is fair, however, to say that the board also did a great deal of good in providing basic services to the Rhymney and Aber valleys. The new township of Trethomas was naturally one of the beneficiaries. The gas main was extended to it from Caerphilly in 1911–12,[14] and eventually, in 1913, plans were made to erect a new gasworks there. This involved the purchase of land, which naturally belonged to W. J. Thomas.[15] The money needed to buy this land, build the gasworks, and provide the gas supply to Trethomas was raised by new share capital. This provision turned out to be something of a drain on the finances of the company, and was still being quoted, in 1918 (together with the war) as one of the reasons for the raising of gas prices by the company (in a Parliamentary Bill that was strongly opposed by Gelligaer Urban District Council).[16]

The Barry Railway Company

In January 1912, Thomas was invited to become a director of the Barry Railway Company. This company (originally the Barry Docks and Railway Company) had been set up in the early 1880s to develop the new port at Barry for the export of coal from the Valleys, and to build the railway that would serve it, thereby bypassing the Bute monopoly in Cardiff, and at the same time competing with the TVR. The name of David Davies of Llandinam (owner of the Ocean collieries) has been above all associated with the scheme, but another prime mover was the Earl of Plymouth, who had purchased Barry Island in 1878. Other colleagues on the original board included Archibald Hood (owner of the Glamorgan Coal Company at Llwynypia), Crawshay Bailey, Robert Forrest (Lord Plymouth's agent), William Jenkins Ystradfechan (manager of Ocean collieries), and T. R. Thompson, a Cardiff shipping magnate.[17] It was Thompson who put forward W. J. Thomas's name at a meeting on 19 January 1912, seconded by Sir Clifford Cory MP, another Rhondda coalowner.

Thomas had joined a powerful group. At his first meeting on 2 February 1912, the following were present: The Earl of Plymouth (Chairman), David Davies MP (David Davies Llandinam's grandson; later the first Baron Davies), Lord Aberconway (the prominent shipowner), Sir Clifford Cory MP, Reginald Cory, Col. William Forrest (who had succeeded his uncle as Lord Plymouth's agent), W. W. Hood (of the Glamorgan Collieries), George Insole (chairman of Insole's), William Jenkins Ystradfechan and T. R. Thompson.[18] Clearly, as a coalowner Thomas now ranked with Davies, Insole, and the Corys, and he appears to have been the representative of the Rhondda Fach valley on the board. Certainly, his Standard collieries were among the greatest users of the Barry railway (and though of course Bedwas was not directly within its catchment area, one of the Barry railway's concerns in this period was to strike through east of Caerphilly from the Rhymney to the Sirhowy valley, on a route that would pass Bedwas).[19]

Thomas was to remain a director of the Barry Railway Company right through the First World War (when the Government took over the railways, guaranteeing profits to the companies), and then in the short post-war period before the Railway Act 1921, which amalgamated all the small companies in Great Britain into the four great ones (GWR, LMS, LNER and SR), and which took effect in January 1923.

Thomas's reputation as an employer

When, in the New Year's Honours for 1914, William James Thomas was created a knight, the *Western Mail*, in its coverage of this, described him as 'The Squire of Ynyshir', and as 'the most popular employer of labour in south Wales'. It listed at length his many benefactions, and stressed his care for his workers:

> Examples of his personal interest in the welfare of his workmen could be multiplied. 'Cordial' is too weak a word to convey the quality of his relations with his men. He is, as he has always been, a 'people's man'. The social and religious interests of his workers have always been his concern.[20]

At the celebrations of his knighthood there appeared to be corroboration of this. The workmen at his various collieries turned out in force. A continuous theme was the good relations that existed between him and his workers. On 19 March, reporting a party in Bedwas, the press said that 'there are a large number of immigrants from Ynyshir at the new coalopolis in Gwent, and one would naturally expect the same warm-hearted feeling for him as exists there . . . The whole of the new Bedwas has been christened in honour of the family, namely Tre-Thomas.' Addressing those assembled, Thomas stressed their friendship: 'Dear Friends, he thought it proper to call them friends, for they ought to be friends – Capital and Labour should be friends (Cheers)'.[21]

A week later, Caerphilly, the town where he had been born, made a presentation to him, the mayor saying that 'The townspeople are justly proud of Sir William's career as a patriotic Welshman, as a sympathetic employer of labour, and as a philanthropist.[22]

By June, it was the turn of the employees of his Ynysfeio colliery, Treherbert. There, John Thomas Fernbank spoke 'of the good feeling that existed between Sir William and his workmen, and as a colliery manager of over thirty years' experience he said that this good feeling was the one essential for the prosperity of a colliery'.[23]

All these statements go far beyond the customary statements of this kind in the admittedly owner-biased press, and therefore deserve to be taken a bit more seriously. There is, however, also a certain amount of evidence that all was perhaps not quite so perfect in the industrial relations of Thomas's collieries. In 1910, for example, at the start of the Cambrian strike, when (as in 1893 and 1898) the Coalowners' Association was calling on its members to issue summonses to those workers who went on strike in breach of contract, Standard collieries had followed this policy; and this nearly led to a further industrial escalation on 1 October:

> The men at the Standard Collieries, Ynyshir, resenting the summonses issued by the company in connection with the recent stoppage, held a mass meeting yesterday with a view to consider whether they should not come out on the notices given in connection with the non-Unionist question.

It took the miners' leader Dai Watts Morgan to defuse the situation. When he had addressed the men, they 'were induced to withdraw the notices tendered, and resume work as usual'.[24] A fortnight later, however, there was another mass meeting 'to deal with the question of the breach of contract alleged to have been committed by the men in coming out on the occasion of the recent dispute'. The amount of damages claimed was £1,000.

Again, Watts Morgan rode to the rescue. He had 'waited upon' W. J. Thomas, he reported, and they had arrived at a settlement:

> The summonses would be withdrawn by the management, who promised to do all they could to prevail upon the Coalowners' Association to accept the arrangement. The solicitors on both sides would be instructed to make the announcement in court that the workmen had agreed to nominal damages of £300 being entered against them, together with the costs of the summonses.[25]

The meeting unanimously accepted the deal, and thanked Watts Morgan for his services.

Now, there are a number of things worth noting in this account. Firstly, how much things had changed since Siamps Thomas had been running the mine. As we have seen, in the 1893 strike, Siamps had remained unaffiliated to the Coalowners' Association, and had declined to follow the hard line being taken by that association. In the 1898 strike, on the other hand, with Siamps safely at his farm in Llanedarne, and the day-to-day running of the mine in the hands of John Thomas, in conjunction with W. J. Thomas, the colliery (and Siamps's other concerns) had joined the Coalowners' Association, and signed up thereby to a tough line with the strikers. Clearly this was still the case and though W. J. Thomas appears to have taken an emollient line when challenged by Watts Morgan, he still obviously felt himself to be in thrall to the Coalowners' Association, and to have to have any 'arrangement' he made approved by them. Also, the 'arrangement' does not seem to have been a generous one. The miners still had to pay a third of the original damages claimed, and to meet the owner's expense of the issuing of the summonses. Above all, the principle of the validity of issuing the summonses seems thereby to have been accepted by the workers and their representative Watts Morgan. Thomas seems to have taken a fairly hard line, despite talk of a compromise. One fails, from a modern standpoint, to see what cause the miners had to congratulate Watts Morgan. But *autre temps, autres moeurs*.[26]

What nevertheless seems clear is that W. J. Thomas, while prepared to compromise, could strike a hard bargain; also, that the relations between workers and management at Standard collieries were not necessarily as idyllic as the newspaper reports at the time of his knighthood appeared to suggest. That being said, Thomas appears, like his grandfather, to have been more accommodating, in relation to industrial relations, than many of his fellow-coalowners. A newspaper article of August 1912, for example, at a time when, in the aftermath of the Minimum Wage Act, many coalowners were being slow to make payments of arrears, shows us something of his methods, similar to those of his grandfather:

> We are asked by an Ynyshir workman to state that there is no difficulty being experienced by the workmen in securing the arrears due to them under the Minimum Wage Act in the Ynyshir Collieries. We are informed that the proprietor has even acted with great benevolence in the matter and extended the benefit to old men beyond the statutory age of sixty-three. Nor has Mr Thomas drawn a fine line over the five-sixths clause, but has paid for the whole of the days worked.[27]

Politics

In the year 1910, W. J. Thomas took a short-lived step into politics. That he should have done so is not surprising, given local adulation for him.[28] He ventured both into local and national politics. Given his lack of success in the latter, it is hardly surprising that he withdrew so rapidly.

In March 1910, he successfully stood as a Liberal, unopposed, for the Glamorgan County Council in the by-election for the Ynyshir seat. The *Porth Gazette* ascribed the lack of opposition to the regard in which he was held by his workmen:

> No finer testimony to the workmen's regard for Mr Thomas than the fact that in the recent County Council election so enthusiastic were the workmen in support of their employer's candidature that the Labour Party saw the folly of attempting direct Labour representation and abandoned the project.[29]

No doubt what support there was from his workmen (and we have already seen how untrustworthy newspaper accounts could be) could be ascribed to the political stance taken by Thomas in the run-up to the general election that had taken place in January of that year. In that election Mabon, the member for the Rhondda seat, who until then had been a member of the Liberal party, stood for the first time in the Labour interest. This was because, in 1908, the South Wales Miners' Federation (and a majority of miners throughout Britain) had voted decisively to affiliate to the Labour party, and by 1909 all Welsh Lib-Lab miners' MPs had joined the Labour benches. This had produced something of a dilemma for the Liberal party in the Rhondda. In the event, they decided to continue to support Mabon's candidature in the 1910 elections (on the basis that he was 'still the same Mabon').[30]

It was at this point that W. J. Thomas came to the fore as a Liberal spokesman. In the campaign he took the Rhondda Labour and Liberal Association's line, and backed Mabon.[31] In fact, he chaired meetings for Mabon, and was heard to claim himself to be a 'Labour man'.[32] This Mabon vouched for, at a meeting chaired by Thomas in Ynyshir on 7 January 1910, when Mabon said that all present, including Thomas, were socialists, and that whereas Lloyd George was a 'practical socialist', he himself was a 'revolutionary socialist'.[33]

At the same meeting, Thomas declared that 'notwithstanding that he was a capitalist of some standing he had no hesitation in coming to show his favour towards the Budget and all its proposals especially the one relating to the old age pensions'.[34] The Liberal party's struggle with the Lords over its budget proposals was of course at the centre of this election, and Thomas was essentially taking a straight Liberal party line; while Mabon, whatever he called himself in party terms, remained the moderate Lib-Lab man he had always been (and hardly a 'revolutionary socialist'). Nevertheless, W. J. Thomas found himself, at such meetings, alongside the representatives of organised Labour, supporting the same candidate. It was he who signed Mabon's election papers, his co-signatory being George Dolling,[35] the Labour activist and Standard collieries checkweigher.

The esteem in which W. J. Thomas was by now held by the Welsh Liberal establishment is shown by events shortly after the January 1910 election. Sir Alfred Thomas, Liberal MP for East Glamorgan (later Lord Pontypridd) had decided to retire. Discussing possible candidates to replace him, the *South Wales Daily News*, the organ of south Wales Liberalism, on 20 April 1910 placed William James Thomas's name at the head of its list:

> Foremost has been the name of Mr W. James Thomas, the proprietor of the Standard Collieries, Ynyshir, whose liberality in support of every deserving cause has won the esteem of all sections of the community. Mr Thomas is an ideal employer, and, as a local man, he is regarded as one of the strongest men who could be found.[36]

The idea was taken up enthusiastically by the local papers in the Valleys, notably the *Porth Gazette* and the *Chronicle for South and Mid Glamorgan*.[37] The *Porth Gazette*, in particular, pointed to Thomas's Welsh patriotism, his Liberal principles, and his claim to be a 'Labour man', while seeing him as the ideal candidate to combat 'rampant Socialism':

> Mr W. J. Thomas, Brynawel, is permeated through and through with the Welsh Nationalist spirit. He speaks his native tongue with a fluency which would hardly be beaten by the Prince of Welshmen from Carnarvon. Moreover, Councillor W. J. Thomas is a native of the constituency and has always been deeply interested in the ideals and aspirations of Wales. Politically, Councillor Thomas fulfils the qualifications to the letter. He is a lifelong Liberal and a Progressive in the best sense of the word. In fact he has in many ways justified his somewhat unique claim to be a 'Labour man'. In the last General Election he occupied the Chair at Mabon's meetings, and was throughout one of the veteran's most ardent supporters. In East Glamorgan the candidate will, in all probability, have to enter the lists against rampant Socialism. As a model employer who has the enthusiastic esteem and affection of his employees, Councillor Thomas is the ideal candidate to oppose Socialism ... He is a wealthy man, and his many wise and thoughtful benefactions prove that he regards the possession of wealth as a sacred stewardship, and not as a divinely-invested right of overlordship over less fortunate beings.[38]

Five weeks later, the *South Wales Daily News* noted that Thomas's name was among those that had been actually submitted; it still placed him as its first preference.[39] On 28 June, a general meeting

of the East Glamorgan Liberal Association was held to arrange
interviews. They had written to invite thirteen of those whose
names had been put forward to appear before them, to address them
on matters which had been communicated to them. Unfortunately,
only three had agreed to do so.[40] One of these three was eventually
chosen for the seat: Clement Edwards, a barrister who had already
been the MP for Denbigh from 1906 to January 1910, but had been
defeated at that election.[41] He had been prominent in the fight for
disestablishment od the Church, and had also been 'instrumental in
saving the position of the Trade Unions by his amendments to the
Trade Disputes Act, 1906'. He was seen as a candidate who 'might
easily succeed in uniting Liberal and Labour forces in a special
way by reason of his knowledge and sympathetic interest in Labour
questions'.[42]

W. J. Thomas, despite being on the shortlist of thirteen, was not
one of the three who had agreed to come forward to the
committee. Why was this? The most likely possibility is that he had
had an inkling of the committee's wish to have a practised politician
rather than a local candidate. (Indeed, it is not unlikely that, as has
often tended to happen in Wales in such circumstances, someone
may have 'tipped him the wink' that the committee had already
made its decision.) Whatever the reason, we hear no more of
parliamentary ambitions on his part.

Though he was to serve for several years, from 1910 to 1919, on
the Glamorgan county council, holding the Ynyshir seat, his interest
in local government appears to have waned too. His attendance at
the council and its committees was poor – in fact the worst of all
councillors and alderman. Of the thirty-six quarterly meetings of
the full council during his tenure, he attended only sixteen. Of sixty-
nine meetings of the Roads and Bridges Committee (on which he
served alongside his Bedwas colleague John Glasbrook and the
veteran W. H. Mathias), he attended only sixteen. And of the
meetings of the other committees to which he had been appointed
(County Rate Assessment Committee, Agricultural Committee, and
Small Holdings and Allotments Committee), he attended not one in
the whole nine years.[43] All in all, he does not appear to have taken
much interest in the council's work. It can have been no great drama
for him when, in 1919, W. H. Mathias's failure to take the Ynyshir

seat on the Council meant that, as Mathias could not be voted in as alderman, there would be no vacancy in the post-aldermanic by-elections. Thomas left the council, and never stood for it again.

A Gradual Exit from the Coal Trade

It is ironic that in the very year, 1914, when all his knighthood celebrations were stressing his good relationship with his workmen, and his skill as an employer, Sir William James Thomas should have been starting his gradual exit from the coal trade. In 1914, he decided to sell the Standard Collieries Ynyshir, the flagship of his grandfather's fortunes. They were sold to the neighbouring National Collieries, Wattstown, with the two properties henceforth becoming known as the 'United National Collieries Ltd'.

Why did he sell Standard? In these, the most prolific years of coal production, nobody could have had the foresight to perceive the coming crisis in the coal trade in the post-war period. It is far more likely that his successful new venture, the Navigation colliery in Bedwas, was, together with Ynysfeio, now seen by him as his major concerns, taking over from Standard, whose output had declined from the highly prolific early days. Indeed, it appears from his statements at the time that the future of Standard had been in doubt, and that the amalgamation was seen as possibly breathing new life into the concern.

As a successful entrepreneur, Thomas had no time for sentiment when it came to selling the mine central to his grandfather's success. In a party given in honour of him and of John Thomas Fernbank by the officials of Standard colliery, in November 1914, he answered their good wishes with an explanation of why they were leaving:

> I wish to explain that my severing of my connection with the Standard Colliery has simply been done for the benefit of Ynyshir generally. We know that there is a possible chance that this is going to add to the life of the Standard Colliery.[44]

We do not know how much he made out of the sale; but the proceeds for him personally must have been considerable.

Though Thomas sold the Standard collieries in 1914, he maintained at that time all his other mining interests. In 1918, however, he and Matthew Cope sold the highly successfulYnysfeio mine at Treherbert.[45] It is hard to assess the reason for this. Admittedly, since February 1917 all coalmining had come under governmental control for the duration of the war; but the prospects for post-war coalmining success (on the basis of the output records created before the war) appeared to be good. For a few years factors such as 'the destruction of the Belgian and French coalmining areas, the French occupation of the Ruhr, and the American coal miners' strike'[46] contributed to keeping up the prosperity of the Welsh coalfield; it was only after 1924 that reality struck home, with the onset of a severe economic depression felt particularly strongly in the southWales mining area because of a substantial loss in markets.

In 1918–19, however, few people were aware of this prospect. This makes it all the more remarkable that W. J. Thomas had proceeded to move so smartly out of the coal trade. For a while he retained his major interest in the Bedwas Navigation colliery. Not for long, however. In 1921, that company went out of existence, and was succeeded by the Bedwas Navigation Colliery (1921) Ltd,[47] a body of which Thomas was not a member, and of which the controlling shareholder and chairman was Sir Samuel Instone. Thomas, of course, retained his mineral rights in relation to the coal extracted from beneath his land in Bedwas and Trethomas.

An abortive venture into shipping

ThatThomas's move out of coalowning did not in any way denote a lack of confidence in the future of that industry, is shown by his next venture. Having moved to Cardiff, he seems to have decided to base his business ventures in that city, branching out into a new area of entrepreneurship intimately connected with the coal trade. And it was in this venture that he was first to feel the effects of the coming recession of the 1920s.

In 1919, in partnership with his cousin John Thomas Fernbank, who like him had moved to Cardiff, he founded a shipping company called the Rhondda Merthyr Shipping Company Ltd.As its name suggests, this company was to be devoted to shipping coal from Cardiff. John Thomas was chairman of the new company, and William James Thomas one of five other directors, the others of whom described themselves on the directors' list as 'merchants' or 'shipowners'. They all lived in Cardiff. The largest shareholder was W. J. Thomas, with 12,000 shares. The other directors ranged between 2,000 and 4,000 each.[48]

The two Thomases appear to have been affected by the euphoria in relation to the future of Cardiff shipping which swept the port in that same year of 1919, when many people 'took it for granted that there would be a surge in the post-war demand for vessels and concluded that ship ownership was a good way to make money', and there was a 'stampede' to set up new shipping companies. The euphoria was shortlived, however. In May 1920, there came a crash. Freight rates descended in a rapid slide because, with this rapid expansion in shipping, there was more cargo space now available than there was cargo to fill it. Then, by the mid-Twenties, the decline in markets for south Wales coal heightened the problems of the shipping companies. From 1922 companies were taking ships out of service, and many were going to the wall.[49]

Sir William James Thomas's venture into shipping at such a time was uncharacteristic of the successful entrepreneur he had shown himself to be in the coal industry. His Rhondda Merthyr company was among those that were forced out of existence. On 15 July 1925, finding that it could not, because of its liabilities, continue its business, it wound itself up voluntarily.[50]

W. J. Thomas was not among those, however, whose personal finances suffered too greatly. Only a small part of his considerable fortune had been vested in the Rhondda Merthyr Company, which was, of course, a limited liability company. Others had a far worse time. Among the people worst hit by the shipping slump was the major operator Owen Williams (who had established for himself a vast estate in the Cowbridge area, having bought, among other properties, 'Crossways' from William James Thomas, and 'Great House' from William Henry Mathias). Williams lost his entire fortune. When he died in 1938, his estate was valued at a nominal five pounds.[51]

This was William James Thomas's last venture related to the coal trade. It appears also to have taught him a lesson. From now on, as the coal recession began to bite, he kept well out of entrepreneurial activity, having retained the greater part of his fortune.

14

'Ynyshir's most noted citizen, the Principality's most noble benefactor': William James Thomas's many benefactions, and later years

While he was to be as concerned as his grandfather with making money, Willie Thomas at a very early stage showed signs of wishing to give it away as well. At first, his munificence was directed at the Christian religion. Shortly after his grandfather's will had been proved in 1902, he gave £600 (almost £40,000 in modern values) to be divided among the chapels and churches of Ynyshir. The largest amount was, of course, given to Saron Welsh Independent chapel; but considerable sums were given to the Welsh Calvinistic Methodists and to two Welsh Baptist chapels, while lesser amounts were given to the Welsh Wesleyans, the English Baptists, the English Wesleyans, and the Church of England.[1] His generosity to the local places of worship was to continue, at intervals, throughout his life.

Hospitals

It was in 1907 that Thomas first started making gifts to hospitals. This was to be the centre of his activities for many years. The main beneficiaries were two institutions: the Porth Cottage Hospital and the Cardiff Infirmary.

The Porth Cottage Hospital had originally been founded in 1894, thanks to the efforts of Dr Henry Naunton Davies, the well-known local surgeon. It was the lack of resources at the time of the Tynewydd disaster that had led Davies to realise the need for an 'accident hospital' that could cope with such situations. Among those whose financial help he had obtained for the venture were Sir William Thomas Lewis and the Crawshay Bailey family. A total of £4,000 were raised.[2] As Steve Thompson has pointed out, in relation to the provision of such hospitals:

> The initial stimulus for hospital movements in certain communities, and most significantly for accident hospitals intended to treat injured workers, came from employers and the middle class as much as it did from workers and the labour movement.[3]

From the start, the Thomas/Mathias clan had been involved with the Porth venture. Charles Jenkins and Son were the contractors who built the hospital, and David Jenkins of that firm was one of the earliest subscribers to the fund.[4] Richard Packer was the first secretary of the hospital, and remained so till his death in 1903, being 'chiefly instrumental in raising the required funds'.[5] By 1902, William Henry Mathias was one of the vice-presidents, alongside Dr Evan Naunton Davies the son of the founder, while on the Ladies' Committee sat Mrs David Jenkins and Miss Thomas of Brynawel (one of W. J. Thomas's stepsisters).[6] There is no evidence, however, of W. J. Thomas himself taking any interest in it until 1908. In October of that year, two new wards were opened. One was dedicated to the memory of Dr Henry Naunton Davies, the other to 'the late Mr James Thomas, of the Standard Collieries'.[7] These two wards had cost £1,060 (equivalent in modern terms to about £74,000), which had been paid with most of the hospital's small capital. Dr Evan Naunton Davies had been asked to open the one, and W. J. Thomas the other.

At the inauguration, Alderman Morgan Williams, the senior trustee, made the opening speech. Given his position as one of the representatives of the workers on the county council, it is interesting to note his praise of old Siamps Thomas, alongside H. Naunton Davies: 'He felt that people could live better in the district as a result of the two gentlemen who were honoured having lived there.' William James Thomas then spoke, and made a flamboyant gesture which was, over the years, to become typical of his style. He said that having enquired how much the ward dedicated to his grandfather had cost, he had brought with him a cheque for that amount, £534

10s 6d (over £37,000 in modern terms), which he now flourished, handing it to Morgan Williams amid much cheering.[8]

W. J. Thomas had already started funding the Cardiff Infirmary. In 1907, he had made the first of many gifts to it, in the form of the endowment of two beds at £1,000 each, one in memory of his father, the other of his grandfather.[9] Endowing an individual bed was one of the preferred methods of charitable giving to hospitals in the first years of the twentieth century. In many areas of south Wales we find prominent local ladies holding 'fêtes, bazaars, soirées, dinners', by which 'worthy citizens were encouraged to give'.[10] As Bynum puts it, 'Voluntarism provided a socially acceptable outlet for the energies of thousands of middle-class women.'[11] The Pontypridd area was no exception to this. In May 1901, for example, a meeting was held in the New Inn Hotel, chaired by Mrs Godfrey Clark of Talygarn House. Among those present were Mr and Mrs Rhys Williams of Miskin Manor. The purpose of the meeting was to 'endow a Pontypridd bed for female patients at Cardiff Infirmary'.[12]

Thomas's gift of two beds was, of course, not the result of a collection, but a personal gift entirely funded by him. He was soon to be involved in even more generous giving to the Infirmary. In this he was one of many prominent figures who were persuaded by Colonel E. M. Bruce Vaughan to support this institution. Colonel Bruce Vaughan is nowadays best known as the prolific architect who built so many of the new churches dedicated in the new urban areas of south Wales in the late nineteenth and early twentieth centuries. His best known (and possibly most successful) is St James, Newport Road, Cardiff, built in 1892–3 just opposite the Infirmary.

At the turn of the century, the Cardiff Infirmary had found itself in a parlous financial state. In 1903 Bruce Vaughan, who lived locally, became chairman of the House Committee, and set about righting the situation with vast energy and enthusiasm. His programme was an ambitious one: 'First to make existing arrangements efficient; secondly, extension; thirdly, increased income; and last, to increase the status of the institution by creating a medical school.'[13] His main talent was that of a fund-raiser, mostly based on personal contacts, though he also made use of circular appeals. Initially, he asked his rich contacts to endow beds, while the 'working class' were asked for weekly contributions. In the first ten years of Vaughan's chairmanship, the Infirmary's financial position improved beyond all expectations. As Neil Evans puts it, 'Bruce Vaughan's appeals depended on the disproportionate response of a few wealthy individuals',[14] who included John Cory, the Marquess of Bute and Sir W. T. Lewis. The most generous of all such benefactors was however William James Thomas, whom the historian of the School of Medicine has described as 'arguably south Wales's most celebrated philanthropist before the First World War'.[15]

The two beds endowed by Thomas in 1907 were a mere beginning. Soon he was to give far more generously to the Infirmary, and eventually to be the principal funder of Bruce Vaughan's dream, a medical school for Cardiff. In late 1908, he contributed to a new extension to the Infirmary by presenting £5,000 (about £350,000 in modern terms) for the creation of a 'William James Thomas Ward'.[16] Colonel Bruce Vaughan presented the sum to the board on 31 December, expressing Thomas's wish that 'his example will be followed by many others in the district who are as well off as himself'.[17] By 1912, Thomas was turning his attention to the project for a new medical school. In July of that year, Bruce Vaughan, in a letter to the Council of the University College of South Wales and Monmouthshire, was able to announce that William James Thomas had donated 10,000 guineas towards the cost of a new physiological block in Newport Road, 'in the hope that other men of means would follow his lead and subscribe the necessary sum, which is estimated to be £50,000, to complete the scheme of buildings of the medical school'.[18] The Council thanked him for 'his generous gift – a gift exceeding in liberality any which the College, throughout its history, has received'.[19] Within a year, Thomas had doubled his contribution to £20,000.[20] Clearly the 'other men of means', some of whom had contributed generously to the Infirmary, had been slow in coming forward for a medical school. By the time the new school had been erected, and inaugurated in 1915, Thomas had contributed over £100,000 (about £5.5 million in modern terms) to the project.[21]

There was, however, one down-side to his generosity. He appears to have believed it to have entitled him to a major role in the planning of the scheme. In the controversy, 'labyrinthine in its complexity', which surrounded the creation of the new medical school, and of which he was one of the main protagonists, he has been described as 'prickly and disconcertingly obstinate about people and procedures'.[22] This obstinacy was to be a constant in his dealing with hospital affairs.

In the meantime, he had endowed many further beds in the Cardiff Infirmary, and at the Royal Hamadryad Hospital, the Royal Gwent Hospital, and the Prince of Wales Orthopaedic Hospital; and he showed an ongoing interest in Porth Cottage Hospital, where he funded important additions, including in 1915 a new 10-bed ward.[23] He also contributed £5,000 to the Welsh National Anti-tuberculosis Fund.

His commitment to hospitals was heartfelt, and dominated his thoughts and his conversation for the rest of his life.

Churches

One of the first things W. J. Thomas had done, when he came into his inheritance, was to give money to the churches of Ynyshir. When made a knight in January 1914, his immediate instinct was to give a vastly greater amount of money to those churches: £3,489 15s 11d in all (almost £250,000 in modern terms), matching their own contributions to their appeals.[24] These two occasions were, however, mere tips of the iceberg. He gave to his local places of religion on many occasions over the years.

There is evidence, throughout his life, of Thomas's strong commitment to Congregationalism. What is interesting, however, is to see alongside his gifts to the various nonconformist chapels, gifts to the Church of England. This is, perhaps, because of his stepsisters' commitment to that Church – surprising given their mother's strong Congregationalist connections, and her benefactions to Saron chapel. Nevertheless, the girls did a great deal of fundraising, and organising of fetes and other events, for St Anne's Church Ynyshir,[25] and they held office in the church's organisations too (Rachel, for example, being president of the St Anne's Church Women's Guild).[26] There is evidence within the church itself which shows how involved with it they were. A massive brass lectern was given to the church, in Advent 1908, in memory of their father

Thomas James Thomas by 'his daughters Elizabeth, Rachel and Maud'. In October 1914 they gave the pulpit, in loving memory of their mother Rachel Thomas. And, even as late as the Thirties, a local paper noted that 'the choice flowers which decorate the altar all the year round, personally arranged by Mr Lewis Morgan, the Brynawel gardener, are the gift of Mrs A.T. James [Rachel Thomas] and Miss Maud Thomas, from the gardens of Brynawel'.[27] Someone who lived in the area when they were still alive has described to me how the sisters used, at infrequent intervals, to come to St Anne's Church and sit in a special pew reserved for them.[28] While we do not know the origin of their connection with the Anglican Church, it does explain why, alongside his generalised gifts to the local nonconformist chapels, Thomas always included the Church of England (and later, after disestablishment, the Church in Wales). His main choice for benefaction was, however, his local Congregationalist chapel in Yyshir, Saron, and later, when he had moved to Cardiff, the Roath Park Congregationalist church in Penywain Road, to which he contributed handsomely.

Netley Welsh Hospital

With the outbreak of war in 1914, Sir William James Thomas found yet another good cause to take up, related to his already strong interest in hospitals. This time, he was concerned for the provision of care for Welsh soldiers wounded at the front. He persuaded the Committee of the Welsh Hospitals, of which he was a prominent member, to establish, in the grounds of The Royal Victoria Hospital, Netley, Hampshire (a Victorian hospital originally built for the Crimean War) a Welsh hospital of 200 beds. This building, set up in October 1914, was built of corrugated iron, and specially designed so that it could be moved to France or elsewhere if necessary. The original cost of construction was £16,000. In the event, Netley Hospital stayed where it was, and as the war continued enlargements were planned, which entailed the need for extensive further funds.[29] W. J. Thomas himself became treasurer of the new project, and persuaded the Earl of Plymouth (whom he knew through the board of the Barry Railway company) to become the chairman of trustees. Other prominent trustees were the brothers William North Lewis and Alfred North Lewis.[30] Thomas was to spend a large part of his time over the next few years drumming up funds for this project.

Some of this consisted of gifts made by himself, as was noted at times in the newspapers. But he also called on others for contributions (a pattern that was from now on to be common in his charitable giving). He saw himself as providing the seed-corn for others to contribute as well. In March 1916, for example, it was reported that he had recently collected £6,000.[31] Everyone he met became fodder for his project, even children at his local Sunday school in the Rhondda. A description of a prizegiving at Saron chapel in June 1916 gives us something of the tone which was to mark many of Thomas's public pronouncements from now on.

'The bounteous donor of Brynawel' was enthusiastically received 'as an old and faithful Sunday School scholar who had attended that Sunday School for many years in his youth.' It was the custom for Sir William annually to present prizes of books, and then to announce the treat that he was giving the children, usually a trip to Barry Island, which was now a flourishing holiday resort for the inhabitants of the Valleys. For the children of Ynyshir, such a trip must have been a great excitement. This year, however, things were different. He started by giving a short sermon in which he exhorted the pupils to 'remember their Creator in the days of their youth'. He then proceeded to tell them about his own important role in public life, and about his devotion to Netley:

> He himself had reached the prime of life, and the many functions which he was continually asked to preside at, made it impossible for him to be as regular as he would like at Saron. Still, he knew he was doing good in another way. He went on to say that the great crisis which we were going through at the moment, required his services. His whole life was given for the sick, 'the wounded and the maimed', and Netley Hospital had become his shrine. He had already endowed a bed there in the name of Saron chapel.

Finally, he came to the crunch. He 'asked them to co-operate with him in his good work, in their little way'. He had 'intended giving them a trip to Barry as usual'. But he had something to ask of them:

He would ask them all a question: 'Which would you prefer, a trip to Barry or a bed at Netley in the name of the Saron Band of Hope?' Then came a chorus of replies from the youngsters: 'A bed at Netley, Sir'. This delighted Sir William and all the audience present. The answer came as a pleasant surprise. The children had been instilled with the same spirit of self-denial as the good knight himself

After this 'good moral test', one of the deacons got up to give Sir William a vote of thanks. 'He mentioned what a good man Sir William was in every respect; he seemed to have an endless amount of virtue.'[32]

One cannot help feeling a little uncomfortable at the unctuous tone of this scene, and of so many other newspaper accounts of Sir William's pronouncements and actions, and the speeches made in his honour. And one wonders what would have happened if the children (who obviously knew what was expected of them) had opted for Barry Island. But we must accept that such a tone was that of the time and of the place;[33] and one is aware, despite it all, of Sir William's own personal generosity, and his enthusiasm for the causes he was supporting.

The Netley Welsh Hospital was a considerable success, and contributed a great deal to the medical war effort. Almost 10,000 soldiers passed through it. Of particular value was its psychiatric wing (where the poet Wilfred Owen was brought in early 1917 with shell shock, before his transfer to the Craiglockhart Military Hospital, Edinburgh).

In the years 1920–5, Sir William was to give another example of his obstinacy, when he undertook five years of protracted litigation in relation to the surplus funds left over from the Netley fund, trying against all the odds, and unsuccessfully, to get the Government to allow those funds to be diverted to the Cardiff medical school. Eventually, costs were awarded against him and William North Lewis, the two plaintiffs. This would almost entirely have depleted the funds in question (unless Thomas paid the costs himself).[34]

The Pentre and Treherbert Tank Fund

Thomas's commitment to the war effort took other forms, as well. One example was the enormous amount, £30,000 (modern equivalent over £1million), he gave to the Pentre and Treherbert Tank Fund in 1918. This caused some feeling, however, in the Porth and Ynyshir area, which had its own tank fund. It seemed to the local inhabitants as though, having sold Standard – and, as we shall see, having also by now left Brynawel – Sir William was neglecting 'this district, which has brought him up', for less worthy recipients 'higher up the valley'.[35] The Treherbert area was, of course, the site of Thomas's successful Ynysfeio mine, which he and Matthew Cope had kept when he got rid of Standard, so the reasons for his choice of this tank fund must have seemed reasonable to him, even if the inhabitants of Porth and Ynyshir felt slighted by his choice. It is interesting to note, however, that in this same year Thomas and Cope sold Ynysfeio.

Baronetcy

In the 1919 New Year's Honours, Sir William James Thomas was created a baronet. His outstanding gifts to charity, and in particular to hospitals and the war effort, would have amply qualified him for such an honour. It was in a sense bad luck that he should have been honoured in a list that had caused considerable controversy.

In this period, considerable suspicion was already growing that Lloyd George was selling honours for money.[36] The New Year's Honours, in this year of 1919, were strangely delayed. A list had been presented in December 1918,[37] but had been withdrawn thereafter. The delay had been caused by concern at some of the names submitted. By February, Lloyd George was being warned that his list in its present form was a grave risk, because 'the bulk of recommendations were for (a) the press, (b) trade, and (c) capitalists'.[38] A new list was eventually presented to the King (by Bonar Law, on behalf of Lloyd George) on 26 April 1919,[39] and was published, together with the Civil Service list, on 29 April. In its eventual form there were no representatives of the press. There were however a large number of capitalists (many of them from south Wales).

It is fair to say that the history of this list means that those who remained upon it were unlikely to have been the doubtful cases that had caused the delay. It is also clear that Thomas was an entirely deserving case for an honour; and indeed no question has ever been raised about the matter. His citation was for 'public and local services, more particularly in connection with the Welsh University'.[40] The *Western Mail*, noting that Sir William had just given another gift to Porth Cottage Hospital of £6,000, also highlighted his services to Netley, for which £80,000 had in all been collected since August 1914, and to the Welsh National School of Medicine.[41]

Thomas's new coat of arms contained a telling image, which reflected his pride in his family's achievements, and the origins of his wealth in coalmining. Prominent on the shield is a mining pick.

Sir William James Thomas's charitable giving

What were Sir William's motives for his immense charitable giving? And how much were they similar to those of other rich men who, in this period both in Wales and in England, also gave generously? Social historians have tended to take a cynical view of such motives. Peter Shapely's conclusion to his study of charity in Victorian Manchester gives us a typically bleak picture:

> Those with the necessary capital and habitus were able to enter the charitable field with most success, and in so doing their capital was transformed into symbolic power. Economic and social standing alone did not make them acknowledged leaders within the community. It had to be legitimized. They had to prove their moral worth in order to gain the recognition of the community ... Public reverence came through the local press and official accolades. Through acquiring a charitable profile it was possible to obtain symbolic power and legitimate domination.[42]

A number of sociologists have similarly come to the conclusion that there is no such thing as an altruistic gift, and that even when donors believe they are behaving in a disinterested manner, their actions are usually performed in the hope of a return.[43] Questions have, however, been raised about such all-embracing theories. Alan Kidd, in particular, while appearing to share the fashionable cynicism when he states that 'charitable giving may have less to do with the wants of the needy than with the needs of the donor',[44] and that 'voluntary charity offered a morally approved vehicle for self-aggrandisement',[45] also questions the use of generalisations about the 'self-interested individual', which he sees as 'of only limited value in understanding social (and indeed economic) behaviour', and roundly states that 'to write of "reciprocity" is not to denigrate the innumerable acts of compassion and generosity of spirit which can often bring meaning to individual lives'.[46]

Kidd's work has led other scholars to doubt the wisdom of the 'concentration on motive' when examining the charity field. Indeed Shapely, despite his cynical assessment of motives quoted above, stresses elsewhere that 'motives are difficult to quantify in any meaningful way', and that 'each individual had his own specific reasons for becoming associated with charities', while 'not everyone who became associated with a range of charities was motivated from a desire to fulfil the criteria for social leadership'.[47]

John Williams went further, in his earlier 1980 essay on the coalowners in *A People and a Proletariat*. Here he pointed out that though the coalowners had given to chapels, churches, schools, libraries, hospitals and workmen's institutes, 'social control' was a most unlikely type of motivation, if only because 'such deliberate manipulation of the community was frequently otiose'.[48] Such an explanation failed to do justice, he felt, to the complexity of the reasons for such behaviour. Prominent among such reasons, alongside the simple concept of 'conscience money', were straightforward religious considerations, and the nonconformist concern with the moral and physical wellbeing of the local population.

Where does this all this leave us, where Sir William James Thomas was concerned? One can see, in some of Shapely's descriptions of the Manchester philanthropists, echoes of Sir William's attitudes. He certainly enjoyed being admired and praised. But it is very unlikely that he saw philanthropy as a way to 'convert his capital into symbolic power'. Everything we see of his behaviour, particularly in the inter-war period, shows him to have been unconcerned with 'social power', however much he may have enjoyed the trappings of success. His strong nonconformist faith may have been the guiding force in his activities. And is it perhaps too simple to suggest, as some of his contemporaries did, that he was to some extent trying to repay a debt to the society that had given him so much?

His coalowning and shipowning contemporaries included a good number of others who contributed generously to good works in south Wales. John Cory, in particular, gave generously to the Cardiff Infirmary. His statue in the gardens in from of the National Museum in Cardiff, with its inscription 'John Cory: Coalowner and Philanthropist', sums up in its way the paradox whereby those who made their money from the toil of others were, by giving some of that money back in this way, able to command respect as men of virtue. Sir William James Thomas stands high in the roll of honour of such philanthropists and, whatever his motives may have been, his money did much more good to the community around him than that of many others had done.

Resting on his laurels by the sea

Throughout the period up to the war, William James Thomas had continued to live at the family home of Brynawel, and, despite his spreading business affairs, remained a local man of the Porth area, much as his grandfather had been. Unlike his grandfather, however, he took a prominent part in local life, sitting on the Pontypridd Board of Guardians, being a diligent JP, chairing the local Chamber of Trade, and taking a major part in many local events.[49]

He was single-minded in his approach both to his business affairs and to his charitable giving, and in the pre-war period had lived a simple life, untainted by show or luxury. He also, though by 1914 he was forty-seven, gave every sign of being a permanent bachelor. His three stepsisters, though slightly younger than him, also remained unmarried.[50]

In November 1916, however, his engagement to Maud Cooper, assistant matron of the King Edward VII Hospital (the new name given to the Cardiff Infirmary), was announced. She was an Englishwoman, from Bexhill-on-Sea. They were married on 11 April 1917, at a quiet ceremony at St Mary Abbot's Church, Kensington.[51]

Whether it was because of his forthcoming marriage, or as a result of his gradual detachment from the Valleys which had started with the sale of Standard, Sir William decided in 1916 to make a clean break with the family home in Ynyshir (despite his grandfather's express wish, in his will, that he should continue to live there),[52] and to move to Cardiff. He bought Birchwood Grange, a mansion off Tŷ Gwyn Road, at the top of Penylan Hill, which had originally been built in 1890 for the architect Sir Charles Jackson. The family home, Brynawel, was retained, but was inhabited only by two of his sisters, Rachel and Maud.

The 'Ruée vers la mer'[53]

In this move to Cardiff, Sir William was merely following in the footsteps of many other people who had made their money in the Valleys. As early as the mid-nineteenth century coalowners and their heirs had bought, and lived in, properties either in the countryside of the Vale of Glamorgan, or in the coastal towns. The same was true, also, of those who had made their money in other ways, as landowners, as tradesmen or as builders. In the twin townships of Cowbridge and Llanblethian, in the Vale of Glamorgan, for example, we find substantial properties being bought in the 1880s by the Revd David Watkin Williams of Treforest,[54] the prominent freeholder of mining properties in the Rhondda Fach;[54] by William Griffiths, grocer, of Appletree, Dinas;[55] and by William Rees, innkeeper, of Graig Ddu, Dinas.[56] They were soon joined by others, including David Powell, hay merchant of Porth,[57] John Rees Evans, provision merchant of Trealaw, and Daniel Enoch, builder from Tonyrefail, to name but a few.

Meanwhile, some of the most affluent scions of entrepreneurial families had been buying country properties, and turning themselves into country gentlemen – the Williams family of Miskin Manor, the Llewellyn family of The Court, St Fagan's, etc. Just before William James Thomas moved to Cardiff, William Jenkins Ystradfechan had retired in 1915 from Ocean Collieries and had gone to live in Herefordshire (The Porch, Westhide), where he listed his recreations as 'farming and breeding Hereford pedigree cattle'.[58]

For many others, the lure of the coastal towns was more attractive. The leafy suburbs of Cardiff (Llanishen, Radyr, Llandaff, Whitchurch, St Mellons), and the prosperous little town of Penarth, at the entrance to Cardiff Bay, became full of those who had made their money in the coal trade, and of their descendants.

The descendants of W. H. Mathias are typical of this trend. His two surviving sons, Richard (who died young) and James, both went to live in Radyr (near which Mathias's colleague Henry Lewis also lived, in a large house called Tŷ Nant). Of his daughters, Maggie accompanied her husband Edward Williams to Cardiff, where they lived in fashionable Park Place; Lizzie accompanied her husband Lemuel Griffiths to the seaport of Barry; May (Dawkin) and Gwen (Penry Evans) ended up living together, as childless widows, in Whitchurch; only Louie's husband Arthur Williams (Louie had died early) continued to live in Porth, at Brynglas, with his daughter Mary and his second wife.

A number of William James Thomas's associates came to Cardiff at the same time as him. In 1916, John Thomas Fernbank bought a large detached house in the fashionable area of Lake Road East, facing Roath Park, just at the bottom of the hill on which Sir William's Birchwood Grange stood. He named the house 'Fernbank', after his Ynyshir home. Edmund Hann, too, moved to the Cardiff at the same time, to a house called 'The Rise', in the affluent suburb of Llanishen, where he was a close neighbour of Alfred North Lewis, William North Lewis, and James Hurman. A neighbour of Sir William's in Tŷ Gwyn Road (at a large house called 'Bronwydd') was his friend and political ally Lord Pontypridd (the former Sir Alfred Thomas, MP for East Glamorgan).[59]

The expatriate Valleys people often tended to stick together. Usually this was facilitated by the chapels they attended, and by certain key figures. In Barry, for example, there was a strong Welsh-speaking middle-class Porth contingent, which gathered around the Welsh Congregational chapel of Bethesda, in High Street. A key figure who linked everyone together was the Porth grocer Evan Walters, who now had a shop in Gladstone Road, and who delivered his goods to people in their houses. In Cardiff, at a slightly higher social level, the 'crachach' gathered around a Congregational church, but in this case an English-speaking one:

Roath Park English Congregational Church in Penywain Road. The minister was the Revd R. E. Salmon, who in the 1900s had been the 'popular young pastor'[60] of the English Congregational chapel in Porth, and who had 'had the call' to the Roath Church in 1913.[61] He had now become the indispensable companion and confidant of the wealthy Congregationalists who had gravitated from the Valleys to Cardiff (a Congregationalist equivalent of the 'society abbés' who played such a role in Parisian high society), at times even accompanying them, in what almost seemed the role of a personal chaplain, on their holidays in Llandrindod Wells.[62] Sir William James Thomas gave generously to this chapel, and was one of the benefactors who funded the building of a substantial church hall in 1927.[63] Possibly the decision to change to an English-language chapel was in deference to his wife, who did not speak Welsh.

Sir William's last years

From now on Sir William lived, in Cardiff, the life of an acknowledged public figure, obviously enjoying the experience, and with it the honours that had been, and continued to be, showered on him. These included the Freedom of the City of Cardiff (1915), an Honorary LLD of the University of Wales (1921), a Vice-Presidentship of the University College of South Wales and Monmouthshire (1921), the Deputy Lieutenantship of Glamorgan (1917), and the High Sheriffship of Glamorgan (1936).

The spirit of entrepreneurship was no longer there, however. After his last entrepreneurial venture, the Rhondda Merthyr Shipping Company, folded in 1925, he remained alongside John Thomas as a director of the Rhymney and Aber Valleys Gas and Water Company; but the only other directorship he took on in this period was, from 1923 to 1943, that of the Great Western Railway. When the railways were amalgamated into the 'Big Four' in 1921, the former Barry Railway had been allowed one director on the GWR Board, which was to start in January 1923. The Earl of Plymouth had been chosen, but in 1922 he died, and Sir William was chosen to replace him. He was one of the most assiduous attenders at the monthly meetings at Paddington Station, and the board, when he retired in 1943, noted that 'his intimate knowledge of industrial conditions in South Wales [had] made his counsels especially valuable in connection with matters affecting that area'.[64] Whether he had any influence upon the decisions of the board (apart from the naming of one of the 'Grange' class of locomotives after his house, Birchwood Grange), is uncertain.

In every other respect, from 1925 onwards, it was as though Sir William had decided to rest on his laurels. He had become a considerable public figure, and appeared in public a great deal, both in connection with charitable giving and in carrying out his public duties as deputy lieutenant and high sheriff. He also encouraged charitable giving in others, and founded various ventures to help with hospital funding.[65]

His later life appears to have been a happy and rather placid one. He and Maud had three children: William James Cooper Thomas (b.1919); Maureen (who married Joseph Gaskell, a member of a prominent south Wales family); and Geoffrey.

Sir William James Thomas died on 3 January 1945, and was buried (in a grave surmounted by another formidable Thomas monument) in Cathays cemetery in Cardiff, not far from the Roath Park Congregational Church. The inscription on the monument lists his honours (JP, Hon. DL, Hon. LLD, Freeman of the City of Cardiff), together with the following quotation:

> None knew him but to love him,
> None named him but to praise,
> He lived to serve others.

He was succeeded in the baronetcy by his son William Cooper Thomas.

Conclusion

Sir William James Thomas cut quite a figure in inter-war south Wales. And he seems to have thoroughly enjoyed his position and influence. Admittedly, to some, his perpetual harping on his own good deeds, and on the worthiness of the hospital causes that he espoused (and which by now he seemed to epitomize) tended to grate somewhat. There is no doubt, however, that despite the sometimes naïve manifestations of his pride in his achievements, he had a genuine enthusiasm for the causes he had espoused, and outstanding generosity in relation to them.

Despite the eminence he had achieved, he remained his grandfather's grandson in many respects. His entrepreneurial activities in the pre-war period had shown him to have been a true chip off the old block. And, like Siamps, he was a man of simple tastes, a hard-headed approach to business matters, and a mulish stubbornness when his desires were thwarted. While an employer in the Valleys he had shared, too, his grandfather's sense of togetherness with the workforce (while of course, like Siamps, nevertheless maintaining his position as the boss). In this, he differed from many of his generation. Even among the admittedly sycophantic newspaper reports about coalowners and their workmen which abounded in the newspapers, the perpetual harping on this theme in relation to him seems to point to something more than the mere mouthing of platitudes. In this, he owed much to his early upbringing, including his work experience as a working miner. But all that, coupled with the simple education he had received, had done little to prepare him for the new social life he had entered in his late forties.

With his marriage and his move to Cardiff he had not only detached himself from the coal trade, but also from the relatively uncomplicated life that, like his grandfather, he had lived in Ynyshir. This is perhaps why, from our distance, he seems something of a fish out of water amid the Cardiff rich. It also, perhaps, explains his ingenuous inability to cultivate the discourse of modesty and self-effacement in the new eminence where he found himself.

Throughout his life, he had differed from his forebears in one important respect: the extent to which he had been prepared to put his wealth to the service of others. His grandfather Siamps had perhaps had too much of a hard battle before making his fortune; he tended to hang on to his hard-earned money. William Henry Mathias did occasionally give to the causes supported by his nephew, but his contributions were sparse in comparison. There were, of course, a considerable number of other wealthy people who had made their money in the coal trade, and who, for what was clearly a variety of reasons, gave generously to public causes, and in particular to the hospitals. Among them, however, the name of William James Thomas stands in the forefront.

Conclusion

Sir William James Thomas's decision to withdraw from active involvement in the coalfield was not an isolated case. Many of those people who had been prominent in the coal industry retired on their laurels at about the same time, as the big combines gradually took over from the smaller individual owners. Before the war the trend towards consolidation had already been under way. From 1906 onwards, D. A. Thomas had formed the Cambrian Combine, which within ten years was producing over a fifth of the Welsh coal output. About the same time David Llewellyn (son of an Aberdare coalowner, Rees Llewellyn), on his return in 1905 from a visit of some years to the United States, 'started acquiring properties', and soon 'owned or controlled one-seventh of the south Wales coalfield'.[1] The list of his directorships and chairmanships, in the 1921 edition of *Who's Who in Wales*, shows us something of the scale of his interests:

Chairman and Managing Director Graigola-Merthyr Co., Gwaun-cae-Gurwen Collieries, Ynisarwed Coal Co., Troedyrhiw Coal Co.; Chairman Bwllfa-Dare Colliery Co., Cwmaman Colliery Co., Tower Collieries, Hirwaun; Director North's Navigation Coal Co., Imperial Navigation Coal Co., Celtic Collieries, Cynon Colliery Co., Cambrian Collieries, Glamorgan Coal Co., Meiros Collieries, and Britannic Coal Co.; Chairman Llewellyn Shipping Co., chief Partner and Chairman, Llewellyn, Merritt and Price (Ltd) ... [etc.][2]

The greatest example of a successful combine was, however, the Powell Duffryn Colliery Company Ltd, which 'by the middle of the 1930s was the largest coal firm in Britain, with over one hundred mines, the majority in Glamorgan, and was in 1935 capable of producing over 60 million tons of steam and other coals'.[3] At the same time the great iron and steel companies, such as Guest, Keen and Nettlefolds Ltd, Baldwins Ltd, and Richard Thomas and Co. Ltd, acquired large coalmining interests.

The day of the individual entrepreneur had thus passed. In a way, such entrepreneurs were lucky that it had done so, because in the disastrous recession that overtook the coalfield from now on, the big companies were able to weather the storm better than the old coalowners could have done.

The decline of the south Wales coal industry was caused mainly by its heavy reliance on the export market. Shipping was turning to oil rather than coal, and the formerly highly prized steam coal now became difficult to sell. (The Royal Navy's consumption of coal ell by over ninety per cent between 1914 and 1930.)[4] Former customers abroad were now turning to their own domestic supplies. The return to the gold standard in 1925, and the resultant over-valuation of sterling, hastened the decline. By the late 1920s, south Wales exports had fallen by 23 per cent, and by the mid-1930s by a further 25 per cent.[5] In the inter-war period, the number of men employed fell from over 271,000 to 112,000. The result for the Valleys societies was disastrous. The grim despair of the region has been captured in many accounts.

By contrast, those employers who had got out of the industry, and their descendants, managed to live comfortably off the gains that they had made in the preceding period. Those who had not moved from the mining valleys when they were employers there, did so now. Some moved to the countryside of the Vale of Glamorgan and rural Monmouthshire. Others moved to Cardiff and its more affluent suburbs, or to seaside Penarth.

Not for their heirs the entrepreneurial spirit of the late nineteenth century. Instead, they were for the most part happy to live on the income from the accumulated wealth that had come to them. Some, such as the heirs of the Davieses of Llandinam, devoted a good deal of their time to public-spirited activities, chairing public bodies and sponsoring good works of various kinds, and giving generously to charity. At the other end of the spectrum, others lived a life of conspicuous waste and extravagance (an extreme example, from another industry, being 'Johnny Millions', the heir of the Richard Thomas steel family). Some drank away the proceeds. Others invested cautiously and badly (War Loan being a typically popular investment). Mostly, however, the heirs hung on to their money without either generosity or personal extravagance. Some undertook prestigious careers, others remained in relative obscurity. The affluent Cardiff roads and suburbs contained many wealthy but retiring relicts and spinsters. The impression given by many of these was one of decent respectability, of lack of ostentation but comfortable affluence – but often of lack of any concept of the realities of the industrial society that had nurtured them.

What had happened to that entrepreneurial spirit? Do these people perhaps just bear out the old saying whereby the first generation makes the money, the second consolidates it, and the third either spends it or sits on it like the bad steward? I think it is more than that. The second half of the nineteenth century had been a period of enormous opportunity, not just in south Wales, but in the United Kingdom as a whole, as the network of railways spread, and heavy industry grew up in the Midlands and elsewhere. In south Wales in particular, it was a period of unremitting activity, in which the entrepreneurial flair of many people, from a wide variety of backgrounds, came into its own. Then, after the first wave of exploitation of the coalfield, other entrepreneurs built on the progress that had been made, and created a network of interest which made of south Wales ports the greatest exporters in the country. All this had now come to an end. Amid the recession of the inter-war period, only the organised might of the great combines could survive, and even then marginally. Even if there were a gene containing the spirit of entrepreneurship, the descendants of many of the families we have been studying never had the opportunities, the scope for invention, that the south Wales 'coal rush' had provided.[6]

It comes as something of a surprise when one realises that the south Wales coal boom lasted for only eighty years. To those living in present-day south Wales, it seems like a monumental past which had always been there. Yet those eighty years of feverish activity came and went within what would be the lifetime of a long-lived individual. From the 1920s onwards, there was a gradual decline in the industry, until now, in the twenty-first century, mining is almost non-existent, and the memory of it has to be preserved in 'heritage parks' and in showcase mines such as Big Pit, Blaenafon.

The communities that mining formed continue to exist. Many individuals have, of course, moved elsewhere in search of work. But the strength of the attachment to these communities is such that, unlike their forebears in the mid-nineteenth century, a good number of the inhabitants of the Valleys remain in the place where employment used to be. The Valleys as a whole have suffered from the artificial nature of the boom followed by slump that the mining industry had provided. The ports, too, suffered, almost their sole trade having been coal. Barry, in particular, went into a steep decline.

Of recent years, south Wales, and in particular cities like Cardiff and Swansea, have been undergoing a kind of transformation, in which the outward signs of prosperity have returned. The diversification of the south Wales industrial scene has helped in this transformation. The same cannot be said of the Valleys. Admittedly, the physical surroundings have changed, in that the formerly black river is now sparkling and clean, the ugly spoil tips have been mostly removed from the mountainsides, and something of the greenness of the pre-industrial valleys has returned to the surrounding environment. But the rows of terraced houses remain, and they have changed for the worse, in that they seem to have become lifeless and desolate. In the valleys towns, there is a sense of defeat and decay. Even in the former hubs of social activity such as Porth, the bustling and prosperous commercial life has disappeared, the shopping centres have become drab and depressing. This is what remains of the legacy of the entrepreneurial society of the nineteenth century.

It is something of a truism to say that the nineteenth century was a materialistic age, and this was certainly true of the south Wales valleys.

The transformation of the Valleys from an idyllic rural landscape to a harsh industrial scene had been brought about by two things: the pursuit of wealth by those entrepreneurs who created the new industry, and the search for a living wage on the part of the multitude of workers who migrated to the district. At the start, it looked as though each might be serving the other's interests. It was only as the century progressed that strife between employers and employed underlined the fact that their interests were, in fact, totally different. The selfish interests of the employers had become more apparent, and the gulf between employers and employed had widened.

This is not to say that the aims of the employers had not, from the start, been selfish. It was in the nature of the society in which they lived that material concerns should have been uppermost in their minds. Coalowners of the generation of Siamps Thomas had often fought their way up, either in their mining career itself or in the other occupations which enabled them to buy into mining, from comparatively humble origins. They had taken the risks inherent in sinking mines. Money was important to them, in the way it usually is to those who have struggled to make it. The 'economical' Siamps Thomas was typical of a great number of his contemporaries. The other side of the coin, however, was that he lived in proximity to his men, and worked alongside them. He could be a hard taskmaster, but he was nevertheless, like many of his contemporaries, closer in spirit to the workers than to the smart entrepreneurs of Cardiff.

William Henry Mathias, on the other hand, was typical of the next generation of entrepreneurs, who had been brought up in the Valleys, and who had settled into the Valleys existence. One of their driving forces was, like that of their fathers, money; but added to that there was a thirst for position, and for the outward trappings of success. Far from the rough simplicity of his father-in-law, Mathias continually strove after the grand gesture, the recognition of his superiority. Where Siamps Thomas had achieved everything by his unaided skills in mining, Mathias, though admittedly a man of great ability who would have succeeded anyway, was helped to his success by the great system of networks within second-generation Valleys society, and by the generally accepted methods of business, many of which would nowadays be questioned.

In Mathias and his contemporaries, the headlong pursuit of wealth was more obvious, because it was not palliated by the simplicity and economy of men like Siamps, nor by their fellow-feeling with those whom they employed. Employers had become more distant from their men, and less understanding of their needs. The companies which ran the mines by the end of the century consisted in large part of absentee directors living in Cardiff or London, many of whom had little knowledge of the realities of mining. Mathias, living in Porth and close to the coal industry, was in some senses an exception to this – but the exception that proves the rule.

The third main character who has been studied in this book, Sir William James Thomas, presents us with something of a mixture of characteristics. In his generosity to good causes, he was typical of a number of other major beneficiaries of the coal trade, in the years of the new century. In the simplicity of his early life, and in his clear attempts to get along with his workers, he appears something of a throwback to a previous age, having more in common with his grandfather Siamps Thomas than with the intervening generation. In his pride in his own generosity, and in the lack of modesty in his public statements, however, he seems to have shared in the desire for public acclaim so typical of the second-generation entrepreneurs. And after his move to Cardiff he became almost indistinguishable from the rest of 'the great and the good' of that city.

How typical were the Thomas/Mathias clan? Their name has not, of course, remained a well-known one, like the Davieses of Llandinam, the Hoods of Llwynypia, Lord Rhondda or Lord Merthyr. They were not on this scale, but were a typical example of the middle-range coalowners who inhabited the greater part of the Valleys. In the Porth area, they and their friends were pre-eminent in local society. The only thing in which they were not typical of the majority of coal entrepreneurs was that, unlike so many others who moved to new pastures, they remained until after the First World War in the Rhondda, as part of the Welsh-speaking, nonconformist, respectable middle-class society of the area.

There is one point of detail that, finally, is worth noting. In our own age, much criticism has been made of the nature of south

Wales business and political methods: the 'shady' deals, the use of insider knowledge, the corruption, of which local government has seemed to be the centre. As one expatriate Welshman once said to me in the 1970s: 'In the north-east they try to hide it. In south Wales they're proud of it.' All this has tended to be blamed on the fact that for a large part of the mid and late twentieth century, south Wales local government was virtually one-party. In other words, it was said that it was all the Labour Party's fault.

What such critics have failed to notice is that when other parties took control of local councils, the same practices tended to continue. And now, in our study of the Mathias family and their friends, we have found that south Wales business and local government produced the same kinds of practice even in the late nineteenth century, and that the people involved could by no means be described as politicians, let alone Labour politicians. This kind of activity has been endemic in the industrial society of this area, for at least a century and a half. What the reasons for this are, it would take another book to explore.

We can find a great deal to criticise in the activities and attitudes of the employers of this period. Their lack of concern, in many cases, for the living conditions of those they employed; their single-minded pursuit of profit; their neglect of safety measures if they interfered with production; their bullying tactics in times of industrial dispute; all these things have caused their reputation to be a bad one. It is all very well saying, in palliation, that these were the *moeurs* of the time; or that if they had not initiated the wealth-producing process, most of the workers would have been starving in the dire conditions of nineteenth-century agriculture. It is abundantly clear that, in almost every case, profit was their single greatest motive, and all else was subordinated to that.

When we look at what became of the Valleys after the First World War, however, we can perceive that there is an even greater thing for which these entrepreneurs can be criticised, and that is lack of foresight. They had created an almost single-industry region, without any thought of what the future might hold once profits ceased; and they had then taken their wealth out of the region, turning their backs on the population that had made their prosperity.

The members of the Thomas/Mathias family were neither better nor worse than the average of such people. They, like their contemporaries, unthinkingly followed the attitudes and behaviour of the society of which they were part. As such they have been eminently worthy of study.

Notes

1 The South Wales Coal Industry

[1] Most of the information in this section (except where otherwise indicated) relies on the accounts in J. H. Morris and L. J. Williams, *The South Wales Coal Industry 1841–1875* (Cardiff: University of Wales Press, 1958), Trevor Boyns, Colin Baber and Dennis Thomas, 'The iron, steel and tinplate industries, 1750–1914', John Williams, 'The coal industry 1750–1914', and Harold Pollins, 'The development of transport, 1750–1914', the last three all in the *Glamorgan County History, Vol. 5: Industrial Glamorgan from 1700 to 1970* (Cardiff: Glamorgan County History Trust Ltd, 1980).

[2] Michael Asteris, 'The rise and decline of south Wales coal exports, 1870–1930', *Welsh History Review*, 13, 26.

[3] Most of the information in this section (except where indicated otherwise) is taken from E. D. Lewis, *The Rhondda Valleys* (Cardiff: University College Cardiff Press, 1984).

[4] Matthew Cope, 'Marriage and industrial enterprise', *Western Mail*, 14 April 1928.

[5] Lewis, *The Rhondda Valleys*, p. 42

[6] D. S. M. Barrie, *The Taff Vale Railway*, p. 8.

[7] 'Bituminous coal working in the lower Rhondda, 1809–1855', chapter 3 of Lewis, *The Rhondda Valleys*, pp. 36–65.

[8] John Williams, 'The coal industry 1750–1914', p. 182.

[9] Morris and Williams, *The South Wales Coal Industry*, p. 111.

[10] Lewis, *The Rhondda Valleys*, pp. 67–9.

[11] Matthew Cope, 'Marriage and industrial enterprise', *Western Mail*, 14 April 1928.

[12] 'Steam coal working by private and joint stock enterprise, 1854–84', part of chapter 4, Lewis, *The Rhondda Valleys*, pp. 69–76.

---

[13]   Chris Williams, *Democratic Rhondda: Politics and Society, 1885–1951* (Cardiff: University of Wales Press, 1996), p. 15.

[14]   'Rhondda', in John Davies, Nigel Jenkins, Menna Baines and Peredur I. Lynch (eds), *The Welsh Academy Encyclopaedia of Wales* (Cardiff, University of Wales Press, 2008), p. 746.

[15]   Lewis, *The Rhondda Valleys*, p. 241.

[16]   Quentin Outram, 'Class warriors: the coalowners', in John McIlroy, Alan Campbell and Keith Gildart (eds), *Industrial Politics and the 1926 Mining Lockout* (Cardiff: University of Wales Press, 2004), pp. 115–16.

[17]   L. J. Williams, 'Capitalists and coalowners', *Glamorgan County History, 6: Glamorgan Society 1780-1980* (Cardiff: Glamorgan County History Trust, 1988), pp. 113–4.

[18]   Williams, 'Capitalists and coalowners', p. 113.

[19]   John Davies, *Cardiff and the Marquesses of Bute* (Cardiff: University of Wales Press, 1981), p. 215.

[20]   Ibid, p. 216.

[21]   Glamorgan Record Office, D.LLE.

[22]   Davies, *Cardiff and the Marquesses of Bute*, p. 217.

[23]   See chapter 5.

[24]   Morris and Williams, *The South Wales Coal Industry*, pp. 116–25

[25]   Davies, *Cardiff and the Marquesses of Bute*, p. 219.

[26]   William Henry Mathias was typical of such people. (See chapters 4 and 8)

2   *'A dogged will, a fixity of purpose, a tenacity of spirit': Siamps Thomas, 1817–1901*

[1]   Elizabeth Phillips states (*A History of the Pioneers of the Welsh Coalfield*, Cardiff, Western Mail, 1925, p. 165) that he was born in the parish of Bedwellty, at a farm called 'Hen Fryn'. Other evidence (including James Thomas's own 1851 census return, his elder sister Ann's 1861 census return, later statements by members of the family, and the position of the farm in which we find the family living at the 1841 census) points convincingly, however, to Mynyddislwyn. Things are further complicated by the fact that at times Thomas, in later life, referred to 'Bedwellty' as his place of origin (e.g. 1891 census). The weight of evidence, however, points to Mynyddislwyn.

[2]   For much of this genealogical information, I am indebted to Miss Mary James, James Thomas's great-granddaughter. Thomas Thomas's date of birth, however, is that given in the 1841 census.

[3]   John Davies and G. E. Mingay, 'Agriculture in an industrial environment', *Glamorgan County History, 5* (Cardiff: Glamorgan History Trust Ltd, 1980), pp. 294–7.

[4]   Phillips, *A History of the Pioneers*, p. 165.

[5]   In the 1841 census, James's father, mother and younger brothers David, Daniel

and Zephaniah, and his sister Harriet, are listed as still living at Hen Graig Penna.

6   For an examination of this phenomenon, see E. T. Davies, *Religion in the Industrial Revolution in South Wales* (Cardiff: University of Wales Press, 1965).

7   See the Revd T. Mardy Rees, *A Mount of God: New Bethel Church, Mynyddislwyn* (Aberdare: Pugh and Rowlands, 1922), p. 21.

8   *Children's Employment Commission 1842: Report by Robert Hugh Franks Esq. on the Employment of Children and Young Persons in the Collieries and the Ironworks of South Wales* p. 37.

9   J. H. Morris and L. J. Williams, *The South Wales Coal Industry 1841-1875* (Cardiff: University of Wales Press, 1958), p. 211.

10   Quoted in R. Meurig Evans, *Children Working Underground* (Cardiff: National Museum of Wales, 1979) pp. 7–9.

11   *Children's Employment Commission 1842: Report*, pp. 80, 61, 66, 69.

12   *Rhondda Leader*, 3 August 1901.

13   Ibid.

14   1841 census.

15   See the Revd T. Mardy Rees, *A Mount of God*; also Gareth Griffith and John J. Lambert, *Set on a Hill: A Story of Two Hundred Years: New Bethel Congregational Church, Mynyddislwyn, 1758–1958* (Tonypandy, 1958).

16   Griffith and Lambert, *Set on a Hill*, p. 17.

17   Most histories of the period wrongly (e.g. J. H. Morris and L. J. Williams, *The South Wales Coal Industry, 1841–1875*; E. D. Lewis, *The Rhondda Valleys*; and the *Glamorgan County History*) call him 'Matthew Cope', having confused him with his son Matthew, who later inherited his mining interests, and whose memoirs are cited in this chapter.

18   Matthew Cope, 'Some worthies of the two ports', *Western Mail*, 21 March 1928.

19   Matthew Cope, 'Marriage and industrial enterprise', *Western Mail*, 14 April 1928.

20   John Williams, 'The coal industry 1750–1914', in *Glamorgan County History*, 5, 189–90.

21   Phillips, *A History of the Pioneers*, pp. 165–9.

22   *Pontypridd Chronicle*, 16 March 1888.

23   The situation remained much the same into the 1870s, as we see from the Ordnance Survey map of 1875 (Map 27/12, GRO),

24   See not only the 1875 Ordnance Survey map (27/8, GRO), but also the illustration of the Tynewydd mine on p. 144, in the background of which one sees the beginning of the Rhondda Fach valley.

25   Phillips, *A History of the Pioneers*, pp. 165–9.

26   Ibid.

27   Morris and Williams, *The South Wales Coal Industry*, p. 129.

28   *Western Mail*, 30 January 1875.

29   Phillips, *A History of the Pioneers*, p. 168.

30 Matthew Cope, *Western Mail*, 14 April 1928.

31 Lewis, *The Rhondda Valleys*, p. 52.

32 Ibid., p. 53.

33 Matthew Cope, 'Marriage and industrial enterprise', *Western Mail*, 14 April 1928 ('The ground landlord and royalty owner was Mr Llewellyn of Neath') See also DLLE 132–133 (GRO), the Papers of the Llewellyn family of Baglan and Cwrt Colman.

34 Lewis, *The Rhondda Valleys*, p. 72.

35 *Rhondda Leader*, 3 August 1901.

36 Lewis, *The Rhondda Valleys*, p. 74.

37 Phillips, *A History of the Pioneers*, p. 166; Lewis, *The Rhondda Valleys*, p. 99.

38 See 1875 Ordnance Survey map 27/8 (GRO), where the house Mount Pleasant figures prominently.

39 See censuses of 1861, 1871 and 1881.

40 *Slaters Commercial Directory, Pontypridd*, 1880.

41 Phillips, *A History of the Pioneers*, p. 205. See also the accounts of the Tynewydd Disaster.

42 *Western Mail*, 30 January 1884.

43 For Daniel Thomas, see pp. 84–85.

44 *Western Mail*, 30 January 1884.

45 See chapter 9.

46 *Kelly's Directory*, 1891.

47 PRO BT 31/2932/16362.

48 See chapter 7.

49 One account of the Standard Collieries (*www.Welshcoalmines.co.uk*) refers to an explosion on 18 February 1887 which killed 39 miners. Examination of the newspapers of the time shows, however, that this disaster took place not at Thomas's colliery, but at the National Collieries, Ynyshir (also known as the National Collieries, Wattstown).

50 In an address made by the workmen to John Thomas, eight years after Siamps's death, their two names were linked in this respect: 'There is an air of confidence and repose amongst the workmen under your supervision and they have an instinctive feeling that the underlying principle of your professional policy is the safety of the workmen. We are not surprised at this when we reflect that this was the guiding principle of the veteran pioneer, the late Mr James Thomas.' (*Porth Gazette*, 29 April 1909).

51 Lewis, *The Rhondda Valleys*, p. 100. Also *Pontypridd Chronicle*, 25 June 1897.

52 See chapter 11.

53 *Pontypridd Chronicle*, 16 March 1888.

54 Kenneth O. Morgan, *Wales in British Politics, 1868–1922* (Cardiff: University of Wales Press, 1963). Paperback edition, 1991, pp. 10–11.

55 *Kelly's Directory*, 1891.

56 *Porth Gazette*, 14 November 1914.

57 Ibid.
58 *Porth Gazette*, 26 August 1911.
59 *Western Mail*, 26 April 1877.
60 1851 census.
61 Ibid. Siamps is listed as 'visitor' and 'miner agent' (no doubt a mistake for 'mineral agent', caused by his semi–illiteracy). His wife and family are listed, in the same census, at his home near the Troedyrhiw mine, his wife being described as 'wife of mineral agent'.
62 1861 census.
63 1881 census.
64 See censuses of 1861, 1871 and 1881. See also *Porth Gazette*, 14 September 1912.
65 1881 census. On the 1875 Ordnance Survey map of the area (27.8, GRO), Danygraig House figures very prominently as the largest house in the Ynyshir area.
66 Information from Mathias family Bible (in the author's possession), and from Miss Mary James.
67 This is one of the most historic chapels in the history of Welsh nonconformism. It was originally built in 1742, under the inspiration of Howell Harris (1714–73) of Trefeca, the great pioneer of Welsh Calvinistic Methodism. Within a short time it had, however, become a chapel of the Independents (Congregationalists).
68 *Porth Gazette*, 14 September 1912.
69 John Newman, *The Buildings of Wales: Glamorgan* (London: Penguin Books, 1995), p. 177.
70 Phillips, *A History of the Pioneers*, p. 169.
71 Elizabeth Phillips (p. 169) suggests that 'though nominally a Congregationalist, he was not a very active one, and concerned himself scarcely at all with religion'. This hardly seems to fit with his devotion to New Bethel Chapel, with his patronage of Saron Chapel Ynyshir, and with the keen religious sense of his daughters and his grandson.
72 *Rhondda Leader*, 12 January 1901.
73 These chapel connections are mentioned on numerous occasions in the *Porth Gazette* and other local newspapers.
74 *South Wales Echo*, 3 January 1945. See also the Revd T. Mardy Rees, *A Mount of God: New Bethel Church, Mynyddislwyn* (Aberdare: Pugh and Rowlands, 1922).
75 *South Wales Echo*, 3 January 1945.
76 *Pontypridd Chronicle*, 16 March 1888.
77 This was the tone of many meetings between miners and employers. And much of the apparent sycophancy, that we shall be seeing in this book at various stages, may have been a subtle way of informing the recipients of what was expected of them as good employers or managers.
78 *Pontypridd Chronicle*, 16 March 1888.

[79]   In the 1881 census, on the sheets for this area, Evan Thomas's house is entry number 42, and James Thomas's house Mount Pleasant, entry number 52.

[80]   All except Maggie figure in the 1881 census.

[81]   1891 census.

[82]   Ibid. His occupation is, strangely, given as 'colliery labourer'. This may, of course, have been for reasons of anonymity, or it may have been because the census official misheard or misunderstood what he was told (as often happened). By 1901, now living with Mary, he was to be listed as 'colliery proprietor'.

[83]   Obituary, *Rhondda Leader*, 3 August 1901.

[84]   1901 census.

[85]   *Rhondda Leader*, 3 August 1901.

[86]   *Porth Gazette*, 20 April 1901.

[87]   *Porth Gazette*, 3 August 1901.

[88]   *Cardiff Times*, 10 August 1901.

[89]   'For many years after its erection a father and son would travel from Italy every seven years to clean it. They would take a week and then return home.' (Len Burland, *A Historical Tour around Mynyddislwyn Mountain*, Abertillery: Old Bakehouse Publications, 2002), p. 296.

[90]   John Newman, *The Buildings of Wales: Gwent/Monmouthshire* (New Haven and London: Yale University Press, 2002), pp. 415–16.

[91]   The Revd T. Mardy Rees, *A Mount of God*, p. 21.

[92]   Will of James Thomas, 1901.

[93]   John Morgan's (the solicitor's) evidence, *Western Mail*, 19 March 1902.

[94]   Ibid.

[95]   When naming the streets in Trethomas, the mining town he built in 1912–13 for the workers in his Bedwas Navigation mine, William James Thomas called them Thomas Street, William Street, James Street (his, his father's and his grandfather's names) – and Mary Street. There is no other Mary in the family (apart from Mrs Mary Ann Packer, whom he is unlikely to have wished to commemorate in this way). Mary appears to have been accepted by him as his grandfather's companion, and wife in all but name.

[96]   For accounts of the hearing (in which the details of the events surrounding the signing of the will were given in full), see the *Western Mail* (19 March 1902), the *Rhondda Leader* (22 March 1902), the *Porth Gazette* (22 March 1902), the *Cardiff Times* (22 March 1902), the *Glamorgan Free Press* (22 March 1902), and *The Times* (19 March 1902).

[97]   'David Williams (Alaw Goch)', in *Dictionary of Welsh Biography down to 1940* (London: Honourable Society of Cymmrodorion, 1959).

[98]   Michael Eyers, *The Masters of the Coalfield: People and Place Names in Glamorgan and Gwent* (Griffithstown: Village Publishing, 1992), p. 97.

[99]   John Williams, *Was Wales Industrialised?*, p. 100.

3 'A blunt, straightforward, and from head to feet an honest man': Richard Mathias (1814–1890)

1   I am indebted, for much of the early information about the Mathias family, to Michael Mathias, who has been undertaking a genealogical study of the family.

2   Genealogical research by Michael Mathias.

3   Marriage record of Richard Mathias and Margaret Evans (research by Michael Mathias).

4   Baptismal record of William Henry Mathias. (research by Michael Mathias).

5   *Pontypridd Herald*, 10 January 1891.

6   Much of the information on the Llancaiach branch (except where signalled otherwise) is taken from Colin Chapman's book *The Nelson and Ynysybwl Branches of the Taff Vale Railway* (Oxford: Oakwood Press, 1997).

7   'Navigation House' itself was a large house built for the officials of the canal company. It later became a hotel, and is still in existence to-day.

8   Chapman, *The Nelson and Ynysybwl Branches*, p. 9.

9   Ibid., p. 6.

10 Ibid., p. 13.

11 1851 census.

12 A son, John Evan Mathias (who was to die as a child), was described on his baptismal record as having been born in Nelson in 1864.

13 See 1871 census.

14 *Pontypridd Herald*, 10 January 1891.

15 *Porth Gazette*, 13 May 1922; *Western Mail*, 9 May 1922.

16 The erection of a skew stone bridge at Eirw (6 April 1870); Nantydall Bridge (13 September 1876); a girder bridge at Maesaril (18 June 1879); and a retaining wall for the Dinas and Cymmer Road (3 July 1878). (Glamorgan Record Office, (GRO) H/Bpp 1).

17 GRO, H/B Pp 1, entry for 31 March 1875.

18 GRO, L/BY 1/1, entry for 25 April 1878.

19 GRO, L/BY 1/1, entry for 25 April 1879.

20 My thanks are due to the Revd Chris Reaney, Rector of Llanfabon, for information pertaining to the parish.

21 For Richard Mathias's activities on the Llanwonno Board, see the minutes of the board 1871–1891 (GRO E/SB/40/1-5)

22 *Pontypridd Herald*, 10 January 1891.

23 *Who's Who in Wales*, 1920. (Cardiff: Western Mail Ltd, 1921).

24 Grant of Letters of Administration of the Personal Estate of Richard Mathias, 14 July 1891 (research by Michael Mathias).

25 See PRO BT 31/3760/23446, for the distribution of his shares in the Aber Rhondda Company.

26 *Pontypridd Herald*, 10 January 1891.

27 Censuses of 1851, 1861, 1871, 1881.

28 See minutes of Rhondda Urban District Council (RUDC), *passim* (GRO).

29 See minutes of Glamorgan County Council (GCC), 1910–12. (GRO).

4 *The Rhondda Second Generation:William Henry Mathias (1845–1922),*
   a Rhondda Notable

1   1861 census.
2   Indenture, 13 July 1861 (Bute MSS XXIII/2) copy in Glamorgan Record Office
    (GRO), D/D CL.
3   Ibid., 30 November 1862.
4   *Western Mail*, 9 May 1922; *Porth Gazette*, 13 May 1922.
5   Marriage certificate of William Henry Mathias and Rachel Thomas (research by
    Michael Mathias).
6   James Mathias's birth certificate (research by Michael Mathias).
7   In the 1871 census, in the area of Troedyrhiw, Mathias's house was entry 56, and
    Siamps's entry 66.
8   See 1881 census onwards.
9   *Rhondda Leader*, 11 July 1914.
10 See Fig. 3.
11 See Fig. 2.
12 Recorded in family Bible (in author's possession).
13 The author's own observation of his great-aunts and his grandparents
    (W. H. Mathias's daughters and son-in-law).
14 *Porth Gazette*, 13 May 1922.
15 *Daily Telegraph*, 12 June 1877.
16 Records of Ystradyfodwg Urban Sanitary Authority (YUSA), 14/12/77. Also
    14/4/82, 26/5/82, 23/5/84. (Glamorgan Record Office, L/BY 1/1, L/BY 1/3,
    L/BY 1/4).
17 Most of the general information in relation to this railway (except where
    signalled otherwise) comes from the chapter 'Treferig Valley Railway,
    1879–1889', in Colin Chapman, *The Llantrisant Branches of the Taff Vale Railway*
    (Oxford, Oakwood Press, 1996).
18 PRO RAIL 1110/461.
19 Minutes of Pontypridd District Highway Board, 22/3/82, 6/9/82, 4/10/82,
    18/10/82, 29/11/82, 27/12/82, 3/1/83, 24/1/83, 7/2/83, 21/2/83, 7/3/83,
    21/3/83, 18/4/83, 16/5/83, 13/6/83, 27/6/83 (GRO, H/B Pp 3).
20 PRO RAIL 1057/1830.
21 PRO BT 285/637.
22 PRO RAIL 1027/175. Evidence of W. H. Mathias.
23 Chapman, *The Llantrisant Branches of the Taff Vale Railway*, p. 30.
24 A full chapter will be devoted to them (chapter 7).
25 *Western Mail*, 9 May 1922.
26 From 1866 onwards, with the creation of the new highways boards, the
    Pontypridd area was divided into two districts. We have records for District No.
    2, comprising the areas to the south and west of Pontypridd, and Mathias's name
    does not appear on them (GRO, H/B Pp). District No. 1 had been a much
    smaller one to the north, for which no records subsist.

[27] GRO, L/B Y 6.

[28] He was not on the list of magistrates in 1891, but figures on the 1895 list (*Kelly's Directory*). We can place his appointment more precisely by looking at the meetings of the Ystradyfodwg Local Board, where he and the chairman, William Jenkins Ystradfechan, were first listed as JPs in April 1893. The first reference to Mathias's name in the regular magistrates' court reports in the *Pontypridd District Herald* came in July 1893.

[29] This question will be examined in chapters 11 and 12.

[30] See chapter 7.

[31] See Memorandum of Agreement, 16 August 1886 (PRO BT 31/3760/23446)

[32] PRO BT 31/3760/23446.

[33] See chapter 12.

[34] John Williams, 'The coal industry, 1750–1914', in *Glamorgan County History*, 5, 185.

[35] Apart from the original directors, most shareholders held small numbers of shares (50, 100, 200, and in some cases merely 10 or 20). William Henry Mathias held 1,500, a figure only exceeded by three of the Directors (Matthew Cope 3,782, Henry Lewis 1,882, Philip Vyvyan-Robinson 3,841) and by Ebenezer Lewis (1,665). (PRO BT 31/31242/33695).

[36] Phillips, *A History of the Pioneers of the Welsh Coalfield*, p. 205.

[37] In the *Times*, 16 April 1877, Cheney, as agent for the Troedyrhiw Company, assured the press that the Tynewydd accident in no way affected the Ynysfeio mine.

[38] Matthew Cope, 'Forestalling Sir William Thomas Lewis', *Western Mail*, 18 April 1928.

[39] *Western Mail*, 18 June 1894.

[40] Ray Lawrence, *The South Wales Coalfield Directory*, 1898, 2, pp. 51–2.

[41] *Western Mail*, 21 August 1893.

[42] *Pontypridd District Herald*, 5 August 1893.

[43] PRO BT 31/16674/70655.

[44] *Who's Who in Wales* (Cardiff: Western Mail Ltd, 1921).

[45] *South Wales Coal and Iron Companies*, May 1910.

[46] *Who's Who in Wales* (Cardiff: Western Mail Ltd, 1921).

[47] PRO BT 31/17065/77933.

[48] Ibid.

[49] Ibid.

[50] R. H. Morgan, 'The development of the electricity supply industry in Wales to 1919', *Welsh History Review*, 11, 317–337.

[51] T. Boyns, 'The electricity industry in south Wales to 1949', *Welsh History Review*, 15, 79–107.

[52] PRO RAIL 1068/247

[53] *Who's Who in Wales*, 1921.

[54] Boyns, 'The electricity industry in south Wales to 1949', 78.

55 For James Hurman, see pp. 116–21.

56 *Weston and Somerset Mercury*, 10 October 2008.

57 For details as to Walter Morgan's involvement in this deal, see Walter Nicholas's evidence to the Select Committee of the House of Lords in relation to the Rhymney Valley Water Board Bill of 1911 (PRO RAIL 1068/250/667).

58 List of Mathias's mineral rights at the time of his death, for probate (research by Michael Mathias).

59 Ibid.

60 PRO MT 6/2408/19.

61 Mathias's Will merely says, 'all my freehold farms and lands situate in the County of Radnor.' Family tradition (and the testimony of Mr Davies of Bryn-y-Groes), makes the number seven.

62 Bryn-y-Groes's seventeenth-century farmhouse is described in detail in Richard Haslam, *The Buildings of Wales: Powys* (London: Penguin Books, 1979), p. 236.

63 Mr Davies, Bryn-y-Groes Farm, in conversation with the author at Bryn-y-Groes, 1980.

64 *Porth Gazette*, 21 December 1907.

65 See chapter 7.

66 Kelly's Directory, 1895.

67 *Pontypridd Chronicle*, 7 January 1898.

68 Thomas Evans, *The Story of Abercynon* (Risca: Starling Press, 1976), pp. 61-2.

69 *Porth Gazette*, 15 June 1912.

70 *Western Mail*, 9 May 1922.

71 WHM was still listed in 1905 as living at Green Meadow. The last Morgan owner was described by the *Porth Gazette* as still owning Tynycymmer Hall in March 1906. Mathias's floral tribute at the funeral of Thomas Griffiths's wife in October 1906 was inscribed 'from Mr and Mrs W. H. Mathias, Tynycymmer Hall'. (*Porth Gazette*, 1 March, 6 October 1906).

72 List of Mathias's properties at his death, for probate (research by Michael Mathias).

73 *Llanblethian Houses and People* (Cowbridge Record Society, 2001), p. 77.

74 'Surrender by Anthony Hanmer Myers, £9,000 split (£4,500 freehold, £4,500 customary hold) of (premises) CROSSWAYS . . . To the intent that the Lord regrant premises to: William James Thomas, Colliery Proprietor, of Ynyshir nr. Porth.' (research by Philip Riden).

75 There are several mentions in the *Porth Gazette* of her living at Crossways, e.g. 14 September 1912.

76 23 Sept. 1911: 'Sold for £2,000 to William Henry Mathias, Gent.' 17 June 1920: 'Sold by William Henry Mathias for £4,000 to Owen Williams of Crossways.' (research by Philip Riden).

77 See, e.g., *Western Mail*, 24 January 1911.

78 *Porth Gazette*, 22 March 1913.

79 *Porth Gazette*, 13 May 1922. 'GOM' was the title originally given to Prime Minister William Ewart Gladstone, the 'Grand Old Man'.

[80] *Pontypridd Chronicle*, 1894.

[81] *Porth Gazette*, 1 September 1906.

[82] *Porth Gazette*, 1 February 1908.

[83] *Porth Gazette*, 31 October 1908.

[84] *Porth Gazette, passim.*

[85] He endowed two beds in perpetuity at the King Edward VII Hospital in 1915, in memory of his wife and the two sons, Richard and John Edmund, who had died before their time, and he was also a generous supporter of the Porth Cottage Hospital (*Porth Gazette*, 13 May 1922).

[86] Princess Louise (1848–1939) was a daughter of Queen Victoria. She married in 1871 the future Duke of Argyll.

[87] *Porth Gazette*, 24 May 1909.

[88] *Porth Gazette*, 29 June 1912.

[89] *Porth Gazette*, 4 July 1914.

[90] W. H. Mathias's Entry in *Who's Who in Wales* (Cardiff: Western Mail Ltd, 1921).

[91] PRO NATS 1/928. Note on 'Exemption of quarrymen in road stone quarries', 2 November 1917.

[92] *Western Mail*, 9 May 1922.

[93] *The Times*, 9 May 1922.

[94] *Western Mail*, 9 May 1922.

[95] PRO RAIL 1068/250/122.

[96] WHM's daughters Lizzie and Gwen, in conversation with the author in the 1950s. This is borne out by some of his recorded attitudes as a magistrate.

[97] *Western Mail*, 24 January 1911.

[98] Ewart Davies, reported in the *Cardiff Times*, 28 January 1911.

[99] See chapter 8.

5 The Rhondda Second Generation: Some Other Major Figures

[1] *Western Mail*, 6 November 1894.

[2] *Western Mail*, 9 November 1894.

[3] *Pontypridd Chronicle*, 16 November 1894.

[4] 1841 census.

[5] 1851 census.

[6] See 1875 Ordnance Survey map 27/12 (GRO).

[7] 1861 and 1871 census.

[8] *Pontypridd Chronicle*, 16 November 1894. For the position of Brynglas, see 1875 Ordnance Survey map 27/12 (GRO)

[9] Her aunts, the surviving Mathias girls, still referred to her as 'Mary Brynglas' in the 1960s.

[10] 1891 census.

[11] 'Morien', in *Western Mail*, 6 November 1894.

[12] *Western Mail*, 6 November 1894.

[13] *Porth Gazette*, 11 April 1908.

[14] *Porth Gazette*, 15 June 1901.

[15] *Western Mail*, 6 November 1894.

[16] T. J. Prichard, "'The Squire of Fairfield": Rhondda on the eve of the industrial revolution', *Welsh History Review*, 11, 516–29.

[17] Prichard, 'The Squire of Fairfield', 524.

[18] Ibid., 527.

[19] 'Morien', *History of Pontypridd and the Rhondda Valleys* (Pontypridd: Glamorgan County Times, 1903).

[20] *Kelly's Directory of Monmouthshire and Principal Towns and Places in South Wales*, 1884.

[21] Prichard, 'The Squire of Fairfield', 527.

[22] *Central Glamorgan Gazette*, 10 August 1877; *Western Mail*, 6 August 1877.

[23] Prichard, 'The Squire of Fairfield', 528.

[24] *Western Mail*, 13 July 1877.

[25] *The Times*, 24 May 1877.

[26] *Daily Telegraph*, 12 June 1877.

[27] Quoted in Prichard, 'The Squire of Fairfield', 528.

[28] *Western Mail*, 8 August 1877.

[29] 'Reminiscences of an 89-year-old native of Eglwysilan' (Glamorgan Record Office, D/D X 181/1,2).

[30] 1861 census.

[31] *Porth Gazette*, 25 February 1905.

[32] 1881 census.

[33] 1881 and 1891 censuses.

[34] Prichard, 'The Squire of Fairfield', 528.

[35] *Porth Gazette*, 25 February 1905.

[36] Regularly reported in the 'Hunting Notes' of the *Western Mail*, as for example in the account of the meet at Crossways, Cowbridge (then occupied by Mr Thurston Bassett of the Bassett family of Beaupre) in November 1894, at which the Master was Blandy Jenkins, and the huntsmen included Theophilus Hamlen-Williams, Herbert R. Homfray of Penllyn Castle, Oliver Jones of Fonmon Castle, Sir Morgan Morgan, Mrs Naunton Davies (daughter of Daniel Owen of Ash Hall) and Miss Williams of Miskin Manor. (*Western Mail*, 8 November 1894)

[37] GRO, D/D X 181 2.

[38] Many of the details in this section (except where it is indicated otherwise), are to be found in the entry 'Gwilym Williams' in the *Dictionary of Welsh Biography down to 1940* (London: Honourable Society of Cymmrodorion, 1959).

[39] See p. 35.

[40] Michael Eyers, *The Masters of the Coalfield: People and Place Names in Glamorgan and Gwent* (Griffithstown: Village Publishing, 1992), p. 97.

[41] See p. 84.

[42] Much of the information about Rhys Williams comes from various editions of *Who's Who*.

[43] See chapters 2 and 8.

[44] *Who's Who in Wales*, 1920 (Cardiff: Western Mail, 1921).

[45] *Who's Who*.

[46] *Western Mail*, 17 July 1894.

[47] Much of the account of Griffiths's early career (except where it is stated otherwise), is based on Richard Watson's book, *Rhondda Coal, Cardiff Gold: The Insoles of Llandaff, Coal Owners and Shippers* (Cardiff: Merton Priory Press, 1997).

[48] GRO, L/B Y 1/3

[49] He had to be called out of those negotiations in order to give his evidence on W. H. Mathias's objection to the proposed Rhymney Water Board Bill, at the Select Committee in the House of Lords in July 1911 (PRO RAIL 1068/249).

[50] The information in this section is mostly taken from Jenkins's entry in *Who's Who in Wales* (Cardiff: Western Mail, 1921).

[51] R. H. Walters, *The Economic and Business History of the South Wales Steam Coal Industry, 1840–1914* (New York: Arno, 1977), pp. 170–1.

[52] Chris Williams, *Democratic Rhondda: Politics and Society 1885–1951* (Cardiff: University of Wales Press, 1996), p. 37.

[53] 1871 census.

[54] GRO, D.LLE, the papers of the Llewellyn family of Baglan and Cwrt Colman.

[55] Elizabeth Phillips, *A History of the Pioneers of the Welsh Coalfield* (Cardiff: Western Mail Ltd, 1935).

[56] From 1881 onwards, the censuses give two separate entries for 'Tynewydd Farm' and 'Tynewydd House', in the latter of which William Morgan and his wife Mary were residing.

[57] *Cardiff Times*, 26 January 1889.

[58] PRO BT 31/3278/19302.

[59] See chapter 8.

[60] 'Morien', *A History of Pontypridd and the Rhondda Valleys*, p. 174.

[61] *Rhondda Leader*, 3 August 1901.

[62] *Porth Gazette*, 26 April 1913. See also Nicholas's *Who's Who* entry.

[63] Chris Williams, *Democratic Rhondda: Politics and Society 1885–1951* (Cardiff: University of Wales Press, 1996), p. 23.

[64] In one of Mathias's 1922 obituaries, Nicholas was referred to as his 'constant and most intimate friend', and Mathias named Nicholas as executor of his will (and left a small legacy to Nicholas's young daughter in it).

[65] Most of the information in this section is taken from Chris Williams, *Democratic Rhondda*, pp. 22–3, and from *Who's Who*.

66 Anne Digby, *The Evolution of British General Practice 1850-1948*, (Oxford: Oxford University Press, 1999), p. 271. Most of the information in this section has been taken from this, and from the entry on 'Henry Davies' in *The Dictionary of Welsh Biography down to 1940* (London: Honourable Society of Cymmrodorion, 1959).

67 *Kelly's Directory*, 1884. See also successive censuses. For the position of Glyn Rhondda House, see 1875 Ordnance Survey map (GRO).

68 'Henry Davies', in *The Dictionary of Welsh Biography down to 1940*.

69 Digby, *The Evolution of British General Practice*, p. 271.

70 Matthew Cope, 'Some famous characters of Cardiff', *Western Mail*, 7 April 1928. R. H. Walters, *The Economic and Business History of the South Wales Steam Coal Industry, 1840–1914* (New York: Arno, 1977), p. 57.

71 Elizabeth Phillips, *A History of the Pioneers of the Welsh Coalfield* (Cardiff: Western Mail Ltd, 1925), p. 203.

72 R. H. Walters, *The Economic and Business History*, pp. 26–7.

73 Phillips, *A History of the Pioneers*, p. 204. Walters, *The Economic and Business History*, p. 27.

74 Walters, *The Economic and Business History*, p. 57.

75 Phillips, *A History of the Pioneers*, p. 205.

76 *Western Mail*, 6 August 1877.

77 Matthew Cope, 'Marriage and industrial enterprise', *Western Mail*, 14 April 1928.

78 Matthew Cope, 'Forestalling Sir William Thomas Lewis', *Western Mail*, 18 April 1928.

79 Ibid.

80 PRO BT 31/31242/33695.

81 See chapter 10.

82 See chapter 12.

83 Phillips, *A History of the Pioneers*, p. 205.

84 *Western Mail*, 30 January 1884.

85 Ibid.

86 Ibid.

87 *Slaters Commercial Directory*, 1880.

88 *Western Mail*, 29 January 1884.

89 'Afterdamp' describes the lethal atmosphere (carbonic acid, nitrogen and steam) produced by an explosion of gas.

90 *Western Mail*, 1 February 1884.

91 *The Times* and the *Western Mail*, 24 April 1877.

92 Walters, *The Economic and Business History*, p. 138.

93 *Porth Gazette*, 29 April 1905.

94 Ibid.

95 Ibid.

96 See Owen Vernon Jones, *William Evans, 1864–1934* (Porth County Comprehensive School, n. d.).

Notes

97 *Free Press and Rhondda Leader*, 6 December 1930.

98 1851 census.

99 Marriage Records, April–June 1869.

100 1851 census.

101 1871 census.

102 Ibid.

103 R. C. B. Oliver, *Bridging a Century: The Hotel Metropole, Llandrindod Wells 1872–1972* (Llandrindod Wells, 1972), p. 20. See also 1881 census.

104 'Public house reminiscences in the Rhondda: the New Inn Hotel', *Pontypridd District Herald*, 9 January 1892.

105 Ibid.

106 *Cardiff Times*, 6 April 1889.

107 *Cardiff Times*, 30 June 1894.

108 *Porth Gazette*, 9 November 1901.

109 Spencer Miles, in conversation with the author in the early 1960s.

110 William Thomas Griffiths, in a number of conversations with the author and his brother Roger Griffiths.

111 Oliver, *Bridging a Century*, pp. 20–1.

112 *Heywood's Guide*, 1891.

113 *Cardiff Times*, 11 June 1910.

114 In the 1901 *Kelly's Directory*, she is listed as the proprietress of the Angel. As late as 1895 the Angel was listed as being run by its previous owners Bland and Savours (*Kelly's Directory*, 1895). Oliver notes that she leased the Angel from Lady Honywood for 20 years (*Bridging a Century*, p. 21). This is puzzling, as Lady Honywood did not start her career as a hotel entrepreneur until the mid-1900s (see below). It may, of course, be that Lady Honywood bought the hotel when Mrs Miles was already the leaseholder.

115 *Kelly's Directories*, 1906 and thereafter.

116 *Porth Gazette*, 13 May 1922.

117 Oliver, *Bridging a Century*, p. 20.

118 Hannah Barker, *The Business of Women: Female Enterprise and Urban Development in Northern England 1760–1830* (Oxford: Oxford University Press, 2006), pp. 94–9.

119 Irene Bandhauer-Schöffmann, 'Businesswomen in Austria', in Robert Beachy, Béatrice Craig and Alastair Owens (eds), *Women, Business and Finance in Nineteenth-century Europe* (Oxford and New York: Berg, 2006), p. 117.

120 Again, a European phenomenon. See the figures for widows among women in retail businesses in Lille, for example, between 1831 and 1890. These vary between 45.7 per cent and 31.4 per cent. (Béatrice Craig, 'Where have all the businesswomen gone? Images and reality in the life of nineteenth-century middle-class women in northern France', in Beachy, Craig and Owens (eds), *Women, Business and Finance*, p. 58).

121 Barker, *The Business of Women*, pp. 72–104.

[122] 'Lewis, Sir William Thomas', in *The Dictionary of Welsh Biography down to 1940* (London: Honourable Society of Cymmrodorion, 1959), p. 564.

[123] Revel Guest and Angela V. John, *Lady Charlotte Guest: An Extraordinary Life* (Stroud: Tempus, 2006), p. 172.

[124] Robert Beachy, 'Profit and propriety: Sophie Henschel and gender management in the German locomotive industry', in Beachy, Craig and Owens (eds), *Women, Business and Finance*, 67–80.

[125] Oliver, *Bridging a Century*, p. 20.

[126] 'Honywood, Lady (Constance Mary)', *Who's Who* entry, 1933.

[127] 'Honywood, Sir Courtenay John', *Who's Who* entry, 1933; 'Honywood, Lady', *The Ladies' Who's Who*, 1930. The Honywoods were married in 1903, and Lady Honywood (the daughter of an Anglican clergyman) started her business career thereafter.

6 *W. H. Mathias and Local Government, 1886–1919*

[1] First meeting of YUSA, 29 November 1877 (GRO, L/B Y 1/1).

[2] Minute of 2 July 1886 (GRO, L/B Y 6).

[3] Minute of 28 April 1882 (GRO, L/B Y 1/3).

[4] See *Porth Gazette*, 1 September 1906, for Mathias's reminiscences of this.

[5] GRO, L/B Y/8.

[6] GRO, L/B Y/11.

[7] See chapter 8.

[8] *Western Mail*, 9 May 1922.

[9] E. D. Lewis, *The Rhondda Valleys.*, p.210.

[10] *Pontypridd District Herald*, 10 September 1892.

[11] *Pontypridd District Herald*, 23 September 1893.

[12] See minutes of meetings on 17 December 1886, 17 February 1893 (GRO, LB Y/6, LB Y/11).

[13] Minutes of 10 May 1895 (GRO UD/R C/1/2).

[14] Minutes of 24 May 1895, 7 June 1895 and 2 August 1895 (GRO, UD/R C/1/2).

[15] Minutes of 4 June 1897 (GRO, UD/R C/1/4).

[16] Minutes of 17 July 1896 and 25 September 1896 (GRO, UD/R C/1/3).

[17] Minutes of 19 October 1888, 23 March 1888 and 12 December 1890 (GRO, L/B Y7, L/B Y8).

[18] *Western Mail*, 9 May 1922.

[19] E. D. Lewis, *The Rhondda Valleys*, p. 212.

[20] *South Wales Daily News*, 17 May 1911.

[21] *Porth Gazette*, 19 March 1904.

[22] *Porth Gazette*, 22 March 1913.

[23] *Porth Gazette*, 4 March 1905.

24 *Porth Gazette*, 22 March 1913.
25 R. C. K. Ensor, *England 1870–1914* (Oxford: Clarendon Press, 1936), p. 202.
26 The list of occupations of the first intake of Councillors, referred to on the next few pages, is taken from the *Cardiff Times* of 26 January 1889.
27 See list of 'The great landowners of Glamorgan in 1873', in Philip Jenkins, 'The creation of an "ancient gentry"': Glamorgan 1760–1840', *Welsh History Review*, 12, 214–25.
28 Interestingly, Cilfynydd was to remain an Albion fief right up to the First World War, with Philip Jones, the Manager of Albion, being its County Council representative in the later stages.
29 See David A. Pretty, 'David Morgan ("Dai o'r Nant"), miners' agent: a portrait of leadership in the south Wales coalfield', *Welsh History Review*, 20, 495–531.
30 *Cardiff Times*, 12 March 1892.
31 *Western Mail*, 9 and 10 March 1892.
32 *Western Mail*, 10 March 1892.
33 GRO, GC/CC 1/3.
34 *Cardiff Times*, 19 March 1892.
35 Information from various Kelly's Directories.
36 GRO, GC/RB.
37 *Porth Gazette*, 8 March 1919.
38 *Western Mail*, 9 May 1922.
39 GCC minutes, 1919–22 (GRO).
40 *Porth Gazette*, 13 May 1922.

7 '*The history of the undertaking is rather peculiar*'. *W. H. Mathias, the Cowbridge–Aberthaw Railway and the Rhondda Connection, 1886–1892.*

1   Information about this, and about the Cowbridge line in general, is taken (except where indicated otherwise) from Colin Chapman's book *The Cowbridge Railway* (Poole: Oxford Publishing Company, 1984).
2   Chapters 1 and 2 of Chapman, *The Cowbridge Railway*, pp. 6–23.
3   'Getting fearfully out of repair', chapter 3 of Chapman, *The Cowbridge Railway*, pp. 24–37.
4   Stan Awbery, *The Story of St Athan and Aberthaw* (Barry: Barry and District News, 1959), p. 43.
5   PRO BT 31/3316/19635.
6   Chapman, *The Cowbridge Railway*, p. 52.
7   Ibid., p. 48.
8   Ibid., p. 52.
9   Ibid., p. 53.
10 PRO BT 31/4048/25849.
11 *South Wales Daily News*, 8 February 1890.

12 Chapman, *The Cowbridge Railway*, p. 53.
13 *South Wales Daily News*, 8 February 1890.
14 Ibid.
15 Awbery, *The Story of St Athan and Aberthaw*, p. 42.
16 Chapman, *The Cowbridge Railway*, p. 61.
17 *South Wales Daily News*, 8 February 1890.
18 *Barry and Cadoxton Journal*, 10 May 1889.
19 Ibid.
20 *Cardiff Times*, 30 August 1890.
21 PRO BT 31/2932/16362.
22 Mathias and Hurman occasionally went on holiday together to the Rock House Hotel, Llandrindod Wells. (See the *Radnorshire Standard*'s listing of guests at local hotels, in August or September of various years in the 1890s and 1900s). And after the Aberthaw venture, Mathias and Hurman were to be close collaborators in a number of other entrepreneurial activities, including the building of the pier at Weston-super-Mare (see p. 58).
23 PRO BT 31/3760/23446.
24 Ibid.
25 PRO BT 31/4048/25849.
26 Much of the general account of this railway is based on Colin Chapman's *The Cowbridge Railway*.
27 Minute Book of the Cowbridge and Aberthaw Railway Company (PRO RAIL 140/1), entries for 19 August and 26 September 1889, and 23 January 1890.
28 *South Wales Daily News*, 8 February 1890.
29 *Kelly's Directory*, 1891.
30 James Mathias's obituary, *South Wales Echo*, 18 November 1940.
31 GRO, L/BY/8-10.
32 John Richards, *The Cowbridge Story: History and Anecdotes of the Ancient Borough* (Bridgend, 1956), p. 100.
33 *South Wales Daily News*, 3 October 1892.
34 Chapman, *The Cowbridge Railway*, p. 67.
35 See T. I. Jeffreys Jones (ed.), *Acts of Parliament Concerning Wales, 1714–1901* (Cardiff: University of Wales Press, 1959), p. 160.
36 PRO RAIL 140/1.
37 PRO BT 31/4048/25849.
38 PRO BT 31/3316/19635.
39 PRO RAIL 140/2.
40 PRO RAIL 140/1.
41 PRO RAIL 140/2.
42 See, e.g., his treatment of the Machen Limestone Company at the meeting of 28/11/90 (GRO, L/BY/8).
43 GRO, L/BY/12.

8 *Further peculiar undertakings: Windsor Colliery Abertridwr and the Parc Newydd Estate*

1   In the list of mineral interests in W. H. Mathias's estate, his interest in the farm is listed as a half share. That the other half was owned by Morgan is attested by various other documents, including Walter Nicholas's evidence to the Select Committee of the House of Lords in relation to the Rhymney Valley Water Board Bill of 1911 (PRO RAIL 1068/250/667).

2   List of mineral interests in W. H. Mathias's estate, produced for probate (research by Michael Mathias).

3   Richard Watson, *Rhondda Coal, Cardiff Gold: The Insoles of Llandaff, Coal Owners and Shippers* (Chesterfield: Merton Priory Press, 1997), p. 112.

4   His barrister Rhys Williams, in evidence to the House of Lords Select Committee in 1911 (PRO RAIL 1068/250).

5   C. Lundie to the Company's solicitors, Bompas, Bischoff, Dodgson, Coxe and Bompas, 16 September 1896 (PRO RAIL 1057/1627).

6   DGA/RA 2/4 (GRO). Also PRO RAIL1068/247–254.

7   PRO BT 31/18021/92371.

8   PRO RAIL 1068/247.

9   In that year, Mathias and Morgan asked the Rhymney Railway Company's permission to run a four inch water-main under the railway. (PRO RAIL 1057/1627).

10 PRO RAIL 1068/248.

11 *Monmouth Guardian*, 2 June 1911.

12 *Bargoed Journal*, 12 January 1911.

13 Petition of W. H. Mathias and Others, PRO RAIL 1068/247.

14 PRO RAIL 1068/247.

15 Minutes of GCC Parliamentary Committee, 1910–1911 (GRO, GCC 1910/2, 1911/1).

16 PRO RAIL 1068/249.

17 PRO BT 31/18021/92371.

18 Minutes of the Rhymney and Aber Valleys Gas and Water Company, 8 February 1915, 23 March 1915, 1 June 1915, 1 May 1917, 22 May 1917, 30 August 1917, 30 October 1917, 3 December 1917, 1 January 1918 and 26 February 1918 (GRO, DGA/RA 2/4).

19 See pp. 214–15.

9 *Heroism or negligence? Siamps Thomas and the Tynewydd Disaster, 1877*

1   The initial account of the inundation is taken from a variety of sources, including: *The Times*; the *Western Mail*; the *Aberdare Times*; the *Merthyr Telegraph*; the *Central Glamorgan Gazette*; Charles Wilkins, *Buried Alive! A narrative of suffering and heroism, being the tale of the Rhondda colliers, as related by themselves* (London: Houlston and Sons, 1877); and Ken Llewellyn, *Disaster at Tynewydd: An Account of a Rhondda Mining Disaster in 1877* (Cardiff: Ap Dafydd Publications Ltd, 1975). The major source is the excellent account in the *Western Mail*.

2   *Western Mail*, 13 April 1877.

3   Charles Wilkins, *Buried Alive!*, p. 75.

4   See *Porth Gazette*, 27 August 1904, and censuses of 1861, 1871 and 1881.

5   *Aberdare Times*, 21 April 1877.

6   *Western Mail*, 16 April 1877.

7   *Western Mail*, 17 April 1877.

8   *Western Mail*, 19 April 1877.

9   *Western Mail*, 20 April 1877.

10 Wilkins, *Buried Alive!*, p. 26.

11 Wilkins, *Buried Alive!*, pp. 43–4. Also *Aberdare Times*, 28 April 1877, *Central Glamorgan Gazette*, 27 April 1877, etc. (with slight variants). If Siamps Thomas's words sound a little stilted, this is no doubt because they were translated literally from the Welsh.

12 *Western Mail*, 23 April 1877.

13 Ibid.

14 *The Graphic*, 28 April 1877.

15 *Western Mail*, 26 April 1877.

16 *The Times*, 24 April 1877.

17 *Western Mail*, 24 April 1877.

18 *Western Mail*, 26 April 1905.

19 *The Times*, 23 April 1877.

20 *The Graphic*, 28 April 1877.

21 *Aberdare Times*, 28 April 1877.

22 *Western Mail*, 26 April 1877.

23 *Western Mail*, 25 April 1877.

24 *Western Mail*, 13 July 1877.

25 *Western Mail*, 25 April 1877.

26 Alexander Macdonald, Liberal MP for Stafford 1874–81. secretary of the Miners' Association for Scotland. President of the Miners' National Association.

27 *Western Mail*, 27 April 1877.

28 *Western Mail*, 1 May 1877.

29 Ibid.

30 *Western Mail*, 5 May 1877.

[31] *Western Mail*, 4 and 5 May 1877.

[32] Thomas Collingdon was to die in 1885, aged ninety-four. In the proceedings of 3 May, Thomas had listed Cope, Lewis and Collingdon as his three partners.

[33] The slippage caused by a fault in the seam could serve as a barrier against water or gas.

[34] *Western Mail*, 17 May 1877.

[35] *Western Mail*, 18 May 1877.

[36] Ibid.

[37] *Western Mail*, 25 May 1877.

[38] William Forsyth, LL.D., QC. Conservative MP for Marylebone since 1874.

[39] *The Times*, 23 May 1877.

[40] See *Western Mail*, 13 July 1877, and *passim*.

[41] *The Times*, 24 May 1877.

[42] *Daily Telegraph*, 12 June 1877.

[43] Ibid., and *Central Glamorgan Gazette*, 10 August 1877.

[44] *London Gazette*, 10 August 1877.

[45] *Western Mail*, 6 August 1877.

[46] *Western Mail*, 14 June 1877.

[47] *Western Mail*, 13 July 1877.

[48] *Western Mail*, 18 July 1877 and *The Times*, 17 July 1877.

[49] *Western Mail*, 19 July 1877.

[50] Ibid.

[51] *Central Glamorgan Gazette*, 27 July 1877.

[52] *Western Mail*, 6 August 1877.

[53] *Central Glamorgan Gazette*, 10 August 1877, and *Western Mail*, 6 August 1877.

[54] Matthew Cope, 'Tynewydd heroes and survivors', *Western Mail*, 28 April 1928.

[55] *Western Mail*, 7 and 8 August 1877, and *Reports of the Inspectors of Mines*, 1877 (HMSO C2003, 1878).

[56] *Western Mail*, 9 August 1877.

[57] *Pontypridd District Herald*, 13 April 1878.

[58] *Western Mail*, 20 October 1877.

[59] *Western Mail*, 8 November 1877.

[60] Joseph Lewis, Jabez Evans, H. S. Davies, Richard Rogers, J. Calvert, Idris Williams. The Revd Bickerton Edwards had originally belonged, but had subsequently withdrawn.

[61] *Western Mail*, 7 November 1877.

[62] *Western Mail*, 10 April 1878

[63] *Pontypridd District Herald*, 13 April 1878.

[64] *Western Mail*, 10 April 1878.

[65] *Pontypridd District Herald*, 13 April 1878.

[66] Ibid.

[67] Ibid.

68 *Western Mail*, 10 August 1878.
69 *Pontypridd District Herald*, 13 April 1878.

10 The Albion Disaster, 1894

1   J. H. Morris and L. J. Williams, *The South Wales Coal Industry 1841–1875*, p. 53.
2   John Williams, 'The coal industry 1750–1914', *Glamorgan County History, V*, 192.
3   Apart from Cope, Lewis and Mathias, the Directors were: Philip Augustus Vyvyan-Robinson (Bute Dock merchant); Thomas Morel (Cardiff shipowner) and Alfred Denton Cheney (6 Crosby Square, London; colliery agent). The initial subscribers were Cope, Vyvyan-Robinson and Cheney, and also Ifor Thomas (Bute Dock Cardiff; ship owner); Philip Morel (Lavernock, nr. Cardiff; ship owner); Chas. Wyndham (Cardiff; banker); and E. C. Hull (4 Fenchurch Avenue, London; merchant, coal exporter) (PRO BT 31/31242/33695).
4   Williams, 'The coal industry 1750–1914', 197.
5   T. Boyns, 'Work and death in the south Wales coalfield, 1874–1914', *Welsh History Review*, 12, 515.
6   Williams, 'The coal industry 1750–1914', 199.
7   Fire-damp is methane gas.
8   R. Meurig Evans, *One Saturday Afternoon: The Albion Colliery, Cilfynydd Explosion of 1894* (Cardiff: National Museum of Wales, 1984), pp. 17–22.
9   The main lines of this description of the disaster are based on R. Meurig Evans's excellent account in *One Saturday Afternoon*. Further details, many of them having bearing on the specific concerns of this book, have been found in the accounts in *The Times*, the *Western Mail*, the *Cardiff Times*, the *Pontypridd Chronicle*, the *Pontypridd District Herald*, and the *Glamorgan Free Press*.
10 *The Times*, 25 June 1894.
11 Evans, *One Saturday Afternoon*, p. 27.
12 Matthew Cope, 'The Albion Colliery disaster', *Western Mail*, 28 April 1928.
13 *Western Mail*, 25 June 1894.
14 *Pontypridd Chronicle*, 29 June 1894.
15 *Pontypridd District Herald*, 30 June 1894.
16 *Cardiff Times*, 30 June 1894.
17 Ibid.
18 Evans, *One Saturday Afternoon*, p. 29.
19 Evans, *One Saturday Afternoon*, p. 31.
20 *Pontypridd Chronicle*, 29 June 1894.
21 Evans, *One Saturday Afternoon*, p. 32.
22 *Pontypridd Chronicle*, 29 June 1894.
23 Evans, *One Saturday Afternoon*, p. 32.
24 *Western Mail*, 27 June 1894. *Pontypridd Chronicle*, 6 July 1894.
25 *Western Mail*, 27 June 1894.

[26] *Pontypridd Chronicle*, 6 July 1894.

[27] Ibid.

[28] *Cardiff Times*, 30 June 1894.

[29] *Western Mail*, 27 June 1894.

[30] *Pontypridd Chronicle*, 6 July 1894.

[31] Catrin Stevens, 'The burial question: controversy and conflict, *c.*1860–1890', *Welsh History Review*, 21, 2 (December 2002), 328–56.

[32] Evans, *One Saturday Afternoon*, p.35.

[33] *Pontypridd Chronicle*, 6 July 1894

[34] Ibid.

[35] *Pontypridd Chronicle*, 13 July 1894

[36] *Pontypridd Chronicle*, 29 June 1894.

[37] *Western Mail*, 25 June 1894.

[38] *Pontypridd Chronicle*, 29 June 1894.

[39] *Pontypridd District Herald*, 30 June 1894.

[40] *Western Mail*, 2 July 1894.

[41] Morris and Williams, *The South Wales Coal Industry 1841–1875*, p. 206.

[42] *Western Mail*, 28 June 1894.

[43] Except where it is notified otherwise, the greater part of this account is based on the detailed reports of the inquest that appeared in the *Western Mail* between 17 and 28 July 1894.

[44] Abel Thomas, QC, MP. Born 1848. Son of a Pembrokeshire clergyman. Educated Clifton College and University of London. Called to the Bar at the Middle Temple in 1875. South Wales and Chester circuits. QC, 1892. Liberal MP for Camarthenshire East from 1890 until his death in 1912.

[45] Sir Samuel Thomas Evans, MP. Born Skewen 1859. Called to Bar 1891. Liberal MP for Mid Division of Glamorganshire from 1890 to 1910, when he was appointed President of the Probate, Divorce and Admiralty Division of the High Court. He died in 1918.

[46] *Cardiff Times*, 30 June 1894.

[47] For most of this information on John Roskill, I am grateful to his grandson, Nicholas Roskill.

[48] *The Times*, 21 August 1940.

[49] Ibid.

[50] See arguments put forward by T. E. Wales in 1879, and his successor J. T. Robson in 1887 and 1888, reported in T. Boyns, 'Technical change and colliery explosions in the south Wales coalfield, *c.*1870–1914', *Welsh History Review*, 13, 172.

[51] *Cardiff Times*, 21 July 1894.

[52] *Cardiff Times*, 4 August 1894.

[53] *Cardiff Times*, 11 August 1894.

[54] *Pontypridd Chronicle*, 21 September 1888.

[55] Quoted in Evans, *One Saturday Afternoon*, p. 58. My italics.

[56] Ibid.

[57] *Western Mail*, 31 July 1894. In the 1921 *Who's Who in Wales* T. Pascoe Jenkins was to describe himself as 'The first Labour Magistrate in Wales . . . for many years Chairman Rhondda Liberal-Labour Association.' His views on the Albion disaster, and his actions as magistrate, seem to show, however, that by becoming a magistrate he must have 'gone native' and produced views more typical of his fellow-magistrates.

[58] Matthew Cope, 'The Albion colliery disaster', *Western Mail*, 28 April 1928.

[59] *Pontypridd Chronicle*, 27 July 1894.

[60] *Glamorgan Free Press*, 28 July 1894.

[61] *Pontypridd Chronicle*, 27 July 1894.

[62] *Western Mail*, 1 August 1894.

[63] *Western Mail*, 31 July 1894.

[64] *Report to the Secretary of State on the Disaster at Albion Colliery Cilfynydd, near Pontypridd, on the 23rd June 1894. By J. Roskill, Esq, Barrister-at-Law.*

[65] Except where stated otherwise, the account of these proceedings is taken from the *Western Mail* of 17–19 October 1894.

[66] Morris and Williams, *The South Wales Coal Industry, 1841–75*, p. 200.

[67] *Western Mail*, 18 October 1894.

[68] A case is defined as a statement of the facts of a matter *sub judice*, for a higher court.

[69] Mandamus: a judicial writ issued in the Sovereign's name from the Court of King's Bench, and directed to an inferior court, commanding something to be done.

[70] T. Boyns, 'Technical change and colliery explosions in the south Wales coalfield, *c.*1870–1914', *Welsh History Review*, 13, 173–5.

11 The 1893 Hauliers' Strike

[1] Much of the general information given here about the strike is based on an excellent article by Michael and Richard Keen, 'The coal war in south Wales, 1893', in Stuart Williams (ed.), *Glamorgan Historian X* (1974), 35–49; and also on E. D. Lewis's *The Rhondda Valleys*, Phoenix House, London, 1958 (reprint, University College Cardiff Press, 1984).

[2] Keen and Keen, 'The coal war', 40–1.

[3] *Glamorgan Free Press*, 19 August 1893.

[4] *South Wales Daily News*, 4 September 1893.

[5] *Tarian y Gweithiwr*, 25 May 1878, quoted in Lewis, *The Rhondda Valleys*, p. 167.

[6] Keen and Keen, 'The coal war', 39; Lewis, *The Rhondda Valleys*, p. 170.

[7] Lewis, *The Rhondda Valleys*, p. 170.

[8] See the Home Secretary, Asquith, in the House of Commons on 22 August 1893.

[9] Keen and Keen, 'The coal war', 44.

[10] McIvor tells us that in the north of England 'Employers resorted to the law courts . . . in an attempt to punish and intimidate, and discourage future strike action and other behaviour regarded by management as "deviant". Amongst others, the cotton and coal employers' organisations encouraged their members to prosecute for breach of contract where workmen had gone on strike without giving notice.' (Arthur J. McIvor, *Organised Capital: Employers' Associations and Industrial Relations in Northern England 1880–1939* (Cambridge: Cambridge University Press, 1996), p. 105.

[11] Keen and Keen, 'The coal war', 42.

[12] Ibid., 44.

[13] See retrospective reports at the time of the 1898 strike (quoted in chapter 12).

[14] Reported in *Pontypridd Chronicle*, 4 August 1893

[15] *Pontypridd Chronicle*, 1 September 1893.

[16] *Glamorgan Free Press*, 12 August 1893.

[17] *Western Mail*, 8 August 1893.

[18] *Pontypridd District Herald*, 12 August 1893.

[19] McIvor notes that judges, too, were often affected by sympathy with the employers. In the north of England, 'The employers were aided . . . by the biased, traditionally conservative, anti-labour attitudes of the bulk of the judiciary.' (McIvor, *Organised Capital*, p. 105).

[20] *Cardiff Times*, 12 August 1893.

[21] *Cardiff Times*, 19 August 1893.

[22] Ibid.

[23] *The Times*, 14 August 1893.

[24] *Western Mail*, 12 August 1893.

[25] *Glamorgan Free Press*, 19 August 1893. It is worth noting, however, that despite such rhetoric Brace issued a statement to the press, on the day the troops arrived, 'denying any personal responsibility for the strike, and disclaiming, on behalf of the Miners' Federation of Great Britain, any connexion with the hauliers.' (Keen and Keen, 'The coal war', 45).

[26] *Pontypridd District Herald*, 12 August 1893.

[27] Keen and Keen, 'The coal war', 45.

[28] Ibid., 42.

[29] *The Times*, 19 August 1893.

[30] Ibid.

[31] Keen and Keen, 'The coal war', 45.

[32] *The Times*, 19 August 1893.

[33] *Western Mail*, 19 August 1893.

[34] *Western Mail*, 21 August 1893.

[35] *The Times*, 19 August 1893.

[36] *Western Mail*, 19 August 1893.

[37] *Pontypridd Chronicle*, 25 August 1893.

[38] *The Times*, 21 August 1893.

[39] *Western Mail*, 22 August 1893.
[40] *The Times*, 23 August 1893.
[41] PRO HO 144/250/A55059B.
[42] See, e.g., *Glamorgan Free Press*, 26 August 1893.
[43] *Pontypridd District Herald*, 26 August 1893.
[44] Keen and Keen, 'The coal war', 45.
[45] *Western Mail*, 22 August 1893.
[46] *Western Mail*, 19 August 1893.
[47] *Western Mail*, 21 August 1893.
[48] Ibid. The same story, almost identically told, can be found in the *Glamorgan Free Press*, 26 August 1893.
[49] *Pontypridd Chronicle*, 25 August 1893.
[50] PRO HO 144/250/A55059B.
[51] *Western Mail*, 22 August 1893.
[52] *Western Mail*, 5 September 1893.
[53] *Western Mail*, 2, 4 and 5 September 1893.
[54] It is surprising to note that despite this, McIvor, in his treatment of employers' strike-breaking tactics in the north of England, does not mention the deployment of the military. (McIvor, 'Strikebreaking', in *Organised Capital*, pp. 92–117).
[55] Jane Morgan, *Conflict and Order: The Police and Labour Disputes in England and Wales, 1900–1939* (Oxford: Clarendon Press, 1987), p. 36.
[56] PRO HO 144/254/A55059N.

12 The 1898 Strike

[1] I am grateful to Dr Andy Croll, of the University of Glamorgan (who is preparing a major article on the 1898 strike) for items of information, and for very useful discussions on this matter. An important source, too, has been the chapter 'The strike of 1898' in John Williams, *Was Wales Industrialised? Essays in Modern Welsh History* (Llandysul: Gomer, 1995), pp. 192–213.
[2] Williams, 'The strike of 1898', p. 192.
[3] See Hywel Francis and David Smith, *The Fed: A History of the South Wales Miners in the Twentieth century* (London: Lawrence and Wishart, 1980).
[4] Williams, 'The strike of 1898', pp. 192–5.
[5] *Western Mail*, 1 April 1898.
[6] *Western Mail*, 2 April 1898.
[7] *Western Mail*, 1 April 1898.
[8] *Pontypridd Chronicle*, 15 April 1898.
[9] *Merthyr Express*, 16 April 1898.
[10] *Pontypridd Chronicle*, 22 April 1898.
[11] Ibid.
[12] *Merthyr Express*, 23 April 1898.

13 Minutes of Board of Guardians of Merthyr Tydfil Union, 23 and 26 April 1898 (GRO, U/M 1/25).

14 He was descended from James Lindsay, 26th Earl of Crawford, from another Lindsay, the 5th Earl of Balcarres, and (through his grandmother) from the Earls of Arran.

15 Jane Morgan, *Conflict and Order: The Police and Labour Disputes in England and Wales, 1900–1939* (Oxford: Clarendon Press, 1987), p. 32.

16 Jane Morgan, 'Police and labour in the age of Lindsay, 1910–1936', *Llafur*, V, 1, 15–20.

17 R. Page Arnot, *South Wales Miners: A History of the S.W.M.F., 1898–1914*, p. 82, quoted in Deian Hopkin, 'Patriots and pacifists in Wales 1914–1918: the case of Captain Lionel Lindsay and the Rev. T. E. Nicholas', *Llafur*, I, 3 (1974), 132–46.

18 Jane Morgan, 'Police and labour in the age of Lindsay', 15–20.

19 PRO HO 144/254/A55059N.

20 Jane Morgan, *Conflict and Order*, pp. 37–8.

21 Chief Constable's Report to Glamorgan County Council Standing Committee, 10 June 1898 (GRO, GC SJ/4/1).

22 *Merthyr Express*, 4 June 1898.

23 See *Cardiff Times*, 4 and 11 June 1898, Captain Lindsay's Diary, 28 May 1898 (GRO), Lindsay's Report of 10 June to the Joint Standing Committee of the Glamorgan County Council (GRO, GC SJ/4/1), etc.

24 Lindsay's Diary, 29 May 1898 (GRO).

25 PRO HO 144/518/X69161.

26 Lindsay's Diary, 8 June 1898; *Merthyr Express*, 11 June 1898.

27 Lindsay's Diary, entries for 18 and 29 May, 9 and 10 June 1898 (GRO)

28 Major H. Morgan, Report to Home Office, 10 June 1898 (PRO HO 144/518/X69161).

29 Chief Constable's Report to GCC Standing Joint Committee, 1 September 1898 (GRO, GC SJ/4/1).

30 *Cardiff Times*, 18 June 1898.

31 *South Wales Daily News*, 11 June 1898.

32 *Cardiff Times*, 18 June 1898.

33 Ibid.

34 Lindsay's Diary, entry for 13 June 1898 (GRO).

35 PRO HO 144/518/X69161.

36 *Cardiff Times*, 18 June 1898.

37 Ibid.

38 PRO HO 144/518/X69161, note of 14 June 1898.

30 Ibid.

40 Report from Lionel Lindsay, Chief Constable for Glamorgan, 18 June 1898 (PRO HO 144/518/X69161).

41 *The Times*, 25 June 1898.

42   Letter from D.A.Thomas MP to Mountain Ash District Council, 1 July 1898 (*Cardiff Times*, 16 July 1898).

43   *Pontypridd Chronicle*, 1 July 1898, and Merthyr Express, 2 July 1898.

44   *Cardiff Times*, 10 September 1898.

45   *The Times*, 17 June 1898.

46   Quoted in John Williams, 'The strike of 1898', p. 204.

47   *South Wales Daily News*, 14 July 1898.

48   *Pontypridd Chronicle*, 1 July 1898.

49   *South Wales Daily News*, 27 June 1898.

50   *South Wales Daily News*, 5 July 1898.

51   Ibid.

52   *Cardiff Times*, 16 July 1898.

53   *Cardiff Times*, 23 July 1898.

54   See pp. 29–30.

55   E. W. Evans, *Mabon (William Abraham 1842–1922): A Study in Trade Union Leadership* (Cardiff: University of Wales Press, 1959), p. 46.

56   Minutes of Board of Guardians of Merthyr Tydfil Union, 23 July 1898 (GRO, U/M 1/25).

57   Ibid., 16 July 1898 (GRO, U/M 1/25).

58   Ibid., 30 July 1898 (GRO, U/M 1/25).

59   Ibid., 21 June 1898 (GRO, U/M 1/25).

60   *Cardiff Times*, 30 July 1898.

61   Report of Captain Lindsay to Home Office, 17 August 1898 (PRO HO 144/518/X69161).

62   Williams, 'The strike of 1898', p. 207.

63   *South Wales Daily News*, 2 September 1898; quoted in Williams, 'The strike of 1898', p. 208.

13 'One of the greatest of the Welsh coalowners': William James Thomas's business interests, 1900–1925

1   *Crachach* can be translated as a self-appointed elite.

2   *Porth Gazette*, 8 November 1902.

3   PRO BT 31/3760/23446.

4   *Porth Gazette*, 29 April 1905.

5   Matthew Cope, 'Marriage and industrial enterprise', *Western Mail*, 14 April 1928.

6   PRO BT 31/18634/100542.

7   R. H. Walters, *The Economic and Business History of the South Wales Steam Coal Industry, 1880–1914* (New York: Arno Press, 1977), p. 60.

8   *The Powell Duffryn Steam Coal Company Ltd, 1864–1914* (n.d.).

9   Walters, *The Economic and Business History*, p. 67.

[10] Alun Burge, 'Exorcising demonologies? Coal companies and colliery communities in south Wales', *Llafur*, 9, 4 (2007), 101–9.

[11] PRO BT 31/18634/100542.

[12] *Western Mail*, 1 January 1914.

[13] Minutes of the Rhymney and Aber Valleys Gas and Water Company, 1898–1906 (DGA/RA 2/1), 1906–1910 (DGA/RA 2/2), 1910-1914 (DGA/RA 2/3) and 1914–18 (DGA/RA 2/4). Also minutes of shareholders' meetings, 1898–1947 (DGA/RA 3), all in GRO.

[14] DGA/RA 2/3.

[15] GRO DGA/RA 2/3, PRO MT 10/1685, and PRO MT 10/1947.

[16] PRO MT 10/1947.

[17] D.S.M. Barrie, *The Barry Railway* (St Albans: The Oakfield Press, 1962), p. 159.

[18] PRO RAIL 23/6.

[19] Barrie, *The Barry Railway*.

[20] *Western Mail*, 1 January 1914.

[21] *Porth Gazette*, 21 March 1914.

[22] *Porth Gazette*, 28 March 1914.

[23] *Porth Gazette*, 13 June 1914.

[24] *South Wales Daily News*, 1 October 1910.

[25] *South Wales Daily News*, 14 October 1910.

[26] Watts Morgan, whom Chris Williams describes as 'following in Mabon's footsteps in his political Liberalism', was after the war to be attacked, by a representative of the new Left in the Rhondda, as 'reactionary . . . both industrially and politically' who 'has no conception of the economics and ethos of socialism' ('Demos', in the *Merthyr Pioneer*, 9 March 1918, quoted in Chris Williams, *Democratic Rhondda*, p. 125. See also Chris Williams, *Democratic Rhondda*, p. 64).

[27] *Porth Gazette*, 24 August 1912.

[28] As early as 1905, the *Porth Gazette* had been suggesting that he should be appointed a JP to succeed the recently deceased Thomas Jones Ynyshir, describing him as 'of irreproachable character' (*Porth Gazette*, 16 September 1905). Soon thereafter he was in fact made a JP.

[29] *Porth Gazette*, 16 September 1905.

[30] To doubts as to whether the Rhondda Liberals were 'pledging themselves to go in for Socialism in the future', a reassuring answer was given at a meeting on 15 December 1909: 'They would all agree, that Mabon was still the same in his principles, and he could not change them even if he tried. They need not fear to give him their undivided support (Applause).' (*South Wales Daily News*, 16 December 1909).

[31] *South Wales Daily News*, 8 January 1910.

[32] Ibid.

[33] Chris Williams, *Democratic Rhondda*, p. 246.

[34] *South Wales Daily News*, 8 January 1910.

35   *South Wales Daily News*, 21 January 1910.
36   *South Wales Daily News*, 20 April 1910.
37   *Porth Gazette*, 23 April 1910 and *Chronicle for South and Mid Glamorgan*, 22 April 1910.
38   *Porth Gazette*, 23 April 1910.
39   *South Wales Daily News*, 26 May 1910.
40   *South Wales Daily News*, 29 June 1910.
41   Allen Clement Edwards, Liberal MP Denbigh District 1906–January 1910; Liberal MP East Glamorgan December 1910–18. National Democratic MP, East Ham South, 1918–22. Had contested Tottenham in 1895, as a 'Progressive Labour' candidate.
42   *Chronicle for South and Mid Glamorgan*, 11 March and 24 June 1910.
43   Minutes of GCC and its committees, 1910–19 (GRO).
44   *Porth Gazette*, 14 November 1914.
45   Matthew Cope, 'Marriage and industrial enterprise', in *Western Mail*, 14 April 1928.
46   Colin Baber and Dennis Thomas, 'The Glamorgan economy, 1914–1945', in *Glamorgan County History, Volume 5: Industrial Glamorgan* (Cardiff: Glamorgan County History Trust, 1980), p. 520.
47   PRO BT 31/18634/100542.
48   PRO BT 31/24731/156141.
49   John Richards, *Cardiff: A Maritime History* (Stroud: Tempus, 2005), p. 118.
50   PRO BT 31/24731/156141
51   David Jenkins, *Owen and Watkin Williams of Cardiff: The Golden Cross Line* (Kendal: World Ship Society, 1991), pp. 336–47.

14 'Ynyshir's most noted citizen, the Principality's most noble benefactor': William James Thomas's many benefactions, and later years

1   *Porth Gazette*, 8 November 1902.
2   *Western Mail*, 18 October 1894.
3   Steven Thompson, 'To relieve the sufferings of humanity, irrespective of party, politics or creed?: conflict, consensus and voluntary hospital provision in Edwardian south Wales', *Social History of Medicine*, 16 (2003), 250–1.
4   *Western Mail*, 18 October 1894.
5   *Porth Gazette*, 27 June 1903.
6   *Porth Gazette*, 27 September 1902.
7   The tablets commemorating these two dedications can now be found in a showcase on the first floor of the Royal Glamorgan Hospital, in the Ely Valley near Llantrisant.
8   *Porth Gazette*, 3 October 1908.
9   *Porth Gazette*, 2 January 1909.

10 W. F. Bynum, 'Medical philanthropy after 1850', in W. F. Bynum and Roy Porter (eds), *Companion Encyclopedia of the History of Medicine*, 2, 1485.

11 Ibid.

12 *Porth Gazette*, 25 May 1901.

13 Much of this account is based on an article by Neil Evans, '"The first charity in Wales": Cardiff Infirmary and south Wales society, 1837–1914', *Welsh History Review*, IX, 319–46.

14 Ibid.

15 Alun Roberts, *The Welsh National School of Medicine 1893–1931: The Cardiff Years* (Cardiff: University of Wales Press, 2008), p. 58.

16 *Porth Gazette*, 2 January 1909.

17 Ibid.

18 *Porth Gazette*, 13 July 1912.

19 *Western Mail*, 13 July 1912.

20 *Western Mail*, 1 January 1914.

21 *South Wales Echo*, 3 January 1945.

22 E. L. Ellis, *T. J.: A Life of Dr Thomas Jones, CH* (Cardiff: University of Wales Press, 1992), p.165.

23 *Who's Who in Wales* (Cardiff, Western Mail Ltd, 1921), p. 474. Also *Porth Gazette*, 3 July 1915.

24 *Porth Gazette*, 17 January 1914.

25 *Porth Gazette, passim*.

26 *Porth Gazette*, 29 May 1909.

27 *Glamorgan Free Press and Rhondda Leader*, 30 August 1930.

28 The Revd Huw Rhydderch, in conversation with the author.

29 PRO T 1/12297.

30 PRO TS 27/611.

31 *Porth Gazette*, 16 March 1916.

32 *Porth Gazette*, 15 June 1916.

33 Hyperbolic praise for the rich and powerful, in relation to their charitable giving, was rife in the industrial areas of England and Wales. Shapely gives us an example, from Manchester. The successful engineer Frank Crossley was described as 'a nineteenth-century saint whom Saint Francis of Assisi might have recognised as a brother of faith and spirit', and a character 'so wholeheartedly and so nobly unselfish' that 'he lived in an atmosphere purer and less tainted by earth than that breathed by ordinary men.' (J. R. Harris, *The Life of F.W. Crossley*, pp. v–vi, and *Manchester Guardian obituary*, 27 March 1892, both quoted in Peter Shapely, *Charity and Power in Victorian Manchester*, Manchester: Chetham Society, 2000, p. 75.)

34 PRO TS 27/611.

35 *Porth Gazette*, 15 June 1918.

36 David Cannadine, *The Decline and Fall of the British Aristocracy* (London: Papermac, 1996), p. 315.

37 A list of honours had been presented to the King on 30 December 1918. On the Prime Ministerial file, all that remains of it are the Civil Service Honours, the list of the other honours to be given having been withdrawn (PRO PREM 2/14).

38 Cannadine, *The Decline and Fall of the British Aristocracy*, pp. 315–16.

39 PRO PREM 2/14.

40 *The Times*, 29 April 1919.

41 *Western Mail*, 29 April 1919.

42 Shapely, *Charity and Power*, p. 85.

43 See, for example, Alan J. Kidd's comments on M. Bulmer, *Neighbours: The Work of Philip Abrams* (Cambridge: Cambridge University Press, 1986) in 'Philanthropy and the "social history paradigm"', *Social History* 21, 2 (1996), 185.

44 Kidd, 'Philanthropy and the "social history paradigm"', 192.

45 Ibid., 189.

46 Ibid., 184–6.

47 Peter Shapely, 'Charity, status and leadership: charitable image and the Manchester man', *Journal of Social History*, 32, 1 (1998), 169. See also Shapely, *Charity and Power*, p. 84.

48 L. J. Williams, 'The Coalowners', in David Smith (ed.), *A People and a Proletariat: Essays in the History of Wales 1780–1980* (London: Pluto Press, 1980), pp. 106–7.

49 *Porth Gazette, passim*.

50 Two of them, Cissie and Maud, were to remain unmarried. Rachel married the barrister Abraham James in 1918.

51 *British Journal of Nursing*, 21 April 1917, p. 275.

52 '[A]nd I request him to use my house called Brynawel as a residence for himself.' Last Will and Testament of James Thomas, 26 March 1901.

53 'La ruée vers la mer', the rush to the sea, is the term given to the rapid development of the trench system across northern France in 1914, as each side, trying to outflank the other, dug themselves in, facing each other, across the country as far as the sea. It seems a good term for the rapid exodus of so many people from the Valleys to the coastal towns and to the Vale of Glamorgan, once they had made their pile.

54 In the early 1880s Watkin Williams bought The Verlands, a Georgian mansion in extensive grounds. (See *Kelly's Directory*, 1884, and Prichard, 'The Squire of Fairfield'). He also bought Broadway Farm, which he let to a local dairy farmer (Cowbridge Record Society, *Llanblethian: Buildings and People*, 2001, p. 88).

55 William Griffiths bought Lake Farm, Cowbridge, in 1884 (documents in author's possession).

56 William Rees bought the Georgian property Kingscombe House, in Llanblethian, in 1886. He came to live there himself, and took up a new life as a dairy farmer. Nine years later he sold the property, and moved to an attractive villa called The Thorne, which he renamed Rhondda Villa (*Llanblethian: Buildings and People*, p. 48).

57 He arrived in the 1890s (*Porth Gazette*, 27 March 1915).

58 *Who's Who in Wales*, 1921.

59 Various editions of *Kelly's Directory*.

60 *Porth Gazette*, 15 January 1907.

61 *Porth Gazette*, 5 April 1913.

62 The author's own observation, in the 1950s.

63 See the commemorative stones outside the church hall, in Penywain Road.

64 PRO RAIL 250/60.

65 For example the 'Hospital Cup' which he gave to the Llandrindod Wells Bowls Tournament in 1932. After his death, it was called the 'Sir William James Thomas Cup'.

Conclusion

1   *Who's Who in Wales* (Cardiff: Western Mail Ltd, 1921).

2   Ibid.

3   Colin Baber and Dennis Thomas, 'The Glamorgan economy 1914–1945', *Glamorgan County History*, 5, p. 527.

4   Michael Asteris, 'The Rise and decline of south Wales coal exports, 1870–1930', *Welsh History Review*, 13, 42.

5   Baber and Thomas, 'The Glamorgan economy', pp. 522–3.

6   An exception to this, in the Mathias family, was William Henry Mathias's great-grandson Derek Mathias Tudor Williams, who made a fortune in the property market in the 1950s and 1960s. Derek died young, leaving a substantial bequest to the National Museum of Wales which is now administered by the 'Derek Williams Trust'.

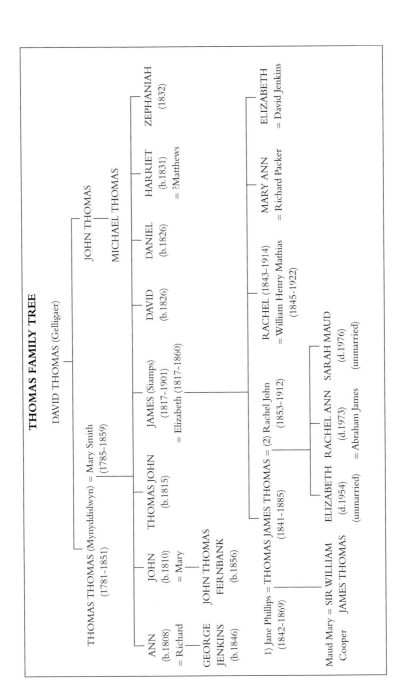

THOMAS FAMILY TREE

DAVID THOMAS (Gelligaer)

THOMAS THOMAS (Mynyddislwyn) = Mary Smith
(1781-1851)   (1785-1859)

JOHN THOMAS

MICHAEL THOMAS

ANN
(b.1808)
= Richard

JOHN
(b.1810)
= Mary

THOMAS JOHN
(b.1815)

JAMES (Siamps)
(1817-1901)
= Elizabeth (1817-1860)

DAVID
(b.1826)

DANIEL
(b.1826)

HARRIET
(b.1831)
= ?Matthews

ZEPHANIAH
(1832)

GEORGE
JENKINS

JOHN THOMAS
FERNBANK
(b.1856)

1) Jane Phillips = THOMAS JAMES THOMAS = (2) Rachel John
(1842-1869)   (1841-1885)   (1853-1912)

RACHEL (1843-1914)
= William Henry Mathias
(1845-1922)

MARY ANN
= Richard Packer

ELIZABETH
= David Jenkins

Maud Mary = SIR WILLIAM
Cooper   JAMES THOMAS

ELIZABETH
(d.1954)
(unmarried)

RACHEL ANN
(d.1973)
= Abraham James

SARAH MAUD
(d.1976)
(unmarried)

MATHIAS FAMILY TREE

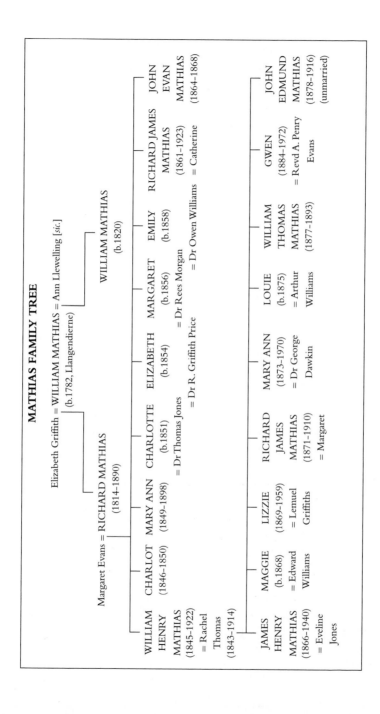

Elizabeth Griffith = WILLIAM MATHIAS = Ann Llewelling [sic.]
(b.1782, Llangendierne)

Margaret Evans = RICHARD MATHIAS (1814–1890)

WILLIAM MATHIAS (b.1820)

WILLIAM HENRY MATHIAS (1845–1922) = Rachel Thomas (1843–1914)

CHARLOT (1846–1850)

MARY ANN (1849–1898)

CHARLOTTE (b.1851) = Dr Thomas Jones

ELIZABETH (b.1854) = Dr R. Griffith Price

MARGARET (b.1856) = Dr Rees Morgan

EMILY (b.1858) = Dr Owen Williams

RICHARD JAMES MATHIAS (1861–1923) = Catherine

JOHN EVAN MATHIAS (1864–1868)

JAMES HENRY MATHIAS (1866–1940) = Eveline Jones

MAGGIE (b.1868) = Edward Williams

LIZZIE (1869–1959) = Lemuel Griffiths

RICHARD JAMES MATHIAS (1871–1910) = Margaret

MARY ANN (1873–1970) = Dr George Dawkin

LOUIE (b.1875) = Arthur Williams

WILLIAM THOMAS MATHIAS (1877–1893)

JOHN EDMUND MATHIAS (1878–1916) (unmarried)

GWEN (1884–1972) = Revd A. Penry Evans

Bibliography

Archives

PRO: National Archives (Public Record Office)

BT 31/3316/19635: Daniel Owen and Company Ltd.

BT 31/2932/16362: Aber Rhondda Colliery Company Ltd.

BT 31/3278/19302: Rhondda and Treferig Workmen's Cottage Company Ltd.

BT 31/3760/23446: Aber Rhondda Coal Company Ltd.

BT 31/4048/25849: Aberthaw Pebble Lime Company Ltd.

BT 31/5974/42128: Llancaiach Collieries Company Ltd.

BT 31/16674/70655: Windsor Steam Coal Company (1901) Ltd.

BT 31/17065/77933: Cardiff and Channel Mills Ltd.

BT 31/18021/92371: Gwernymilwr Land Company Ltd.

BT 31/18634/100542: Bedwas Navigation Colliery Company Ltd.

BT 31/24731/156141: Rhondda Merthyr Shipping Company Ltd.

BT 31/31242/33695: Albion Steam Coal Company Ltd.

BT 285/637: Treferig Valley Railway Company.

HO 144/250/A55059B: Home Office files, 1893 strike.

HO 144/254/A55059N: Report of Interdepartmental Committee on Riots.

HO 144/518/X69161: Home Office files, 1898 strike.

MT 6/2408/19: Taff Vale Railway: New siding at Fforest Wood Quarry, Llanharry, 1915.

MT 6/442/9: Taff Vale Railway: Church Village Station.

MT 10/1685: Rhymney and Aber Valleys Gas and Water Bill, 1914.

MT 10/1947: Rhymney and Aber Valleys Gas and Water Bill, 1918.
NATS 1/928: Road Stone Control Committee.
PREM 2/14: Delayed New Year's Honours, 1919.
RAIL 23/6: Barry Railway Company.
RAIL 23/7: Barry Railway Company.
RAIL 250/50–60: Great Western Railway Board Minutes.
RAIL 684/154: Agreement between TVR and Treferig Valley Railway Company, 1881.
RAIL 1057/1627: Rhymney Railway Company: Parc Newydd Estate.
RAIL 1057/1826: Cowbridge Railway Company.
RAIL 1057/1830: Treferig Valley Railway Company.
RAIL 1057/1832: Cowbridge Railway Company.
RAIL 1057/1833: Cowbridge Railway Company.
RAIL 1068/247–254: House of Lords Select Committee: Rhymney Valley Water Board Bill.
RAIL 140/1: Cowbridge and Aberthaw Railway Company.
RAIL 140/2: Cowbridge and Aberthaw Railway Company.
RAIL 1057/2856: History of Llancaiach Branch.
RAIL 1027/123: Dispute between Rhondda UDC and Taff Vale Railway Company, 1905–7.
RAIL 1027/175: Arbitration between Rhondda UDC and Taff Vale Railway Company, 1907.
RAIL 1110/461: Treferig Valley Railway Company.
T 1/12297: Sale of Netley Hospital.
TS 27/611: re Welsh Hospital (Netley) Fund: Sir William J. Thomas v. the Attorney General.

GRO: Glamorgan Record Office

DGA/RA: Minutes of Rhymney and Aber Valleys Gas and Water Company.
D/D CL Bute XX111/2: Apprenticeship Records.
D/D X 181 1.2: 'Reminiscences of an 89-year-old native of Eglwysilan.'
D/LLE: Papers of the Llewellyn family of Baglan and Cwrt Colman.
E/SB/40: Minutes of Llanwonno School Board.
GC/CC: Minutes of Glamorgan County Council.
GC/LG: Minutes of Glamorgan County Council Local Government Committee.
GC/RB: Minutes of Glamorgan County Council Roads and Bridges Committee.

GC/SJ: Minutes of Glamorgan County Council Standing Joint Committee. (Reports of Chief Constable, etc.)
H/B Pp: Minutes of Pontypridd District Highway Board.
L/B Y: Minutes of Ystradyfodwg Urban Sanitary Authority.
UD/R C: Minutes of Rhondda Urban District Council.
U/M: Minutes of Board of Guardians of Merthyr Tydfil Union.
U/Pp: Minutes of Pontypridd Board of Guardians.
Diary of Captain Lionel Lindsay, Chief Constable of Glamorgan.

Other Unpublished Sources

Wills, Probates, etc.
Baptism and Marriage Records, and Birth and Death Certificates.
Mathias family Bible (in author's possession).
Mathias family photographs (in author's possession).
List of possessions of W. H. Mathias at death (provided by Michael Mathias).
Monuments and gravestones in the graveyards of Groeswen Chapel, New Bethel Chapel Mynyddislwyn, St Mabon's Church Llanfabon, Glyntaff Cemetery (Pontypridd) and Cathays Cemetery (Cardiff).

Official Reports, etc.

Censuses of 1841, 1851, 1861, 1871, 1881, 1891 and 1901.
Children's Employment Commission 1842: Report by Robert Hugh Franks, Esq., on the Employment of Children and Young Persons in the Collieries and the Ironworks of South Wales, the district of Merthyr Tydfil, the collieries of Monmouthshire, Glamorganshire and Pembrokeshire, and on the State, Condition and Treatment of such Children and Young Persons. Edited by Ian Winstanley (Wigan: Picks Publishing).
Reports of the Inspectors of Mines, 1877 (HMSO C2003, 1878).
Report on the Albion Colliery Explosion, by J.T. Robson, Henry Hall and Joseph S. Martin (1894).
Report to the Secretary of State on the Disaster at Albion Colliery Cilfynydd, near Pontypridd, 23rd June 1894. By J. Roskill, Esq., Barrister-at-law (1894).

Newspapers

Aberdare Times.
Bargoed Journal.
Barry and Cadoxton Journal.
Barry Dock News.
British Journal of Nursing.
Cardiff Times.
Central Glamorgan Gazette.
Chronicle for South and Mid Glamorgan.
Daily Telegraph.
Free Press and Rhondda Leader.
Glamorgan Free Press.
The Graphic.
Illustrated London News.
London Gazette.
Merthyr Express.
Merthyr Telegraph.
Monmouth Guardian.
Pontypridd Chronicle.
Pontypridd District Herald.
Porth Gazette.
Porth Gazette and Rhondda Leader.
Radnorshire Standard.
Rhondda Leader.
South Wales Daily News.
South Wales Echo.
The Spectator.
The Times.
Western Mail.
Weston and Somerset Mercury.

Directories, Maps, etc.

Burke's Peerage, Baronetage and Knightage (various editions).
Butcher's Cardiff District Directory, 1880–1.
Debrett (various editions).
The Dictionary of Welsh Biography down to 1940 (London: Honourable
   Society of Cymmrodorion, 1959).

Kelly's Directory of Monmouthshire and South Wales, 1884, 1891, 1895, 1901, 1906, 1910, 1914 and 1920.

Heywood's Guide, 1891.

Ladies' Who's Who.

Lawrence, Ray, *The South Wales Coalfield Directory*, 1998.

Ordnance Survey Maps, 1875.

Oxford Dictionary of National Biography (Oxford: Oxford University Press, 2004)

Rees, Ivor Thomas, *Welsh Hustings 1885–2004: A Who's Who of Parliamentary, European and Assembly Candidates in Wales*. (Llandybïe: Dinefwr Press, 2005).

Slaters Commercial Directories, 1880.

South Wales Coal and Iron Companies (various dates).

South Wales and Monmouthshire Directory and Buyers' Guide, 1907.

W.E. Owen and Co's General, Topographical and Historical Directory for Glamorganshire, Monmouthshire, etc., 1878.

Western Mail Ltd, Pontypridd and District Directory, October 1913.

Who's Who.

Who's Who in Wales, 1920 (Cardiff: Western Mail Ltd, 1921).

Who's Who of British Members of Parliament (2 vols.), M. Stenton (ed.) (London: Harvester, 1976).

Published works

Arnot, R. Page, *South Wales Miners: A History of the S.W.M.F., 1898–1914* (London: Allen and Unwin, 1967).

Awbery, Stan, *The Story of St Athan and Aberthaw* (Barry: Barry and District News, 1959).

Barker, Hannah, *The Business of Women: Female Enterprise and Urban Development in Northern England 1760–1830* (Oxford: Oxford University Press, 2006).

Barrie, D. S. M., *The Barry Railway* (St Albans: The Oakfield Press, 1962).

Barrie, D. S. M., *The Taff Vale Railway* (St Albans: The Oakfield Press, 1950).

Burland, Len, *A Historical Tour around Mynyddislwyn Mountain* (Abertillery: Old Bakehouse Publications, 2002).

Cannadine, David, *The Decline and Fall of the British Aristocracy* (New Haven: Yale University Press, 1990. Reprinted, London: Papermac, 1996).

Chapman, Colin, *The Cowbridge Railway* (Poole: Oxford Publishing Company, 1984).

Chapman, Colin, *The Llantrisant Branches of the Taff Vale Railway* (Oxford: Oakwood, 1996).

Chapman, Colin, *The Nelson and Ynysybwl Branches of the Taff Vale Railway* (Oxford: Oakwood, 1997).

Chapman, Colin, *The Vale of Glamorgan Railway* (Usk: Oakwood, 1998).

Cowbridge Record Society, *Cowbridge Buildings and People* (Cowbridge, 1999).

Cowbridge Record Society, *Llanblethian Buildings and People* (Cowbridge, 2001).

Davies, E. T., *Religion in the Industrial Revolution in South Wales* (Cardiff; University of Wales Press, 1965).

Davies, John, *Cardiff and the Marquesses of Bute* (Cardiff: University of Wales Press, 1981).

Davies, John, *A History of Wales* (London: Allen Lane, 1993).

Davies, John, Jenkins, Nigel, Baines, Menna, and Lynch, Peredur I. (eds), *The Welsh Academy Encyclopaedia of Wales* (Cardiff: University of Wales Press, 2008).

Davies, Russell, *Hope and Heartbreak: A Social History of Wales and the Welsh, 1776–1871* (Cardiff: University of Wales Press, 2005).

Digby, Anne, *The Evolution of English General Practice 1850–1948* (Oxford: Oxford University Press, 1999).

Edwards, H. W. J., *The Good Patch* (London, 1938).

Ellis, E. L., *T. J.: A Life of Dr Thomas Jones, CH* (Cardiff: University of Wales Press, 1992).

Ensor, R. C. K., *England 1870–1914* (Oxford: Clarendon Press, 1936).

Evans, E. W., *Mabon (William Abraham 1842–1922): A Study in Trade Union Leadership.* (Cardiff: University of Wales Press, 1959).

Evans, Elias, *The Aber Valley: The Story of a Mining Community* (Cwmbran: Village Publishing, 1987).

Evans, R. Meurig, *Children Working Underground* (Cardiff: National Museum of Wales, 1979).

Evans, R. Meurig, *One Saturday Afternoon: The Albion Colliery, Cilfynydd Explosion of 1894* (Cardiff: National Museum of Wales, 1984).

Evans, Thomas, *The Story of Abercynon* (Risca: Starling Press, 1976).

Eyers, Michael, *The Masters of the Coalfield: People and Place Names in Glamorgan and Gwent* (Griffithstown: Village Publishing, 1992).

Francis, Hywel, and Smith, David, *The Fed: A History of the South Wales Miners in the Twentieth Century* (London: Lawrence and Wishart, 1980).

Griffith, Gareth, and Lambert, John J., *Set on a Hill: A Story of Two Hundred Years: New Bethel Congregational Church, Mynyddislwyn, 1758–1958* (Tonypandy, 1958).

Griffiths, Roger, *A Life at the Chalk Face*. (Spennymoor: The Memoir Club, 2002).

Haslam, Richard, *The Buildings of Wales: Powys* (London: Penguin Books, 1979).

History of the Barry Railway Company, 1884–1921 (Cardiff, 1923).

Guest, Revel, and John, Angela V., *Lady Charlotte Guest: An Extraordinary Life* (Stroud: Tempus, 2006).

Hutton, John, *Taff Vale Railway Miscellany* (Yeovil: Oxford Publishing Co., 1988).

James, Brian Ll., and Francis, David J., *Cowbridge and Llanblethian Past and Present* (Barry and Cowbridge: Brown and Sons, 1979).

Jeffreys Jones, T. I. (ed.), *Acts of Parliament Concerning Wales, 1714–1901* (Cardiff: University of Wales Press, 1959).

Jenkins, David, *Owen and Watkin Williams of Cardiff: The Golden Cross Line* (Kendal: World Ship Society, 1991).

Johns, Rev. B. D. (Periander), *Early History of the Rhondda Valley* (Pontypridd: Ford, n.d.)

Jones, Owen Vernon, *William Evans, 1864–1934* (Porth County Comprehensive School [1982]).

Lambert, W. R., *Drink and Sobriety in Victorian Wales, c.1820–c.1895* (Cardiff: University of Wales Press, 1983).

Lewis, E. D., *The Rhondda Valleys* (London: Phoenix House, 1958; reprinted by University College Cardiff Press, 1984).

Llewellyn, Ken, *Disaster at Tynewydd: An Account of a Rhondda Mining Disaster in 1877* (Cardiff: Ap Dafydd Publications, Ltd, 1975).

Lowe, J. B., *Welsh Industrial Workers Housing 1775–1875* (Cardiff: National Museum of Wales, 1977).

Mardy Rees, The Revd T., *A Mount of God: New Bethel Church, Mynyddislwyn* (Aberdare: Pugh and Rowlands, 1922).

Morgan, Jane, *Conflict and Order: The Police and Labour Disputes in England and Wales, 1900–1939* (Oxford: Clarendon Press, 1987).

Morgan, Kenneth O., *Wales in British Politics, 1868–1922* (Cardiff: University of Wales Press, 1963; paperback edition, 1991).

Morgan, Kenneth O., *Rebirth of a Nation: Wales 1880–1980 (History of Wales Vol. VI)* (Oxford: Clarendon Press and Cardiff: University of Wales Press, 1981).

'Morien', *A History of Pontypridd and the Rhondda Valleys* (Pontypridd: Glamorgan County Times, 1903).

Morris, J. H., and Williams, L. J., *The South Wales Coal Industry 1841–1875* (Cardiff: University of Wales Press, 1958).

Newman, John, *The Buildings of Wales: Glamorgan* (London: Penguin Books, 1995)

Newman, John, *The Buildings of Wales: Gwent/Monmouthshire* (New Haven and London: Yale University Press, 2002).

Oliver, R. C. B., *Bridging a Century: The Hotel Metropole, Llandrindod Wells 1872–1972* (Llandrindod Wells: Sayce Bros., 1972).

Phillips, Elizabeth, *A History of the Pioneers of the Welsh Coalfield* (Cardiff: Western Mail Ltd, 1925).

Powell, Don, *Victorian Pontypridd* (Cardiff: Merton Priory Press, 1996).

The Powell Duffryn Steam Coal Company Ltd, 1864–1914 (n.d.)

Pride, Emrys, *Rhondda My Valley Brave* (Risca: Starling Press, 1975).

Rees, Rosemary, *Poverty and Public Health 1815–1948* (Oxford: Heinemann, 2001).

Richards, John, *The Cowbridge Story: History and Anecdotes of the Ancient Borough* (Bridgend, 1956).

Richards, John, *Cardiff: A Maritime History* (Stroud: Tempus, 2005).

Roberts, Alun: *The Welsh National School of Medicine 1893–1931: The Cardiff Years* (Cardiff: University of Wales Press, 2008).

Shapely, Peter, *Charity and Power in Victorian Manchester* (Manchester: Chetham Society, 2000).

Stephens, Meic, *Pontypridd: a Town with no History but one Hell of a Past* (inaugural lecture, University of Glamorgan, 2001).

Thomas, Ivor, *Top Sawyer: A Biography of David Davies of Llandinam* (London: Longmans, Green, 1938).

Vaughan, C. Maxwell, *Pioneers of Welsh Steel: Dowlais to Llanwern* (Risca: Starling Press, 1975).

Walters, R. H., *The Economic and Business History of the South Wales Steam Coal Industry, 1840–1914* (New York: Arno, 1977).

Watson, Richard, *Rhondda Coal, Cardiff Gold: The Insoles of Llandaff, Coal Owners and Shippers* (Cardiff: Merton Priory Press, 1997).

Weekes, Philip, *A Great Wealth of Lack of Knowledge* (Cardiff: BBC, 1990).

Wilkins, Charles, *Buried Alive! A narrative of suffering and heroism, being the tale of the Rhondda colliers, as related by themselves.* (London: Houlston and Sons, 1877).

Williams, Chris, *Capitalism, Community and Conflict: The South Wales Coalfield, 1898–1947* (Cardiff: University of Wales Press, 1998).

Williams, Chris, *Democratic Rhondda: Politics and Society 1885–1951* (Cardiff: University of Wales Press, 1996).

Williams, John, *Was Wales Industrialised? Essays in Modern Welsh History* (Llandysul: Gomer, 1995).

Ystradowen: Portrait of a Village: A Brief History (historical notes compiled to accompany the exhibition held at Old Hall, Cowbridge, 17–22 June 1983).

Articles, and Chapters in Collective Volumes

Alderman, Geoffrey, 'The anti-Jewish riots of August 1911 in south Wales', *Welsh History Review*, 6 (1972–3), 190–200.

Alderman, Geoffrey, 'The anti-Jewish riots of August 1911 in south Wales: a response', *Welsh History Review*, 20 (2000–1), 565.

Asteris, Michael, 'The rise and decline of south Wales coal exports, 1870–1930', *Welsh History Review*, 13 (1986–7), 24–43.

Baber, Colin, and Thomas, Dennis, 'The Glamorgan economy, 1914–1945', in *Glamorgan County History*, 5 (1980), 97–154.

Bandhauer-Schöffmann, Irene, 'Businesswomen in Austria', in Robert Beachy, Béatrice Craig and Alastair Owens (eds), *Women, Business and Finance in Nineteenth-century Europe* (Oxford and New York: Berg, 2006), pp. 110–25.

Beachy, Robert, 'Profit and propriety: Sophie Henschel and gender management in the German locomotive industry', in Robert Beachy, Béatrice Craig and Alastair Owens (eds), *Women, Business and Finance in Nineteenth-century Europe* (Oxford and New York: Berg, 2006), pp. 67–80.

Boyns, Trevor, 'Work and death in the south Wales coalfield, 1874–1914', *Welsh History Review*, 12 (1984–5), 514–37.

Boyns, Trevor, 'Technical change and colliery explosions in the south Wales coalfield, c.1870–1914', *Welsh History Review*, 13 (1986–7), 155–77.

Boyns, Trevor, 'The electricity industry in south Wales to 1949', *Welsh History Review*, 15 (1990–1), 79–107.

Boyns, Trevor, Baber, Colin, and Thomas, Dennis, 'The iron, steel and tinplate industries, 1750–1914', *Glamorgan County History*, Vol. 5 (1980), 97–154.

Burge, Alun, 'Exorcising demonologies? coal companies and colliery communities in south Wales', *Llafur*, 9, 4 (2007), 101–9.

Bynum, W. F., 'Medical philanthropy after 1850', in W. F. Bynum and Roy Porter (eds), *Companion Encyclopedia of the History of Medicine*, 2, pp. 1480–94.

Cope, Matthew, 'Eighty-five years in Cardiff and Newport: recollections of men and incidents of the old days' (Sixteen articles in the *Western Mail*, between 21 March and 9 May 1928).

Craig, Béatrice, 'Where have all the businesswomen gone? Images and reality in the life of nineteenth-century middle-class women in northern France', in Robert Beachy, Béatrice Craig and Alastair Owens (eds), *Women, Business and Finance in Nineteenth-century Europe* (Oxford and New York: Berg, 2006), pp. 52–66.

Davies, John, and Mingay, G. F., 'Agriculture in an industrial environment' *Glamorgan County History*, 5 (1980), pp. 277–310.

Evans, Neil, '"The first charity in Wales": Cardiff Infirmary and south Wales society, 1837–1914', *Welsh History Review*, 9 (1978–9), 319–46.

Glaser, Anthony, 'The Tredegar riots of August 1911', in Ursula Henriques (ed.), *The Jews of South Wales: Historical Studies* (Cardiff: University of Wales Press, 1993).

Holmes, Colin, 'The Tredegar riots of 1911: anti-Jewish disturbances in south Wales', *Welsh History Review*, 11 (1982–3), 214–25.

Hopkin, Deian, 'Patriots and pacifists in Wales 1914–1918: the case of Capt. Lionel Lindsay and the Revd T. E. Nicholas', *Llafur* I, 3 (1974), 132–46.

Jenkins, David, 'Cardiff, coal and shipping metropolis', *Wales Past*, 3 May 2005.

Jenkins, Philip, 'The creation of an "ancient gentry": Glamorgan 1760–1840', *Welsh History Review*, 12 (1984–5), 214–25.

Keen, Michael and Richard, 'The coal war in south Wales, 1893' in Stuart Williams (ed.), *Glamorgan Historian X* (1974), 35–49.

Kidd, Alan J., 'Philanthropy and the "social history paradigm"', *Social History* 21, 2 (1996), 180–92.

Morgan, Jane, 'Police and labour in the age of Lindsay, 1910–1936', *Llafur*, V, 1, (1988), 15–20.

Morgan, Kenneth O., 'The new Liberalism and the challenge of Labour: The Welsh experience, 1885–1929', *Welsh History Review*, 6 (1972–3), 288–312.

Morgan, R. H., 'The development of the electricity supply industry in Wales to 1919', *Welsh History Review*, 11 (1982–3), 317–37.

Outram, Quentin, 'Class warriors: the coalowners', in John McIlroy, Alan Campbell, and Keith Gildart (eds), *Industrial Politics and the 1926 Mining Lockout* (Cardiff: University of Wales Press, 2004), pp. 107–35.

Pollins, Harold, 'The development of transport, 1750–1914', *Glamorgan County History*, 5 (1980), pp. 421–64.

Pretty, David A., 'David Morgan ("Dai o'r Nant"), miners' agent: a portrait of leadership in the south Wales coalfield', *Welsh History Review*, 20 (2000–1), 495–531.

Prichard, T. J., '"The squire of Fairfield": Rhondda on the eve of the industrial revolution', *Welsh History Review*, 11 (1982–3), 516–29.

Prothero, Iorwerth W., 'The port and railways of Barry', in Donald Moore (ed.), *Barry: The Centenary Book* (Barry: Barry Centenary Book Committee Ltd, 1984) pp. 209–70.

Roberts, R. O., 'The Smelting of non-ferrous metals since 1750', *Glamorgan County History*, 5 (1980), pp. 47–96.

Roderick, Gordon, 'Self-improvement and the Welsh mineworker', *Llafur*, 7, 3–4 (1998–9), 35–49.

Rubinstein, W. D., 'The anti-Jewish riots in south Wales: a re-examination', *Welsh History Review*, 18 (1996–7), 667–99.

Shapely, Peter, 'Charity, status and leadership: charitable image and the Manchester man', *Journal of Social History*, 31, 2 (1998), 157–78.

Stead, Peter, 'The town that had come of age: Barry 1918–1939', in Donald Moore (ed.), *Barry: The Centenary Book* (Barry: Barry Centenary Book Committee, 1984), pp. 367–428.

Stevens, Catrin, 'The burial question: controversy and conflict, *c.*1860–1890', *Welsh History Review*, 21, 2 (December 2002), 328–56.

Thompson, Steven, 'To relieve the sufferings of humanity, irrespective of party, politics or creed?: conflict, consensus and voluntary hospital provision in Edwardian south Wales', *Social History of Medicine*, 16 (2003), 247–62.

Williams, L. J., 'The Coal industry 1750–1914', *Glamorgan County History*, 5 (Cardiff: Glamorgan County History Trust, 1980), pp. 155–210.

Williams, L. J., 'The Coalowners', in *A People and a Proletariat*, David Smith (ed.) (London: Pluto Press, 1980), pp. 94–113.

Williams, L. J., 'Capitalists and coalowners', *Glamorgan County History, 6: Glamorgan Society 1780–1980* (Cardiff: Glamorgan County History Trust, 1988), pp. 109–129.

Index

The Rhondda Valleys, and the towns of Porth and Pontypridd (all of which figure in the title of this book) are mentioned with such frequency in the text that it has been found best not to list them in the index, except where specific local bodies or institutions are concerned.

Many people, in this index, have the same, or similar, names. In large part, they can be distinguished either by their occupations, or by their mines or houses, or by the area from which they come. The numerous similarly-named members of families are categorized by their relationship with certain key figures. For this purpose, the following initials have been used: ST for James 'Siamps' Thomas; WJT for William James Thomas; WHM for William Henry Mathias; HGL for Henry Gore Lindsay.